OPTIMISTIC, EVEN THEN

OPTIMISTIC, EVEN THEN

The Creation of Two Performing Arts Institutes

Mark Featherstone-Witty

THE SCHOOLS FOR
PERFORMING ARTS PRESS

© The Schools For Performing Arts Press 2000

First published in 2001 by The Schools For
Performing Arts (SPA) Press
Crockers Oswald Hickson, 66 Lincoln's Inn Field
London WC2A 3LH

Distributed by Gazelle Book Services Limited, Falcon
House Queen Square Lancaster, England LA1 1RN

The right of Mark Featherstone-Witty to be identified
as the author of the work has been asserted herein in
accordance with the Copyright, Designs and Patents
Act 1988.

British Library Cataloguing in Publication Data
A catalogue record for this book is available from the
British Library

ISBN 0-9539423-0-9

Typeset by Amolibros, Watchet, Somerset
This book production has been managed by Amolibros
Printed and bound by T J International Ltd, Padstow,
Cornwall

Contents

List of Illustrations

25 Staff rejoice – the building is finally ours.
Picture: Liverpool Daily Post & Echo

26 A moment during the Inauguration.
Picture: Michael McCartney
Copyright: Michael McCartney 2000
Printed by Reg Phillips at the Liverpool Art School

Photographs not otherwise credited taken by and copyright Mark Featherstone-Witty.

Acknowledgments

For their help in the creation of this book, I want to thank: Sir Paul McCartney, Sir George Martin and Alan Parker for providing their cover quotes; Sir Paul McCartney, Shelagh Jones, Paul B Winn, Geoff Baker, Rupert Grey and Anthony Field for commenting on the manuscript; Celia Brayfield and Barry Turner for their general comments; Jim Dimmock for providing the financial detail of the Postscript; Mike McCartney for providing his photographs; John Axon and Maureen Bowtell for identifying all the attendees at the Performing Right Society fund-raising lunch; Jeremy Harrison and John Morley for identifying all the attendees at the Brussels lunch; Laura Oldham for proof-reading the typescript; Mark LeFanu for introducing me to Jane Tatam and Jane for managing the publishing process and Alison, my wife, for just about everything, but here her comments on the manuscript – as well as her undimmed love.

The Title

One evening I was telling a LIPA director that I had come across my childhood copy of Hans Christian Andersen's *Fairy Tales*.

The first story had been 'The Fir-Tree' – a cautionary tale about a discontented tree unable to take pleasure in what it was naturally given: sunshine, the ground and the fresh air. It longed for what others had: the older trees for their height, the birds for their journeys to lands far away and even the trees that were cut down, because the sparrows had told it that they were dressed up in the most splendid manner and placed in the midst of warm cosy rooms.

Before long, this fir-tree too was cut down and enjoyed an evening of Christmas glory before being thrown into an attic. In early summer, it was dragged out of darkness into daylight. It believed that life was beginning again and cried, 'Now I shall live!' For the first time, it rejoiced in the sunshine and fresh air, but when it saw the fresh flowers and the trees in blossom and then looked at itself, its branches withered and yellow, it wished it were back in the attic. It bitterly regretted not having enjoyed what it had once been given while it could.

After the children had happily trampled the branches, it was burnt. As it burnt, it sighed so deeply that each sigh sounded like a pistol shot.

The moment after the tree said, 'Now I shall live!' the rest of the text had been crossed out. The nine-year-old me had added 'and he did live happy ever after'.

Roger Morris smiled and said, 'So, you were optimistic, even then.'

The Start

I'd fatally fallen for musicals ever since watching, no – gazing rapt, at *42nd Street*. One evening when I was eight, my mother had taken me to the National Film Theatre in London. Someone tutted as we emerged, opining that it wasn't right to take someone so young to see such a film. Little me was surprised at finding a stranger talking to us. Years later, I visited the Empire Theatre, Leicester Square, London on 26th November 1980 to watch *Fame*.

As the film unwound, it was as if my life had travelled backwards. Backwards to the time I left school with one enthusiasm: producing and acting in plays – with my parents aghast at the possibility of yet another out-of-work member of the extended family spending serious time showing off; my student performances and tours in England and my professional work in the United States, eventually performing in a film alongside Dina Merrill and the stalwart Hollywood character actor, Leon Ames; my experiences tutoring Sir Laurence Olivier's (as he then was) son, Richard, and so spending time with the grand master at The National Theatre (always stressing the risk of his craft compared with the mechanised certainty of personality-driven television performance – a fair point given the general preference for faultless mediocrity rather than flawed brilliance); talking with his friendly wife, Joan; the confidence I had gained starting three small-scale independent education and training institutions from scratch, sometimes alone, sometimes with a friend and, with yet another friend, taking part in the creation of a tiny television ideas company which went on provide the ideas behind one of the first handful of a series developed by the general public for Channel Four Television (and, of course, there were also activities which seemed to be marking time and so didn't spring to mind).

42nd Street had sown two seeds: the excitement and intensity of performance (where the artificial can be really felt) and that, despite all, it was possible to achieve a goal – given judgement and perseverance. During my life forward, I felt exhilarated when someone overcame the odds to reach a dream – any dream. I was as excited by some artistic achievement or invention as I was by *The Dam Busters*.

'It is good to have an end to journey towards,
but it is the journey that matters, in the end.'

Why Write This Book?

Although you might occasionally, perhaps ruefully, consider Soren Kierkegaard's observation that 'life must be lived forwards, but it can only be understood backwards', it does help when you find yourself relieved that you were glad you didn't know what you were getting into or what needed to be endured, but as the script of Disney's *Aladdin* has it: 'It's surprising what you can live through.'

This story is about a journey, what it entailed and how it was lived – from just my point of view, the person who started walking first. Those who joined in will have their own perception of events and may, one day, make them public as well.

The reason for this book is to add this story to the others where someone has a dream and lives to see it become a reality. David Puttnam told me once: 'People should have many dreams and as few illusions as possible.' I could not have said this better; in fact I wish I'd thought of it myself! I believe in endeavour so I hope what you are about to read feeds your dreams and starves your illusions.

I also belatedly appreciate our time is short and can be even shorter.

Three years ago I was part of a car accident which left me with a reconstructed face, no sense of smell, tiny taste and tendency to see double after a few drinks. One of my reactions on returning home was to throw out anything I didn't actually need. I was driven by a desire to simplify. Then I came across the BRIT School and LIPA papers. They were on their way to the dump when I was struck by the cost of the experiences that would be going to waste. So I kept them to write this.

Now, there's a beguiling temptation to describe the past (particularly your part in it) in a way which makes you look pretty good. You become what you want people to see. I have tried to avoid this. The method I stumbled on was to write the book in the third person, which allowed me unaffectedly to describe events through the personality I was then. I'm somewhat different now. Aside from being older, I know more and I'm not as single-minded. (I then transposed the text into the first person.)

Writing about your personal history when you know the result is just not how life is lived. Many actions have finely balanced potential outcomes. It's so tempting to be the person who later on says: 'Oh, I always knew that it was/was not going to be possible to...' and yet conveniently forget that, at the time, that was only just one of many potential outcomes. Witness many political memoirs. I have tried to present life as it happened, when I couldn't be sure what would happen next, in other words – the 'me' in the action.

The way I've written this also tries to give you some experience of *my* experience. It may mean that, at times, it's tricky keeping all the threads in your mind. Well, that's what it is often like. Aside from running my existing colleges, I was participating in one project and leading another simultaneously. One moment you are dealing with fund-raising and then, in quick succession, marketing, strategy, individuals who simply turn up (and the individuals on board or you are hoping will come on board) corporate image, Companies House and the Charity Commission, national government and European funding agencies, architects, designers and the list goes on. And on. And on some more. The process charts which help you plan a project, do show simultaneous activities, but they cannot show, by definition, the unexpected, nor can they show what happens when an activity starts late or overshoots the allotted timespan. If there's no one else around (and generally start-up teams are small, even tiny), then, somehow, you've got to move around even faster, while working longer hours. I've tried to give you some sensation of what this can be like.

Story-telling is often an application of order so there's another beguiling temptation: to provide a sequence that shows uniform progression from one stage to another, while life is shapeless, unpredictable and open-ended.

This book is my chance to recognise a host of people who got their hands dirty. In the process of creating LIPA, I met Sir Paul McCartney's brother-in-law, John Eastman, who give me a quote I've not forgotten: 'successful orphans frequently find they have many fathers', which is another way of saying that strangers suddenly pop up when a creation is presented to the public to claim some sort of credit.

I'm aware that this story's interest, perhaps even for you, will be its connection with well-known names and, of course, these are unusual people. Politically and commercially, their influence is profound, not to forget the credibility they lend to what they touch. The hours they spend can be small in comparison with others, but they are decisive. They are also the people the press like to cover, but 'Branson's Fame School' or 'Macca's Fame School' (or 'Macca's Cash-strapped Fame School' – as LIPA was portrayed for a fair while) cannot begin to convey what went on or the contribution of the many genuine participants.

I've discovered that too many names in a text is confusing. So I've had to balance reasonable clarity with inclusion; reasonable clarity – key names in the text; inclusion – a cast list on pages 251 to 255.

I'd like to share the nature of perseverance. Columnists and now the current government seem captivated by the nature of creativity. When Edison used to say, 'Invention is 1% inspiration and 99% perspiration,' he was pointing out that inspiration is just the very tip of a particular iceberg. What happens after the spark appeared? Ah, that's the part that isn't talked about.

Motivation has to be a fascinating topic. When I'm asked about mine, I recall myself at sixteen in chapel, listening to the school vicar as he conducted a service of remembrance for another sixteen-year-old from my school who had been killed in a car crash. As the vicar recited the conventional words about 'a life cut short' and 'promise unfulfilled', I flinched in my pew. With that acute sense of fairness that can afflict youngsters, I was appalled by the thought that it was possible to drop dead before you might be able to accomplish anything. On a superficial level, I now suspect I was thinking about sex and the misery of missing making love with anyone. But on another level, I was considering the gift of life and, just as I was coming to terms with what gorgeous possibilities it held, having it snatched away. It seemed then (as now) the very epitome of unfairness.

In a way, it would not have mattered what enterprise I started. I had loads of ideas, many of them in the early days either low-cost copies or hugely grand (purchasing film rights for books that appealed to me – *The Chocolate War* by Robert Cormier was an early example, as was creating a national franchise of nursery schools along the lines of the US creation *Kiddie Kolleges*).

I was an avid reader of the *Business Ideas Letter*, a monthly publication of The Institute of Small Businesses, full of the practicality of business start-up ideas. I had hoped that with the confidence I'd gained, I'd eventually move onto something rather more original and do-able. It wasn't for a while that this came into the mix; in fact I was thirty-four. I've recently come across one of the 'No Fear' posters that said 'Beaten paths are for beaten men'; harsh, because a minute percentage of the world's population has a choice, but, if you do, ah, do you exercise it? To step, not into someone else's footsteps, but to make some of one's own, seemed to me the very reason for working.

At one point in my life I would have said 'living', which shows me that I've have trouble with priorities, but, unlike 'The Fir Tree', I'm coming to grips with the problem, rather late on – as so often it seems. My family, the quality of relationships, the connection with people, the warmth and rejuvenation of friendship is where my heart now fully is, but, without the story you are about to read, I would feel I'd missed a major slice of life.

Chapter One

*'Fame' – how the concepts behind the BRIT
School and LIPA were created – the reaction of
practitioners – meeting George Martin, Bergen
Peck and Anthony Field – a fantasy in
Southwark*

I discovered later that the staff of the New York High
School of the Performing Arts had greeted the '80s' film
Fame (which portrayed them, and when it was screened
for them) in silence. It was a film about their school,
but they were shocked. Richard Klein, the then provost
of the New World School of the Arts in Miami, Florida,
whom I later met during the years of research, recalled
what happened.

'When it stopped running, there was no comment in
the viewing theatre. And I mean no comment –
although we were expected to be wildly enthusiastic.
Our emphasis had always been on self-discipline. We
were appalled by some of the things we saw on film.
The boy pulling down the bookshelf would have been
out. We would never allow a parent into an audition.
That would have stopped it dead. We met with Alan.
He listened and told us not to worry. He would make
us famous. And he did. People just didn't appear to be
worried about what we saw.'

In the States, six schools in California, three in
Texas and three in Ohio were started along similar
lines. In England, I gazed at the screen, enchanted
by the energy and vitality of the unfolding stories. I
longed to teach in a place like the New York school.

1

Then I wondered about starting one up in my own country.

I'd taught for a year at The Italia Conte Stage School in London, so there seemed little point in starting up a carbon copy, particularly when there must be many parents (aside from my own) who knew that some eighty-four per cent of actors registered with their union, Equity, were out of work at any one time. 'Why train for unemployment?' as Margaret Thatcher (prime minister at the time and reminding me later of Angelica Houston as head witch in *The Witches*) had crossly asked me.

Currently, of the sixteen per cent of actors in work, sixty per cent take home less than £10,000 a year. In America, the statistics are grimmer still: in 1999, fifty-five per cent of the profession made less than £2,000. *Spotlight,* the actors' directory, was the size of a slim notebook in the mid-1930s; today it runs to eight volumes, each thicker than the *London Yellow Pages.* 18,000 actors are within.

How the concepts were created

A new concept was needed.

In a moment of clarity, the concept created itself. Why not ask people who had made it in the arts and entertainment economy just how *they* had made it? With an extra question: 'Looking back from where you are now, what would you have liked to have known *then?*'

Did this seem a good starting point, I asked Alan Parker some months later in his Pinewood offices? Alan, with his warm face and manner, leant back, agreeing, and suggested visiting as many existing schools in the United States as I could afford. The States were, unlike the British, unembarrassed about having an industry called entertainment. Learn from the competition.

Which was why I began my US visits, the first to the Fiorello La Guardia High School for the Performing Arts in New York (which was what the New York

School of the Performing Arts had become), quickly followed by the New World School, before others. What surprised me was the separation of disciplines.

In *Fame*, a girl being auditioned said to other girls, hoping to gain entry, that they had to be able to sing, dance and act. So, I was baffled not to find the reality I'd been led to believe existed.

When I visited the New York school, you entered as a dancer and you left with no other performing arts training, other than dance; the same for musicians, actors and artists. How did that relate to *42nd Street*, where performers could act, sing and dance? Or even Christopher Walken, who was not an American actor you would associate with dancing or singing and yet did just that, with style and aplomb, in the American version of *Pennies from Heaven*? And if you could act, sing and dance, surely you could be employed, yes in musical theatre, but as an actor, singer and dancer in other environments. Years later, Cameron Mackintosh (theatre producer of such shows as *Cats, Les Miserables, The Phantom of the Opera* and *Miss Saigon*) told me about The Triple Threat: an American expression for performers who could do just that: sing, dance and act.

Here then was the first idea: a school for versatile performers with a music element concentrating on the popular music styles of the twentieth century.

As it happened, Simon Garfield's (then rock critic of *Time Out*) book, *Expensive Habits,* had come out. Whether artists had music training or not, the one element they wished they had known something about was the business. Although someone, somewhere says s/he wasn't going to be ripped off, someone somewhere forgets.

The latest example appears to be Sir Elton John. In the midst of giving evidence in his contract battle for disputed expenses, he proclaimed he had no flair for, or the slightest interest in, his business affairs. 'I'm a performer, an artist, I don't know about these things.'

It seemed as if the apocryphal story was true: a group of musicians decide to form a band. They rehearse enthusiastically, day and night and the time in between. Then they perform. They know at one gig that an A & R man is going to be there from a major record company. They play their hearts out. There's a sign of genuine enthusiasm from our record company man. Since they are busy with more gigs and have an ambivalent attitude towards business, they pick on the roadie, or better still their van driver, to negotiate. Years later they'd discovered that that casual decision was the most important they'd ever made, and often disastrous for their careers.

It was not as if muscle was involved; the book described self-inflicted wounds. OK, there were a few outright villains, but villainy wasn't needed because the victims were willing to play right into their laps.

Nowadays this familiar story is being joined by another: as a band succeeds, band members spot the revenue flowing from song-writing royalties and, regardless of who did this fundamental work, decide it should be shared amongst them in the joint spirit they all began. Ah, but who actually wrote the song? In the rush to sign the first record deal, the legal relationships between band members were not uppermost in people's minds, anyone's mind.

So here came the second idea: artists should understand they are entering a business and so develop some savvy. This was not to dampen the artistic impulse, but to avoid being a business virgin.

Alongside this there needed to be, I felt, some preparation for the emotional strain of coping with the tough employment life in this area of work – tough in the sense of not having an audience when you wanted to communicate with strangers and tough in the sense that you could, in a twinkling, be turned into being public property. When Kurt Cobain was still alive, I'd read that fame had come too quickly for him. 'If there was a course on being a rock star,' Kurt had said, 'I'd go on it.'

The third idea was also central: collaboration. An institution would put on a show and that virtually every element would be provided by the students – acting, dance, light, sound, the lot – all working together. Since I was focusing on a school, staff would have to join in, which was one part of breaking down age divisions.

The fourth idea was pragmatic: that there should be a series of safety nets which would have encouraged people like my parents to accept the idea of attending a school like this; in other words, enough secondary skills which would allow easier changes of a career if the dream career didn't take off. After all there were loads of occupations in the performing arts' world that few had heard about, let alone understood.

Years later this idea was simply illustrated by reading through the internal tour booklet for Paul McCartney's 1993 'New World Tour', where, for the six members of the band on stage, 176 members of the band and crew party were listed. You could work in the area of activity that interested you most, despite not achieving your dream role.

When the appeal document appeared, the founding principles became known as 'a practical philosophy' with seven key elements: versatility across the three vocational studies; extensive practical performance training; the opportunity to work and study across age ranges and peer groups; preparation for the real world of work; emphasis on the popular and contemporary; a socially and ethnically mixed pupil intake and work in the local community. Translating these into a curriculum was yet to come.

Another step was to address finance, although it was a whole staircase, largely because I'd decided, for the first time in my life, to create a charity rather than a commercial enterprise. The reason for the charity was the need for a mountain of money to get the thing going (when I knew no one). I thought I'd find it easier convincing others to donate if I wasn't in it for personal financial gain.

But first I needed someone with whom to talk over the ideas who wasn't a friend. It happened to be a near neighbour, Nigel Morgan, who lived with his family just two doors away in Bishops Stortford (an hour north from London by train). It turned out that Nigel taught music at the local secondary private school and a comprehensive and, more tantalisingly, had been a student at the Julliard School in New York.

I asked Nigel to provide a curriculum for music, which made me realise that I needed to produce a document that laid out the essence of the school. I would need to find people to provide a dance and drama curriculum. I would have a crack at the main curriculum, which would be designed to take up fifty per cent of the pupils' time. Producing this document alone, in the midst of a full-time job, took me six months.

Although I was almost damp with excitement, I thought forward and considered what would happen next. A dream without money would remain a dream, but how on earth was I going to raise, what? Enter the only friend I had made in two years of being an accountancy articled clerk (my parents deciding that if I wasn't going to be on the stage of The Royal Shakespeare Company, I might find some pleasure in looking after their finances), John Maloney.

Providing the financial element extended the document for a further four months and made me realise that nearly £4,000,000 was needed to set it up and get it running. The first business I had started required £9,600 raised from friends, which had seemed a lot at the time. (My mother had confidently predicted that this was a mechanism that would help me lose all my close friends in one fell swoop – fortunately it didn't happen; the financial returns had surprised and delighted them – and me too, if it comes to that.)

When I thought about £4,000,000, I was optimistic enough to feel that the idea alone would be strong enough to encourage donors. It was just a matter of explaining it with enough energy and enthusiasm, of finding the right key.

From where I am now, I wonder how I could have possibly imagined the idea would become a reality. Part of this, I suppose, was the certainty of youth (or in my case, middle youth!). If someone came to me now, I'd be saying have you thought of this, that and the other – a risk assessment, the market, competitive analysis and so on? Have I lost a necessary blindness? Or put it another way, can you know too much (or think you do); in effect, suffer from analysis paralysis?

However, before I tackled the finance to make the ideas a reality, I had to first see if the ideas could carry any weight in the professional world. It was all very well to have an idea, but would it make sense to the people who spent their lives working in the arts and entertainment world?

I had the concept. I had the two questions. Now I needed to test them. I also realised that as a nonentity, I needed to find well-known people to endorse the concept with their names as patrons.

To achieve the entire patronage list I roughly wanted would take three years. It was like creating the best imaginable alumni party. If they were in a room at the same time, they could be the dream former pupils of the school. Whenever possible, I chose performers who were multi-skilled and even where people in the classical field were chosen, like Sir Kenneth Macmillan, it was on the strength of popular culture (I'd read that Sir Kenneth had become a choreographer on seeing a Fred Astaire movie). The letter I wrote, together with a slim outline of the idea, could not, at the start mention other patrons – there weren't any. Later there were, but I felt that they should be simply asked to comment on and hopefully support an idea.

Only one potential patron ever asked who else had become a patron, Melvyn Bragg. My meeting with Melvyn graphically reminded me of the cliff to climb. At one point, Melvyn gently inquired how far the concept had reached. I pointed to the documents I had sent him. 'That's it,' I said brightly and suddenly realised how paper-thin the project was. It was literally a few sheets of paper. 'Of course we are still in the development stage,' I added, which filled the silence, but not the awareness planted in my mind. I left London Weekend Television a touch less jaunty than when I went in.

David Puttnam would courteously give me two hours of his time in a comfy room in front of an open grate in his mews office in Kensington and was the only patron who, with Patsy his wife, spontaneously donated (£1,000 as it happened).

I happened, through my colleges, to know a vicar who knew Jeffrey Archer, who also donated. £100 this time and hoping, tongue-in-cheek, that this would count towards his salvation.

Thinking back, I now remember spotting Jeffrey Archer as he was crossing a street in Soho and hurrying across to thank him for his donation. He had stepped back as I approached; after all, I was a complete stranger. I realised then that it's an odd meeting between the well-known and the unknown. After all, you know more about them than they know about you, which makes you feel you know them quite well – when you don't. For one person there's an artificial sense of familiarity.

Although he stopped being a patron after suggesting real ideas, Pete Townshend was arresting. I'd taken along one of my most talkative friends, Jo Moriarty, and even she had fallen silent.

It's tricky to define charisma, felt as it is. But that morning in Air Studios, as it then was – perched above Oxford Circus, Pete had his share. As he described his life and the learning along the way, we were silenced by the authenticity of his observations. He warned us: 'My abiding metaphor for the rock industry is people rushing to throw themselves onto a bonfire.'

The reactions of practitioners

Almost three years later, Pete distinguished himself by being the only patron who put his thoughts on education on paper, which included what he called 'the divine balance' for achieving the greatest benefit for students. The balance included a fundamental emphasis on performance; teachers with 'as few musical phobias and preferences as possible'; 'encouraging students to listen to music' and, finally, the 'recognition of the terrible truth that in this modern world, a composition may be conceived, performed, recorded and broadcast to millions of people all over the world within a month'.

In time, over thirty well-known people representing the broad canvas of the arts and entertainment allied themselves as patrons. It was still just an idea.

It was just as possible to learn from people who were not keen on the idea as from the people who were.

In the former category was Trevor Nunn, then artistic director of the Royal Shakespeare Theatre (now the leading The Royal National Theatre).

'Alas I cannot share your enthusiasm or sense of urgency for a School for Performing Arts. The experience of most employers in theatre and television is that when they have need for young performers, they would rather give a wide berth to the current existing stage schools, because of the "professional attitudes" that are to be found somewhat disturbingly and charmlessly amongst so many of the pupils. How is a child to decide on a career in the performing arts? Usually the decision lies with an ambitious or vicarious parent. In what way could this premature conditioning of the young mind and potential be different in the circumstances you describe?' (I of course wrote back and told him, but he was not to be budged.)

While agreeing musical and dance talent needed nurturing young, Nunn felt 'if one is to end up as an actor or a director, the last thing in the world to prepare one for the task is an early education devoted to aspects of the theatre. Well, that's where my thinking has arrived. Forgive this hasty expletive, but I am unable to spend as much time thinking of your ideas as I would like.'

Vangelis was concerned that teachers would do little else than create copies of themselves. We earnestly discussed this in his mews flat off the Edgware Road. It wasn't easy to keep the conversation on track though. He had one of the first wall projection television screens which was transmitting the news at the time. So I was conscious that, just behind my head, were huge pictures of pile-ups on the M1 and his attention kept flickering. His studio was covered, it seemed, by gold disks – in his case for the same music, since he created and engineered his recordings.

By February 1985, I had spoken with roughly 120 practitioners.

The single meeting which was to kick off both the BRIT School in London and The Liverpool Institute for Performing Arts (LIPA) was imminent.

Meeting George Martin, Bergen Peck and Anthony Field

Across the road from Bond Street underground station in London were the then offices of Chrysalis. Amongst the letters I had sent off, looking for meetings and guidance, was one to George Martin. I'd seen Mr Martin's picture many times in those Abbey Road Recording Studio shots, either looking professional behind a recording desk with one or two of the Beatles looking on or looking bewildered and strained as relationships between 'the boys', as he called them, teetered between creativity and destruction.

Shirley Burns, Mr Martin's PA, was the first person I saw as I walked in. A warm, alive soul with a glorious, throaty voice, she was going to act as both a professional confidante, during lunches that followed, as well as giving me seminars on the music industry. This much was clear: of all the performance arts, the music industry was the wealthiest and the more I could learn about its workings and the personalities who drove it forward, the better.

George was unfailing gentle and courteous. I could

never completely rid myself of my first impression: that of a public school housemaster, slightly distant, but imbued with the, perhaps old-fashioned, characteristics of a gentleman. Occasionally I mixed George up with my own father. After all, here was a visitor with little else but an idea. George could have been a patient listener and sent me on my way. In fact, he was the reverse. He had had a classical music education from Guildhall School of Music and Drama and so recognised the value of study. As we talked together, I felt I had come across the first person who could significantly help the project. After all, he sympathised with the idea and knew so many people, not least the Beatles themselves.

As it happened, George always had a record on the go or was off to Monserrat in the Caribbean, where he had a studio or was creating the new Air Studio in Hampstead. Shirley was going to be George, when George wasn't there.

I dimly realised that meeting and discussing the philosophy, which would later lead to the curriculum, was but one leg of the three-legged stool which needed to be created; aside from raising the sheer finance, there was the administrative structure which would carry it forward.

As it happened, another person I'd met locally was Bergen Peck (who at that stage was Head of Music at a local Bishop's Stortford comprehensive school) and had decided to pursue a further degree. In time, Bergen told me that his MA supervisor was someone I had to meet.

Anthony Field, aside from the starting the first arts administration Master of Arts degree at City University, had been finance director of the Arts Council for some twenty years, accounting for budget which had grown from some £500,000 to some £21,000,000 during this period. Here again was an industry stalwart, someone you'd be unlikely to hear about, but someone who made it work. We met for lunch near Theatre Projects, where Anthony worked. He turned out to be a man for whom retirement was another stage of his working life. He turned up with his springy step and ready smile. He told me that, while he was at the Arts Council, Tommy Steele had approached them with an idea for a showbiz school.

Here was a man who began life as a skiffle-board player and in later life starred in *Singing in the Rain* at the London Palladium, having to learn by hard experience how to act, sing and dance. Although Tony and his then secretary-general (Sir Roy Shaw) were enthusiastic, the Treasury told them in no uncertain terms to concentrate on performing arts companies and not education or training.

As it happened, Tony fixed up a meeting with Tommy for me to see if he was still interested. The basement in Soho that Tommy had in mind was no longer available to him, so he'd rather gone off the idea, but liked the general tenor of what he heard.

Tony had helped Cameron Mackintosh with one of his first shows (a revival of *My Fair Lady*) and told me that Andrew Lloyd Webber had also entertained a similar idea when he was thinking about buying the Palace Theatre. So the idea of a school for versatile performers was not new to him. As a long-time backer of shows (called 'angels' in the business because heaven was where the reward for backing shows was usually received), he had himself understood the difficulty of finding (or witnessing) performers who were strong in the three main performing skills.

A fantasy in Southwark

Through an estate agent I knew well, I had been alerted to a property in Borough, Southwark, a disused factory, which might suit. Without trifling with such trivia as a business plan or fund-raising, I hurried off to see it. There is a moment, which I suppose all entrepreneurs experience, when bricks and mortar are seen and the spaces fill in the dream. It was almost as if the school was there.

I hadn't, with Bergen, gone through the business of creating a draft timetable and then seeing if the space could accommodate the activity. No, nothing like that. I saw the space and peopled it. From the roof of the building, I could see Tower Bridge and fantasised about having a student canteen on the roof. I saw the open factory floor with the clean bits where the machines had once stood and saw multi-purpose studios and wondered how high the ceilings should be for dancers. I marked out in my mind teaching spaces, office and storage spaces before realising I was deeply into fantasy. Oh my God, I thought, as I shut the factory door: what am I thinking of?

I totted up where things were. There was a blueprint for the curriculum of the school, as well as financial forecasts. The basic ideas had not only withstood the research but had been reinforced by it. I'd formed a new charity, The School for Performing Arts Limited. A possible building was in existence.

I'd met Kenneth Robinson, the author of the influential Gulbenkian Foundations Report, *'Arts in Schools'* (Chair of the current government's National Advisory Committee on Creative and Cultural Education), who had started a magazine for performing arts teachers – *Arts Express* (gone and missed) and had, with his agreement, plagiarised the magazine's sponsors, gaining a virtual promise of £4,000 from Chevron Petroleum. I had funded the enterprise to date and needed to offload some of this responsibility if I could.

Now the business of creating the school had to begin. But I still knew no one, (although Tony seemed a good bet in a net working sense) who was rich enough to turn the dream into reality. The chance of bumping into Paul Getty (if only I knew what he looked like) was remote and, even if I did, what was I to say? 'Oh, nice to meet you. I've got an idea you might be interested in supporting...' It was daft, even in fantasy, despite my natural optimism.

But, I was raring to go, just raring to go.

Chapter Two

*The first meeting of The Schools for Performing
Arts Trust – initial financing talk – meeting
Terry Ellis, co-founder of* 'Chrysalis' *– Terry's
fund-raising idea –altruism – more on finance –
Harvey Goldsmith rethinks – George Martin
becomes appeal chairman*

So I settled down and wrote letters when ever there was
time to do so (late, late night, early, early morning) and
arranged meetings if there was a glimmer of help
possible. By the time, the first meeting for The School
for Performing Arts Trust took place on 16th September
1985, I had written some three hundred letters and
attended some sixty meetings.

The letters, introducing the concept, ranged widely
from educators (amongst them Robin Howard – the
founder of the London Contemporary Dance School,
Avril Dankworth – the sister of John Dankworth, the
saxophonist and who founded their unique music
summer school, John Hosier – the former principal of
the Guildhall School of Music and Drama who went on
to be the founding Principal of the Hong Kong School
of Performing Arts, Peter Fowler – the head of The Arts
Educational Schools, Anna Sher – the founder of the
Anne Sher Children's Theatre Workshop, John
Stephens – the London drama inspector for schools);
advisors; National Charities (amongst them: The
National Association for Gifted Children, Charity
Projects, British Film Institute, Greater London Arts
Authority , The Arts Council, The National Jazz

Centre); employers; columnists (among them, Jan Murray of *Cosmopolitan*); teachers; friends (amongst them Mary Allen – to be Chief Executive of The Arts Council) and potential funders.

This had to be fitted around managing three London-located private education/training institutions: Capital College (this was the first business I had started up with finance from friends); the London School of Insurance (with Rajendra Sampat, a staff chemistry teacher and avid entrepreneur, who had interested me in the idea and subsequently ran it) and the London School of Publishing (which I housed).

I had a focused life, buoyed up by the adrenaline of enterprise...and dreams. So simple had my outlook become that I took as my mantra conversation that I saw in the film *Flashdance*. This was the moment when the female steel-welder is facing her doubts about being a dancer – her lifelong ambition. She is on the edge of giving up. Her boss and lover simply says, 'If you give up your dream, you die.' Yes, give up your dream, you die, I thought, you're right.

The first meeting of the Schools for Performing Arts Trust

The first meeting of The Schools for Performing Arts took place in a classroom of my first college in Holborn, London. Of the fourteen people present, seven were my friends with specific skills that could be helpful to the project; three were helpful strangers and then there was Tony Field and Alison, my wife.

Listening to the tape of that first meeting, I wonder at the generosity and confidence of the trustees and observers, as well as reflect on the great good fortune of strong, noble friendships. It makes me feel anything is possible, given enough faith and hard work. And friendship.

The test was about to begin.

Initial financing talk

The first meeting concentrated on reviewing the activities to date and outlining what had to be done next. And the first priority was money. Denise Fiennes, a seasoned fund-campaigner for appeals I had come across, told us that roughly £500,000-£600,000 was needed to convert the Southwark building, just shown to the meeting on slides. And that this would take twenty-one months to raise. There were a raft of committees to set up and the key appointment of a fund-raiser to be paid between £8,000 and £10,000 a year, depending upon how generous the National Westminster Bank chose to be. The other key element was the chairman of the appeal committee.

As Denise mentioned well-known business women and benefactors as Pamela Harleck, Jennifer d'Abo, Anouska Weinberg and Vivienne Duffield, I wondered how these excellent names, which doubtless hid busy people, were going to be passionate about an area of work they might only know tangentially. I felt the idea would have greater appeal for the economies most set to benefit (or the artists who were their public faces). I knew next to nothing about well-connected women; I had never been near their circle and felt out of my depth when I considered the reality of raising money that way. I admit this influenced my point of view.

A week later I met the manager of the SPA bankers who told me that, unless there were a large or several large donations to enable the SPA to acquire a building and start conversion work, the bank would not advance money against the security of a building, and, even then, he would only be able to action this with permission from the highest level within National Westminster Bank. The more solid the scheme looked and the higher the level of professional expertise and presentation, the better. This was conveyed to the next meeting.

The estate agent who had introduced the Borough property to me, told the meeting that the building was being offered for £275,000 freehold for roughly 25,000-30,000 square feet; a more realistic price would have been £500,000 upwards; the vendor wanted a quick sale and his agents had already received an unconditional offer with contracts to be exchanged within six weeks and completion within two months. I wondered, not for the first time, if my enthusiasm had run away with me; on the other hand, the property housed my dream when I slept at night. Here was the property; where was the money? Did anyone know of trusts and foundations who might be prepared to house the SPA, or even a big London landlord?

It was decided to write to everyone. Which was fine, except that I remained the only worker for the SPA while I was still busy running the colleges in the daytime, alongside administering the other which used the building in the evening – all the while living in Bishop's Stortford. I realised the pace would be set simply by the amount of time I could devote.

The building was a major hurdle and, by the end of December 1985, we began to wonder if we should be concentrating on an alternative aim: starting a smaller appeal, running a smaller school in a shared building and, in effect, showing potential donors what could be achieved and what might be achieved if only there were significant stand-alone premises. I wasn't at all keen, partly because I couldn't see how it would work and partly because I couldn't bear what seemed to me a half-, no, a quarter-start. Meanwhile, The Church Commissioners, the University of London and the Crown Commissioners were written to.

Then, all of a sudden, a breakthrough.

Meeting Terry Ellis, co founder of 'Chrysalis'

Seven months earlier, George Martin had mentioned to me that Terry Ellis (the co-founder with Chris Wright of Chrysalis Records) might be worth approaching. Here was a music industry man (who also introduced the cartoon character, Max Headroom, to the UK) reputedly worth £13,000,000 after a split with his co-founder and with, currently, little to do. Within days, I had sent Terry a letter with a covering note asking Gillian Weldon, his PA, to present when she judged the moment was right. I had polished my letter until it shone. Concentrating on the music angle, I wrote: 'And despite the huge financial revenues generated by the popular music industry, no one appears to have had the vision to put "something back in". The opportunity this presents a pioneer benefactor is huge and I am writing to you in the hope that the idea of the LSPA may fire your imagination and support.'

Hearing nothing for three months, I'd assumed the familiar, until Gillian wrote back. There was the one sentence I'd been longing to see: 'Mr Ellis has indeed read your letter concerning the School and has expressed great interest.' This was the first time that anyone with the financial means to make the LSPA (the idea was to call it 'The London School for Performing Arts') happen had expressed 'great interest'.

Later that year, when Terry had returned from holiday in the West Indies, we met. Terry's office was in Brook Street, just off Bond Street. It seemed to be one good-sized room off a small office where Gillian worked. I was struck by his height, by the thinness of his socks and the curiously removed way in which he spoke. It was difficult to decide if he wasn't quite listening or taking his time to think. I was eager to make a positive impression, so it was easy for me to feel confused.

What did I expect him to do? Sign over a cheque for £500,000 forthwith, with, maybe, just a few riders? Oh dear, I did.

Terry's fund raising idea

Despite my naïve expectation, the meeting went rather well. Terry had already thought forward and emerged with a fund-raising idea. With his chum, Harvey Goldsmith, this was to be a celebrity event at The Royal

Opera House. Artists would be contacted and asked who they would most like to sing a duet with. The audience would pay Covent Garden-like ticket prices to attend; the whole event would be filmed for an American audience (Terry had good contacts there) so additional revenue would be generated. It would also have the potential benefit of mixing musical genres.

As it happened, George and Shirley worked around the corner. After my first Terry meeting, I shot across to find out if Shirley knew anything about Terry and his achievements. As it happened, Billboard had produced a celebration, *The First Ten Years*, about the partnership between Ellis and Wright. It was bedtime reading. I spotted that Air Record Group, which George chaired, had merged with Chrysalis, which was why George was sitting in Chrysalis' headquarters. I fantasised on the way home that this was the man who was going to make the LSPA happen. As I read the Billboard issue later that evening, I wondered about Terry's wary detachment about his co-founder when he said, 'Looking back it does seem strange that we should have joined up. I was certainly a very independent spirit and it is hard to imagine my having wanted to go into partnership. Presumably we must have felt some sort of good chemistry.' The rest of the long piece had pictures of the two partners with just about everyone significant they had worked with.

By the first Trustees' meeting of 1986, Terry Ellis had agreed not only to become a trustee, but the chairman of the appeal. We were thrilled and were looking forward to the outcome of the meeting between Tony, Denise, Terry and me early the following month. Additionally, Tony thought it might be possible to hold a charity performance of *The Phantom of the Opera* for the benefit of the SPA. There was a definite breeze with the music and stage industry providing the puff.

Two months later, I wrote round to all trustees urging a full house to impress Terry Ellis, only Terry was indisposed. He was, however, still planning his event at the end of 1987 and an appeal committee of twelve to include Richard Branson – the founder of the Virgin group of companies, Lady Mary Russell, Maurice Saatchi – the co-founder of the advertising agency of the same name, Terence Conran – the founder of Conran and Habitat home furnishing shops, Andrew Lloyd-Webber – the composer, Elizabeth Maxwell – the wife of Robert Maxwell (whose sons I had once taught), George Martin, David Puttnam – the film producer, Wayne Sleep – the dancer, Olga Politski, Michael White – the theatre impresario and Nigel Dempster – the newspaper columnist, with Jennifer d'Abo – the MD of Rymans, the stationers, and Anoushka Weinberg in reserve. A fund-raiser had emerged as well. Her name was Susan Davenport and she'd worked with Denise before.

The names mesmerised us. (Yet to come was the fact that the committee was never formed and so never met.)

I was to see Terry again about a building, another building. When the Southwark building was snapped up, the estate agent had come up with an alternative; this time in Old Street. It was an abandoned school, one of those handsomely built 1920 jobs. I nipped along one lunch-time, took slide pictures and again found it hard not to populate the building.

Two weeks later I was showing them to Terry in his office, all the while wondering if Terry would be prepared to advance a loan secured on the building. The building would cost roughly £500,000 and the renovation a further £750,000. Terry watched the slides in virtual silence. At the end, he turned to me and said in his languid way, 'Well, you don't have the money, do you?' I resisted saying, 'Well, you maybe you do or know how to get it.' A month or so later, another building emerged as part of Terence Conran's conversion of Butler's Wharf. Terry never heard about it, since the whole shebang would have cost £2,500,000. Two months later, the trustees decided that there wasn't much point trying to find buildings when the finance hadn't got off first base.

Altruism

I recall now a breakfast meeting I had with Terry at Claridges. That was the meeting when Terry ruminated over the motives for giving money. I nattered on about the value of giving something back to the next generation, not just money, but expertise and experience as well. Terry asked me to think of anyone who had given without expecting anything in return. I went through a number of well-known examples, before alighting on Jesus Christ. Terry wasn't having it and I left the meeting reflecting that altruistic giving was pretty much a contradiction, in this sense: the moment that giving became known, you were receiving a benefit. So, continuing on the same line of thought: you could never produce an example of altruistic giving. As the great Sufi would say, 'A saint is one until he or she knows it.'

More on finance

Over the next year or so, the key issue was finance; the document which might help to secure it and the mechanisms to achieve it. Most immediately, Tony, it turned out, was a friend of Leonard Bernstein (the American composer and conductor) and was arranging a West End salute to the man, through which the SPA received a quarter of the proceeds in addition to one of the premieres of *The Phantom of the Opera*.

Later in June 1986, Terry turned up to his first Trustees meeting. He reported that George Martin had agreed to be vice-chair of the appeal and that he was meeting with Harvey Goldsmith the next day, together with George, to decide the date of the Gala and the composition of the committee. He felt that between £1,000,000 and £2,000,000 could be raised by selling the Gala to American television. I could barely contain myself.

Meanwhile Susan Davenport had began getting a hit list of possible donors together with the help of Robert

Davies, an old friend of mine with extensive experience of the voluntary sector and then working for the Prince of Wales's *'Business in the Community'*. As I reviewed her first report, I noticed that much of her report was about the potential *Phantom* Gala, as well as her cheerful choice of a royal patron for the event, while considering a post-performance reception at the night-club, *Stringfellows*. Was this what fund-raising was about?

Despite Terry's auspicious start, months silently passed. Finally, with Gillian's help I finally managed to get Terry to concentrate upon the reality of helping the LSPA into life. Gillian had been telling her boss to decide once and for all, whether he was going to help the SPA or not.

There are few more important people to form a relationship with than the personal assistant of the person you are dealing with. In the critical matter of timing, when to pitch, few can help more.

Gillian told me that Terry was going off the boil.

Harvey Goldsmith rethinks

Part of the problem for Terry was that his central fund-raising idea hadn't taken off. He'd met with Tony, George and Harvey Goldsmith at some point. George and Tony had decided that the theme would be a 'meeting of different worlds' (in other words, the worlds of rock'n'roll, ballet, drama, opera, sport and pop) which they felt would attract a wide audience. George had agreed to speak with the leading artists he knew. Since Harvey was late, Tony and George had left. When the new idea was explained to him, Harvey felt that there was little mileage in the associations between new and old art forms and sport. On top of that, American television would not be interested unless there was an outstanding line-up of commercial stars. He finished by saying that it would be better to defer the concert until the school had opened since it would easier to persuade performers to participate.

When I finally managed to meet Terry, he had

launched into the story of his life, which had included a difficult and demoralising separation from Chris Wright and a bout of drug addition, which had nearly finished him off. Life simply hadn't been the same since. As a fellow human being, I sympathised; as a person trying to get the London school off the ground, I needed to keep to myself the frustration I felt that my hopes of Terry had been so extensive (and naïve).

Within a further month, Terry resigned as chair of the appeals committee.

George Martin becomes appeal chairman

I appealed to George to take over. He responded, 'Sorry to hear of Terry's abdication. In view of your time problem I will do anything I can to help. My reluctance to accept chairmanship has been purely because of my many other commitments – not least of which is earning a living. But I would be delighted to accept if you can obtain someone to bear the brunt of the work.'

The sale of the Gala to US TV had proven impossible, so the Gala itself was remote. Harvey Goldsmith had resigned from the non-existent appeal committee that had, to date, just two members, Tony Field and David Puttnam. Our one rich hope had given up. We asked Terry if he'd stay on as a trustee. He took a further two months to agree.

So, a year on from the first meeting, all eyes were on Susan Davenport and her mate, Denise Fiennes and indeed, George Martin.

There was nowhere else to go.

Chapter Three

The fund-raisers leave – an alternative financial model – City Technology College Chief advises against the scheme – the Investment Memorandum – the British Phonographic Industry's fight for copyright – the links between Richard Branson, Kenneth Baker, the BPI, the CTC Trust and the SPA – the problem with the word

The next meeting saw the first and only SPA Appeal Document; George Martin getting to work with his appeal committee and the soon-to-be-dreaded mention of cultivation evenings as a fund-raising ploy. There was a general sense in which we supported a gradual testing of the water amongst people likely to be friendly towards the idea of the SPA, rather than a launch. After all, this appeal was not on a par with global or national hunger or illness, so a major push by way of a press conference would largely be an excuse to see and hear a particular speaker rather than a rush for cheque books.

There was also a sense in which both we and the fund-raisers had inflated hopes about each other. As a sense of realism grew, so did a sense of dismay. We had hoped we were paying for a ready access to cash, while the fund-raisers felt the SPA, with its illustrious patronage, should be further along and helping do it; they were doing what they could, but this was not a 'final touch' exercise. It was turning into 'do most of it all'.

The fund raisers leave

There was a sense in things were going on and on. During one session, the SPA Trustees again reviewed what had been achieved; yes, the Appeal Document; yes, the research; yes, the *Bernstein* and *Phantom* evenings and then things started to slow – the formation of the appeal committee and some visits to potential donors. Looking at the list, we became aware that too many of the successful activities were the result of the trustees' own work. At this meeting the next idea had its first outing: to put the capital project out to commercial investment, while retaining the charity for the school itself and the sponsoring of students.

The frustration over slowness and the way in which what little money had been raised was being spent on those who raised it and who largely seemed to be compiling voluminous reports, made us determined that Susan and Denise be set a deadline to appraise the success of money-raising by charitable means. There was also a sense in which we wondered about the lone fund-raiser approach, the level at which an approach was made and the involvement of key trustees who could make a difference. Susan was told to provide copies of all correspondence and to answer questions, but in truth, it was a chance to review her working methods thoroughly. She resigned a month later, securing a similar job with The Royal Shakespeare Company. Denise left a month after that.

1987 began with an evening meeting of the appeal committee at Chrysalis. I felt the meeting crystallised the impotence of the current fund-raising effort. Five people attended, none – apart from Terry (who was feeling a bit odd since this was the first time he had stepped back inside the Chrysalis building after his split with Chris Wright) – had any money. Tony Field chaired it and aside from Terry, Shirley Burns (there on behalf for George who was overseas) and I, there was just James Platt – a man who had helped found the

European Jazz Orchestra and who had introduced me to The Caloutse Gulkenkian Foundation. What were they going to say to each other? They all knew the project and, despite Susan's work, which had included contacting some 250 organisations, not a single potential donor turned up.

To show the no-showers what I had in mind for the school, I ran the final sequence of *Fame*. It was the end-of-year show, following graduation, where the students performed a piece which included dance, classical music as well as rock music, choral as well as solo singing.

What the watchers did not know was that my spirits had been dropping and, whenever they did, I showed myself this sequence on my home video, again and again. It was this sequence that reminded me of the horizon, lifted my spirits and encouraged me to write another letter. Watching the other faces in that room, it seemed that, in essence, nothing had really happened. Of course, it was raining as the small meeting broke up with pleasantries. Not for the first time, I wondered if I was being stupid, self-indulgent, blind and, yes, stupid. Was this just another version of wanting to be an actor?

An alternative financial model

At the following trustees' meeting, there was a long discussion about the viability of fund-raising along the route so far taken. The traditional form just hadn't worked; there were any number of reasons. Again, we returned to Tony's idea of using the charity for bursaries and assistance with student-funding, while creating a commercial company to fund and run the school. The key element here was the return on capital which investors might justifiably expect. In the original estimates, profitability had been planned at ten per cent of turnover. It was felt that those prepared to provide risk capital would be expecting a return nearer to twenty per cent. While the tail end of the old fund-raising strategy was taken over by Shirley – a charity performance of *High Society,* Tony offered to speak with KPMG, as well as Guiness Mahon, the city merchant bankers, for their advice. Everyone agreed.

By the next meeting, there had been a positive meeting between Tony, me and his chums at Guiness Mahon, the latter believing that a commercial plan for the building was feasible. The first step was to prepare a business plan. This fell to me. Rupert Grey, my oldest friend and a lawyer, also joined the Trust, since the appointed lawyer had been relocated elsewhere in the country. Rupert explained how the commercial company might be structured with seventy-five per cent of the shares being held by the SPA Trust and the remaining twenty-five per cent being held by fifteen subscribers; each contributing £100,000 as a prestige investment.

Rupert had raised an issue which was going to keep him busy for some time and pre-occupy the founders for years: how could we even maintain sufficient control to enable our aspirations to be met, when it was generally acknowledged that who pays the piper calls the tune?

Two months later when the business plan was complete and sent to Guiness Mahon for their reaction, this issue surfaced again. Would loan stock be enough or would investors want a controlling share? In which case, what would happen to us? I was also wondering what would happen to me.

By July, 114 approaches to investors had been sent with the following results: definite turn down: 33; 'not on this occasion': 7; possibly: 3.

City Technology College Chief advises against a CTC for the SPA

By the next meeting a month later, I had investigated a new government initiative called City Technology Colleges. This seemed to have some philosophical connection with US magnet schools, where either a specific secondary school specialised in a given skill (performing arts, sport, or technology for instance) with pupils from neighbourhood schools being bussed in for an afternoon or day of concentrated teaching of that skill or, within a given district, most schools would be enabled to teach a particular specialism and pupils would attend full-time.

I visited Cyril Taylor, the man identified with getting this off the ground for the government. Mr Taylor had advised me that this was not the route to go down: dealing with government bureaucracy was energy-sapping, independence would vanish and, anyway, the scheme was geared around technology. Computing seemed to be a main focus.

The Investment Memorandum

What was now being called the Investment Memorandum was available. We were struck by many facts, most of them financial: all the costs had greatly increased the original figure. While climbing the mountain, albeit slowly, the mountain had grown higher.

Within a month, we had to recognise that cold sending was not about to work. Personal contact, both with key network people and potential donors known to them, would be the way forward. Tony would set up a meeting with Lord Goodman, former Chair of the Arts Council, to try out the feasibility of the Investment Memorandum and see if he could suggest further contacts. Meanwhile a hit-list of contacts was also drawn up.

Two months later saw a trustees' meeting with just two trustees present, with Bergen observing. Despite the work on the Investment Memorandum, just two people had been contacted: George Martin had asked Richard Branson for a £250,000 loan, investment or donation or a combination. Lord Goodman had been impressive to meet, but silent on action. By this time, 277 trusts, foundations and companies had been approached. The tally was now 115 uninterested; 162 yet to respond. It was decided that December would see the review of this new initiative. In the meantime, I was worried that the steam was truly leaving the kettle with even my friends losing interest. Tony, meanwhile, took it all in good heart, but I felt that if Tony left, the dream would be over.

A month later the trustees were urging me to devote myself full-time to the SPA, as long as the SPA could guarantee my current salary for five years. This put me in an unenviable situation. While I was the originator of the SPA and longed for its success, I was also the originator or part-originator of the three existing colleges. The first two were achieving financial and educational stability, but neither was a given and needed wholehearted commitment to maintain. A month later, I'd reached my decision: I could not leave my original creations, but, if the commercial route proved successful, the SPA might offer shares to my main college in recompense.

A suggestion from Robert Davies had borne fruit: Prudential Assurance had offered a secondee for a year, so Margaret Bown came on board. The Prudential was also prepared to allow Margaret to continue if the commercial route flourished. 3is and Charterhouse Development and well as the Greater London Enterprise Board were due to be met. Glyn Johns, the record producer, seemed interested in the commercial route, as was Richard Branson. I had suggested to George that Paul McCartney, George Harrison and Elton John might be people worth contacting for a loan or donation.

1988 dawned. The brightest light was Glyn Johns, who thought the idea and the investment memorandum were excellent. He suggested he might invest £300,000 subject to attracting other investors, in which he would play a part. It was time to contact all the existing patrons to share the thinking and obtain their approval. Yamaha Kemble had offered £5,000 of equipment and Isaac Tigrett of Hard Rock Café fame offered a launch party.

By March, Greater London Enterprise expressed 'strong interest' in the project. Tony had met an old chum of his who made offers of help in three areas which included being an investor, helping to find a suitable building and donating management time. All of a sudden, there was another breeze; the Greater London Enterprise Agency were next in line. Even Terry Ellis attended the March Board Meeting seriously challenging the possibility he might break his 1997 record of attending one meeting a year.

Then it happened.

I was busy recruiting students in Sulawesi, West Malaysia, when Margaret sent me a telex:

DEAR MARK

MAIN POINTS FROM TONY FIELD'S LETTER:-

GEORGE MARTIN HAD LUNCH LAST THURSDAY WITH RICHARD BRANSON, HIS HEAD OF FINANCE AND CYRIL TAYLOR (CIVIL SERVANT RESPONSIBLE TO THE CABINET FOR CTC GRANTS).

BRANSON SUGGESTED HE SHOULD PUT UP £1M WHICH CYRIL TAYLOR SAID HE WOULD 'MATCH' WITH £4M. IN FACT, HE WOULD FIND GOVERNMENT FUNDING OF 80 PERCENT OF THE TOTAL REQUIREMENT UP TO MAXIMUM £9M. BRANSON WOULD NOT BE DRAWN ON FURTHER FUNDING AND WANTED THE INVOLVEMENT OF OTHER SPONSORS, HE DID NOT CLARIFY WHETHER HIS FUNDING WAS TO BE GROSS OR NET OF TAX.

GOVERNMENT'S CONDITIONS:-

1 NO FEE PAYING STUDENTS SINCE GOVERNMENT WOULD PROVIDE £2,000 PER ANNUM PER PUPIL.

2 SCHOOL SHOULD ACCOMMODATE APPROX 1,000 STUDENTS SINCE THIS WAS CONSIDERED THE MOST ECONOMIC UNIT AND IT WAS ASSESSED THAT THE INFRASTRUCTURE REQUIRED FOR MANY LESS STUDENTS WOULD BE THE SAME AS FOR 1,000.

3 SCHOOL SHOULD BE BUILT ON THE BASIS OF 90,000 SQUARE FEET IN A 'LIVING AREA' OF APPROX 5 ACRES. THIS WOULD RULE OUT THE CENTRE OF LONDON. IT WAS SUGGESTED A 'DEPRESSED AREA' SUCH AS BRENT OR HARINGAY WOULD BE DESIRABLE.

4 GOVERNMENT WOULD INSIST ON A STUDENT STARTING AGE OF 11.

GEORGE MARTIN THOUGHT THAT ON THIS BASIS HE COULD BRING IN FURTHER FINANCIAL AID (EG FROM YAMAHA) AND WISHED TO TALK TO US BOTH IMMEDIATELY ON YOUR RETURN SINCE IT WAS INTENDED THAT THESE PROPOSALS SHOULD GO TO CABINET LEVEL WITHIN ABOUT 2-3 WEEKS AND HE NEEDS FAST REACTION.

LETTER ENDS

LOVE MARGARET

How had this come to pass?

The British Phonographic Industry's fight for copyright

One of, if not, *the* key issue in 1987/8 for The British Phonographic Industry (BPI – essentially the trade association of the British record industry) was copyright. The issue coalesced around an outdated 1956 Act, the anomalies of which had come to light as had the wish to strengthen the hand of copyright owners against infringers.

Part of the drive was a blank tape levy. At a meeting with MPs, BPI Director General, John Deacon had explained that nine out of ten blank tapes were used for copying music. When the Copyright Bill was revealed at the Department of Trade and Industry on the 30th October 1987, the blank tape levy was not included. In the BPI's newsletter, he lamented 'the record industry is…seen as a cultural soup kitchen in which everyone may eat irrespective of their needs'. He was particularly irritated because government appeared to be supporting the introduction of a levy – in a Green Paper, White Paper and in many policy statements.

On the horizon were two other allied dangers: DAT and CD rental shops, the latter became summed up within the general heading of a rental right (the right to authorise or prohibit rental). The legitimate protection that the industry was seeking would be impossible without political support and therefore action. Clearly cultivation was needed, but time was short.

During the Second Reading debate about CD rental shops, Lord Winchilsea said that '95% of those who rent, copy the rented album at home. Retail outlets in areas with record shops have seen sales decline by up to 60%'. He was referring to the CD rental situation in Japan. I had been told that Richard Branson had flown Lord Young, the then Secretary of State for Trade and Industry, to Japan to witness this first-hand. By the time the Copyright Bill received its third and final reading in the House of Commons, copyright owners had an unfettered rental right. Richard then turned round to the industry and, in effect, said, 'I've got you out of your hole, now please support the school I am a patron of.' It's said he got a grudging OK.

The links between Richard Branson, Kenneth Baker, the BPI, CTC Trust and the SPA Trust

There was a connection between Richard and Kenneth Baker. All of a sudden, a number of pieces fitted together: an approach to the BPI by George Martin, the need for the BPI to cultivate political friends, a response from the BPI to Richard and Kenneth Baker, the then Secretary of State for Education, need (and so Cyril Taylor's need) to breathe life in the flagging City Technology College initiative.

The catalyst was the School for Performing Arts.

At our May 1988 meeting, the SPA's trustees cautiously decided to move forward with the CTC idea. On the one hand, there was relief that at last there seemed a chance that we could set up our first school; on the other, there were reservations about the CTC concept, the criteria used, educational compromises that might have to be made and the reservations Cyril Taylor himself had frankly outlined.

Meanwhile, 3is had indicated they were disinterested in equity funding since the SPA's projected return was not high enough (nearer the thirty per cent to forty per cent was their mark), but could be interested in property finance.

I went to the Unites States again, this time visiting Richard Klein in Miami as Principal of the New World School of the Arts in Miami.

I'd wandered into a voice class with Richard in the New World School. It was a break. The instructor was out. The student pianist began playing; the lead singer began singing; other voices joined in and, within moments, the whole class was performing for us. It was impossible to say where art and reality separated; it seemed as if I was witnessing *Fame* for real. Even more telling was Richard's response outside the classroom. You'd have to know that he'd spent some time complaining to me about the effects of the film: endless phone calls, a surge of applicants and so audition work, misapprehensions about the ethos and nature of the school. Outside the classroom, all this was forgotten. Richard's eyes were moist and dancing as he said, 'That's *Fame!*'

The problem with the word

A 'fame school' has now become synonymous with a performing arts school at a variety of levels: school, college or university. The mixed feelings that the New York staff experienced are experienced today. Whenever LIPA is described as a fame school, some degree-teaching staff cringe. They cringe because the undergraduate work LIPA expects is disciplined, has depth and requires the skills needed to complete a university degree; they cringe because it belittles the motivation that students bring; they cringe because students' work is designed to feed a life, not just a short-term, possibly blind and likely to be ignoble hope.

Malcolm McClaren believes that attempting to be famous is not the starting point; you would simply be copying the familiar. The starting point is recognising the peculiarity of what the inner you wants to express. The first he calls kareoke; the other, authentic.

On the other hand, the film and the television series, which followed Alan Parker's film (from Christopher Gore's book) raised the profile of and popularised the work of performing arts schools to a new level – a level some would argue is not deserved – after all we are not saving lives (although, on occasion, exercising imagination can have this humanising effect). This may be the pact that has to be made to achieve recognition. And in education and training, including LIPA, you can even find people wary about a simple word like 'showbiz' because it doesn't sound serious. LIPA's working title for the main degree was a Bachelor of Arts in Entertainment – which staff felt wasn't serious enough – so it was dropped. Then there's the subjective spectrum between high and low artifice which applies to every creation. The best, by offering most of us something, can be both. How would you classify Edward Elgar or Raoul Dufy or Elmore Leonard or W Somerset Maugham or Fred Astaire?

Chapter Four

The UK government's response to Britain's employment problems – how City Technology Colleges emerged as one solution

The SPA was about to become part of a broader scene, without realising it. While we were trying to turn our dream into reality, research, opinion and the government of the day were contemplating the relevance of existing education and training for the role they envisioned Great Britain taking in the future.

This chapter is about the context of British education and training in the 1980s, which you are welcome to skip because it's inevitably diagnostic. If you do, the story continues in the next chapter. On the other hand, millions of taxpayer pounds went into one solution: city technology colleges and it might interest you to know why they did.

The problem facing Britain in the 1980s was its relatively poorly educated and trained population in comparison with leading European and some Far Eastern countries. The key lay in children of average and below average ability, using attainment in core subjects, particularly three: native language, mathematics and a foreign language. Research was showing that in basic arithmetic seventy-five per cent of German pupils from their secondary modern schools could correctly answer a sum involving addition and subtraction of decimals; the British equivalent was twenty-five per cent and the problem was getting worse. This was gloomy enough, but when allied with limited vocational training, it made the British workforce uncompetitive. School pride resided in academic high flyers. Vocational skills were considered 'training' rather than 'education' and so were usually undertaken after leaving school – again a feature not paralleled in competitor countries. The television series, *Aufwiedersein Pet* was a paradigm: other countries were having to import unskilled workers to do the simple jobs, and Britain was one of the places they were coming from.

Politicians were shifting their focus – away from the education business towards the marketplace. Kenneth Baker said that 'education can no longer be led by the producers...education must be shaped by the users'.

Two government departments addressed themselves to the problem, not always in collaboration, but with success.

The first was the Department of Employment and its agency, the Manpower Services Commission, brought together job placement and industrial training, trying to improve the second for young people and adults, particularly the unemployed. Training for Opportunities (TOPs), Youth Opportunities Programme (YOP), Skillcentres and Open Techs (for home based training), The Youth Training Scheme (YTS) and the Technical and Vocational Educational Initiative (TVEI) were the main instruments used.

As is so often the case, individuals brought their own passions to bear. David Young (the same Lord Young flown to Japan) who was chair of the MSC from 1982 to 1984 and was Secretary of State for Employment from 1985 to 1987 had a long association with the Organisation for Rehabilitation through Training (ORT). Started in Tsarist Russia, ORT was an organisation designed to provide technical training for young Jews and became an international force for technical and technological education. Its fundamental outlook was to combine the practical and the theoretical, the educational and the vocational. The key for the MSC was the integration of training with education, during secondary education.

And the key implement was the Technical and Vocational Initiative because it moved directly into secondary schools by improving the technical and vocational education of fourteen-to-eighteen-year-olds and linking this with employment needs. For pupils on the scheme, learning and work experience schemes took up twenty-five per cent of their timetable.

By 1985, the government introduced a Certificate of Pre-Vocational Education (CPVE) a one-year course combining general education, practical skills and work experience. By 1986, the government announced a National Council for Vocational Qualifications (NCVQ) to bring vocational qualifications within a new national framework and to ensure standards of competence.

The second was the Department of Education and Science (DES) who replaced the old Certificate of Secondary Education (CSE) and the General Certificate of Education (GCE '0' levels) with the General Certificate of Secondary Education (GCSE) in 1986. It was designed to test practical skills as well as knowledge and to apply to a wide ability range.

There was also a change in the way schools were run. Governing bodies were required to have greater parental representation and wider responsibilities. Local management schemes were made mandatory; under these, schools were to draw up and be responsible for their own budgets. Schools, as long as parents wanted this, were able to opt out of local authority control to be directly grant-aided by the government (Grant Maintained Schools).

The third area of reform was the direct involvement of the government with the school curriculum. From the early '40s, there was just one area of prescribed curriculum by law – religious education; by 1988, there was a mandatory national curriculum imposed on local authority schools by the Education Reform Act, together with the compulsory testing of pupils to national criteria at seven, eleven, fourteen and sixteen. The idea was that it was to be phased in gradually, and was not to be in full operation until 1996.

For City Technology Colleges (CTCs), new schools in effect, it seemed that the national curriculum was a fact of life from day one. The national curriculum then was not the national curriculum we have now. The problem for new CTCs was how to fit in all they were planning to do within a school day and within a school year that was about to be circumscribed.

Other schemes too, on a national scale, were being developed. One was the compact scheme, operated in the USA, notably in Boston. Under these, employers guaranteed jobs to pupils who achieve agreed standards. The first British example was operated in London, involving Whitbread and the Inner London Education Authority (ILEA). The Department of Employment then started funding and promoting the scheme elsewhere.

The point was that CTCs were introduced at a time of education and training change. In a sense, they were the sons of TVEI: why not have an entire school offering a TVEI type of curriculum – a good general education with a technological emphasis and a bias towards vocational skills and the world of employment?

They were also to be the British version of American magnet schools – the New York High School for Performing Arts (which Kenneth Baker had visited) being just one example.

The stage was set.

By the time Kenneth Baker took over as Secretary of State for Education, he could build upon some of these initiatives and ideas for a new kind of technical and vocational school which had been floating around the DES during Sir Keith (later Lord) Joseph's time and was contained in a key paper provided by Robert Dunn, MP, Minister of State for Education in February 1986.

There was four ways in which these new schools, CTCs, would be unique: their status, their funding, their curriculum and their location. Each one was a red rag to any number of bulls; each one involved the founders of the BRIT School in debate, advocacy and publicity.

First then, status.

Each CTC was to be a registered independent school for about 1,000 eleven-to-eighteen-year-olds, controlled and managed by its own promoters. Yet no fees were to be charged. So CTCs were outside local government control and yet part of the publicly provided education system since fees were supported by national taxation.

Next, funding.

This was to come partly from the promoters (private companies, trusts and foundations, or individuals) and partly from the government. There was a distinction between capital and revenue costs. Promoters were expected to meet the costs of the buildings and equipment 'or to contribute a substantial part of those costs'.

Next, the curriculum.

This was directed in the early years by the national curriculum and, post-sixteen, by a heavy vocational emphasis.

And, finally, location.

The location of CTCs in inner city areas was motivated by inner city regeneration. Catchment areas became key – the idea was an inner city catchment area of about five thousand secondary age children. Parents were also expected to commit themselves to the school ethos and to doing what they could to keep their children at school beyond sixteen.

That's about as far as I need to take you before you witness the creation of a new school, the first non-fee-paying school, devoted, the SPA hoped, to the performing arts in London.

Chapter Five

The key meeting between the SPA Trust and the CTC Trust – my first journey to the Croydon site – Richard Branson's negotiations with the Department of Education and Science (DES) – the creation of a city arts and technology college category and its presentation to parliament – Richard's private-sector funding idea – the first hint of curriculum difficulties – the first set of architects get going – the BRIT Trust – the Abbey Road press conference – the Liverpool initiative gets its first airing

Apart from noticing Cyril Taylor's white hair and the fact that he wasn't particularly old (for some reason, I hadn't been paying attention to such details the first time around), I spotted that, behind Cyril's desk, he had framed letters he'd received from Margaret Thatcher. Only a particular kind of man does that, I thought, without coming to a conclusion about what kind of man that might be. In fact, there was hardly the time. Cyril absorbed such psychological space that it was difficult to recall what you wanted to say.

Margaret Bown, (complete with a list of questions) and a representative from the DES, also attended this first key meeting.

The significance of this meeting (and the minutes that were agreed by those attending) was that this was the information on which we decided to create the first and only-to-date CCTA. To assess how the school diverged from the original philosophy is only possible against original statements and this meeting provided them.

Cyril launched into the two major problems facing CTCs – finding sponsors and finding a site, the latter was a particular problem – most urban councils were Labour-controlled, the last thing they wanted was a conservative initiative in their midst. (This difficulty meant the CTC Trust had at times to exercise some subterfuge.) If Richard Branson and co-sponsors could come forward with £2.25 million, the government could match this with some eighty per cent uplift to create a total of £11.25 million for the site and the building. There had to be minimum investment of £1 million. Which site seemed to be a site being purchased for another CTC in Croydon. The site was large enough to accommodate two schools, in particular one with performing areas and studios. The sponsors for the other CTC were Phil Harris of Queensway Carpet fame and David Lewis of the Hampton Trust.

A decision had to be made soon. He wanted to meet Richard Branson, the sponsors of the other Croydon CTC, myself and members of the SPA Trust the following week. He added that should the SPA share a site with another CTC, it would be possible for pupils to receive their academic education from eleven at the CTC and start their vocational training with the SPA at thirteen.

He also explained that as things stood, the SPA could not exist as a CTC since it did not meet the criteria, so an amendment to the Education Act was due to be presented in parliament, which would allow the SPA to exist as a City Arts College. It would, initially at any rate, be the only school of its kind.

The meeting agreed that the SPA should set its aims high. It should be a national school with evening classes and a resource centre for performing arts teachers.

From this it followed, the SPA could accept pupils from any part of the country, provided they found their own accommodation. However, the high demand for places would probably mean that there would not be pupils from outside London, so any initial worry about the possibility that there might not be enough pupils of sufficient quality was groundless.

There was no problem with the use of part-time professionals for the vocational courses, nor would auditions be a problem. They would merely replace the aptitude tests used by CTCs. Selection was to be the major bone of contention and ran against the ethos of CTCs because CTCs deliberately chose a representative sample from across the ability range. I felt that mixed ability for vocational pupils was unlikely to ensure employment in what was a highly competitive area of work.

On the legal side, Cyril recommended starting a new company limited by guarantee. The sponsors would become the founder shareholders and would own the school. They would appoint the school governors to represent a cross-section of the public in the catchment area. The governors would appoint key staff and expect them to be responsible for the day-to-day running of the school.

The SPA, as an independent school, would not have to comply with the national curriculum but give certain assurances to obtain government funding. These assurances would have to contain the core subjects of English, Maths and Science. Religious education was mandatory but could be included as part of another subject, such as ethics.

My concern about the higher-than-average expense of delivering a performing arts curriculum was met by an observation that fees could be charged for individual instrumental tuition as was already happening in maintained schools.

It's easy now to see how I and other SPA members were later both relieved and delighted. Despite initial misgivings, we could create the school we'd been planning for years. There might need to be some marginal adjustments, given the needs of the major funders, but these weren't going to be significant.

My first journey to the Croydon site

Two weeks later, I found myself on the first of my many train journeys to Selhurst, near Croydon, south of London. I was to meet Richard Branson, Cyril Taylor and Donald Naismith (Chief Education Officer for Croydon) on site. It was now a shared site, a site that formed part of an existing further education college. The staff and students were bemused seeing a media-rich figure like Richard wandering unannounced around their campus. For me, it was an encounter with the surreal.

Later it appeared that the visit was being impelled by political necessity and the pressure upon the CTC Trust to demonstrate results. Locally, and this was exemplified by the local press the next day, there were parallel universes; pleasure at seeing Richard, dismay about what could be happening to the site.

Branson had travelled down by car with Naismith and Taylor so that he could be briefed. I travelled down alone by train, inevitably feeling somewhat sidelined; a bystander. I was the first to arrive. Once the others rolled up, brief introductions took place, before Branson was whisked off for a tour of the site. Taylor's imperative was to maintain the CTC momentum and he dominated the visit. I took the snaps.

At the end of the visit, after the shaking of hands, Naismith asked Branson if he'd mind signing an autograph for his daughter, who was a fan of his. The switch from politics to show business made an impression on me and was to happen again and again.

There was nothing more for the major players to say to each other, without the benefit of reflection, so Richard had decided to take a train back to central London, which meant that, as I was set to do the same, I could have some undivided time with the man everyone felt held the key to their goals.

This was the first time I spent time with Richard alone. As the train rattled towards Blackfriars Station, and putting to one side Richard's physical resemblance to my all-time favourite American singer/songwriter, Carly Simon, I began to pour out my hopes. Richard didn't seem to be listening to me; most of the time he gazed at a point above my head. I inwardly quailed; I was having no impact at all. After a while I decided that Richard was probably trying to avoid the inevitable gaze of strangers when faced with a national figure sitting on their suburban train. At the time, I was filled with the sensation of an opportunity completely missed.

Once the press had hold of the story, (a picnic compared to a year later) I was responding on Richard's behalf to letters he was receiving asking for help with other performing arts projects. At the moment, it seemed that the SPA was achieving its goal, I was busy on a millionaire's behalf turning down everyone else's.

Richard's negotiations with the Department of Education and Science

I next met Richard on *Duende*, his houseboat moored in Little Venice. This was a unique business venue that doubtless charmed most who stepped on board. However disarming the surroundings, Richard promptly settled down to business.

He had to decide whether he was prepared to support an arts CTC so that an amendment to the Education Bill going through parliament could be introduced to accommodate this departure from the CTC model. Over a series of May meetings, Richard decided he would, but there would be terms. The letter he wrote Kenneth Baker began by confirming his agreement to be a major sponsor for a City Arts College, although he did not want any publicity about his possible sponsorship until seven issues were decided:

1   determination of the location of the
    CAC and determination of the cost of
    building a building with a decent
    auditorium;

2 determination of the annual revenue
   funding payment, bearing in mind the
   higher than average cost of providing a
   performing arts curriculum, particularly
   for sixth formers;

3 determination of the time payment spread
   of his sponsorship;

4 agreement that sponsorship, plus interest,
   would be returned if the school was
   abolished;

5 determination of that curriculum would
   support the breadth the SPA Trust had in
   mind;

6 agreement that, like existing specialist
   performing arts secondary schools in the
   United States, there would be an equal
   spit between academic studies and
   vocational training;

7 agreement that professionals within their
   fields could teach at the school, despite not
   being qualified teachers.

There were other concerns that didn't make the
letter:

1 how the existing trustees of the SPA could
   be woven in to the model memorandum
   and Articles of Association of a CTC;

2 determination of selection of pupils:
   restriction to the local catchment area
   might not achieve the level of ability
   required.

This later point did arise once again soon afterwards
when the name of the school was considered. Debate

about the name (indeed the generic name as well: was it to be a City College for the Technology of the Arts? A City Arts Technology College? A City Arts College?) was to continue for many months. Cyril Taylor suggested 'The National College for the Technology of the Performing Arts'. Richard and I wanted 'National School for the Performing Arts', or 'college' in place of 'school' if that was a problem.

The creation of a city arts and technology college category and its presentation in parliament

The generic name was decided by civil servants and had its first outing through the amendment to the Education Reform Bill. The amendment was proposed by Lord St John of Fawsely in the House of Lords on the 27th June 1988. He began by noting a gap in the CTC programme 'which would, at any rate to a small extent, be remedied by my amendment'. He then went on to say to the House:

> This amendment would establish a new institu-
> tion – a city arts and technology college (CCTA)
> – which would specially acknowledge the impor-
> tance of technology in the arts. It is an offshoot
> of an idea which I also support – a school for
> the performing arts – in which the curriculum
> of drama, dance and music in a specialised
> way would proceed in parallel with an all-
> round general education. I think that this is a
> marvellous idea, but unfortunately it has not
> as yet made very much progress.
>
> A city arts and technology college, in order to
> come under the CTC umbrella, would have to
> differ somewhat from the original SPA
> concept. Students at such a college would
> have the opportunity to study a curriculum
> which emphasises the technological and
> practical aspects of, for example, the

performing arts. Within the framework of a broad curriculum, this would also provide an excellent vocational training, and preparation for sectors of employment which are growing fast.

For example, there are jobs in new types of music: the area of composition and production is one in which we are among the world's leaders but which in fact is fiercely competitive. There is the film industry, in which our set designers and actors are renowned throughout the world but in which the field of computer-aided special effects is now dominated by the United States. There is computer-aided graphics design, which is increasingly irreplaceable in the worlds of film, television and music. There are satellite and cable television, which are complementary to the existing information technology emphasis in CTCs. There is also set and stage design, one example of which that immediately comes to mind is the revolving stage at the National Theatre, which has added so much to the quality if its great productions.

Within a broad curriculum students in such an institution no doubt would also have the opportunity to pursue talents in dance, music and drama performance. This amendment would at least push the door open, which is important because it will encourage a wider enjoyment of the arts and involvement in them by young people.

The debate that followed was lively, although there were complaints about the timing of the amendment. Lord Beloff noted: '...that at Report stage, at 9.50 p.m., the House of Lords should invent a new kind of School...is asking rather a lot.'

Re-reading this speech today, there wasn't a minute chance a school could deliver the range of instruction being presented in the amendment.

A month or so later, after Richard and Kenneth Baker had met, Kenneth Baker responded by pointing out that inevitable boarding costs, even if 'national' could be agreed, would be a cost sponsors would have to meet, but 'national' could not be considered. Under the terms of the Education Reform Act, a CCTA would have to provide education for pupils 'who are wholly or mainly drawn from the area in which the school is situated'.

He also remained concerned about the balance of the curriculum: the title could not, in the light of the assurances he had given parliament, give the impression that the CCTA was solely about the performing arts. (Richard had noted on a draft of the original letter to Baker: '...don't have to follow school curriculum – the spirit of it.')

Richard's private sector funding idea

Thinking about private-sector finance, Richard was clear in his own mind that, as an industry school, the whole music business needed to support the venture. George Martin, as Appeal Chair of the SPA, contacted all the major record labels asking each for £350,000. Initial reactions: EMI and CBS were enthusiastic. WEA wanted to pay less than asked; Polygram was uncertain, while RCA and MCA felt pretty much the same. Over the next few months, this became a serious issue. The three existing supporters felt the same: if all the majors, plus some medium record companies, did not come in, they would withdraw, because everyone would benefit – not just them.

Despite the unanswered questions, the Education Reform Act came into being by August 1988. Croydon Council were grappling with a CCTA on the Selhurst site; first within their Education Committee. As time went on, this became another major issue.

I had tried to see how the unanswered questions might be resolved during a meeting at the DES with Will Whitehorn (representing Virgin).

The DES wanted ' performing' to be removed. Will insisted it remained. The catchment area question was interpreted within the law to be as least fifty-one per cent of the local area, but the local area was not defined. I thought this rather neat but Will insisted on a national intake. On the funding side, the DES pressed for a fifty-fifty split (Treasury: private sponsors); Will insisted on the eighty-twenty as originally specified. Over the curriculum, the DES defined the balance between national curriculum and vocational work thus: 'CTCs must have due regard to the National Curriculum.'

Over the months, Bergen and I, admittedly skating over thin ice, managed to draft a curriculum which achieved a near fifty-fifty split (academic to vocational). The name of the school was to be 'the BPI School of Performing Arts and Technology' apparently. It was also unclear quite how the existing FE college on the Croydon site would interact with the CCTA.

The first hint of curriculum difficulties

While the SPA was drawing up its preferred curriculum, a different version was being prepared by the DES. This appeared in October.

There was minimal mention of performance skills and no sight of the fifty-fifty split. In fact, 'it would share the aims and many of the characteristics of a CTC, but, within the framework of the national curriculum, it would emphasise the applications of technology in the performing and creative arts. It is the emphasis on the technology of the arts which sets a CCTA apart from a CTC.' Where performance emerged was within, as the document put it, 'flexibility about how to organise the teaching'.

Technology was still paramount. 'Indeed a CCTA curriculum should give emphasis to arts technology in the teaching of the core and foundation subjects through the teaching methods adopted, through emphasis on particular aspects of content (e.g. acoustics through physics) and via projects and themes.'

After the high voltage of private enterprise, this was to be my first experience of the low wattage of bureaucracy, low in the sense of aversion to innovation and low in the sense of ability to backtrack. Thinking back, why didn't we firmly grip this divergence at this point? I simply didn't recognise it for the problem it was. I trusted the assurances we had been given and thought it was just a blip.

The first set of architects get going

Despite the fundamental absence of an agreed curriculum, November saw the consultant architects for the new venture completing an exercise which was based upon dual occupancy of the site of the CCTA and Croydon College. The DES then stated that, on the basis of available finance, both colleges would have to integrate. Virgin wasn't keen, feeling this would not attract other possible sponsors. Three alternatives presented themselves: more sponsorship money (which could include hardware counting as cash); more government money or an alternative site.

On the legal front, the CTC Trust had agreed that the SPA's Memorandum and Articles of Association could be adjusted to incorporate a CCTA. The SPA Trustees felt that we should suggest a tripartite set of members for the new school: sponsors, the government and the SPA. The proportions should remain equal with additional members from one group balanced by an increased proportional representation from the others.

A month later, the record industry could still not resolve its group support for the school. In fact, polarisation had taken place. Phonogram could not be persuaded to support proposed CCTA, while CBS favoured lending their financial support, rather than donating money outright. On the positive side, Virgin,

EMI and WEA had suggested support of £350,000 each, while A&M were prepared to contribute £25,000. It took another month for a definite resolution.

The BRIT Trust

After a while, the existing six major record companies pledged £150,000 each; the four medium-sized companies a further £25,000 each, with contributions coming in from minor and independents. It had also been decided that the BPI would set up a trust: The British Record Industry Trust, BRIT for short, to fund the industry's present and future charitable initiatives, the first being the school.

At first glance, this looked excellent; at closer inspection, this funding would leave the school short. The project cost regarded by government was roughly £5,000,000 – with £2,000,000 coming from sponsors.

Despite this, the BPI was busy organising a press conference at Abbey Road Recording Studios (the famous Studio Number 3, where the Beatles, amongst others, recorded) on the 6th February 1989 to be followed by an announcement at the BRIT Awards on the 13th February at the Albert Hall.

No curriculum and no corporate structure didn't seem to be an impediment. As can often happen, an impending press conference can be a spur to focus in on issues, well, one issue at least: what exactly was the corporate structure and how would the SPA fit into it?

The lawyers for the main parties (BPI, CTC Trust and the SPA Trust) met, for the first time, on the 12th January 1989. The focus was to be the company that was entrusted with the project – a subject close to our heart.

Although this was a first meeting, the BPI lawyer described the school as a BRIT concept. How so? wondered Rupert (for the SPA) out loud and proceeded to remind everyone present whose concept it was. The BPI lawyer conceded the history but went on to observe that we had been unsuccessful in getting the project off the ground. How so? (again) wondered Rupert out loud, observing that the BPI's support inclined him to take the view that the SPA's efforts had been moderately successful. He went on to say that we saw the school as a partnership between the arts world as represented by the SPA and its patrons and the world of commerce represented by the BPI. If the school was to succeed in this marriage, it should be an equal partnership.

The lawyers then started to construct the new company without instructions from their clients. The model chosen was one where they were two sponsors (the SPA and the BPI), each empowered to appoint primary members (three each) with the secretary of state appointing the seventh. Together they would appoint the Board of Governors. The lawyers also established that there was an immediate need for two personnel: a Project Director and an Educational Advisor. The meeting broke up with people promising to consult with their clients.

When Rupert contacted me, he warned me that the BPI had little natural inclination to give us suitable representation in the running of the new school and if we weren't careful and active, we would be left behind.

I called an extraordinary SPA meeting at once. A raft of initiatives and meetings were decided with the intention of ensuring that the originators were not legally sidelined. The key matter was our representation on what came to be called the primary members – the people who had the power to control the new school.

The BPI was being advised by the CTC Trust that sponsors (who would have the power to appoint primary members) were cash investors. Rupert had pointed out that the proposed school grew from a different point than other CTCs; they were government initiatives which had sought private sponsors to support them; the London school had been conceived and developed, not by government, but by a charity with the support of both charitable funds and hard unpaid work and as such could be seen as a contribution equivalent to financial sponsorship. In this, Rupert, on behalf of the SPA's Trustees, was anxious to protect the thinking which had given rise to the project; it was this, after all, that the patrons were supporting. There was some comfort in the likely outcome of two immediate posts for the project: a Project Manager to manage the physical aspects of the thing and a Senior Education Advisor to look after the curriculum, publicity, funding, academic direction, appointments of staff and pupil enrolment. However, this was likely to be temporary; we sought an ongoing relationship with the project we had fostered.

Clearly a face-to-face meeting was needed. Time was running out. At the end of January, John Deacon, Director General of the BPI, Peter Jamieson, the Chairman of the BPI, George Martin, Rupert and I met. After a certain amount of general chat and a résumé of the project to date, Rupert pointed out that the current proposal of one SPA place amongst the primary members did not constitute a partnership between the BPI and the SPA. Peter Jamieson disagreed and went on to point out that it was important for the BPI to protect its investment. George felt 'investment' was a curious word to use; it was a donation. Rupert pointed out that the lawyer working on behalf of the government had already make it clear that there was no difficulty in the SPA being granted the status of a sponsor and having three primary members on the board. The government was prepared to leave this matter to the BPI and the SPA to sort out amongst themselves. This led on to a discussion about the composition of the management committee, which could not be formed until the primary member issue had been agreed and they appointed the management committee.

The Abbey Road press conference

The other matter that also pre-occupied us was how we were going to be represented at the press conference.

The speakers were Kenneth Baker for the government, Peter Jamieson for the BPI and George Martin for the industry and for us. Since the industry seemed uncertain about us and George was a natural diplomat, something else needed to be done. We had received the first version of Virgin's press release for the event and found...we were nowhere to be found. Michael Church, then literary editor of *The Times Education Supplement* and a friend of mine, had no hesitation in urging that we ensured that proper recognition of our work, our philosophy and our interest by briefing journalists in advance. He also advised a swift meeting with Will Whitehorn to adjust the impending press release. Will agreed to include a sheet about the history of the project.

The press release itself was tricky. Fundamental gaps existed between the DES, the CTC Trust, the BPI and the SPA about any number of aspects of the proposed school. At this juncture, it seemed that any number of spins were being put onto the project and even if there were mutually exclusive elements, the imperative was to get the show on the road and sort out the details later.

So the release, written by Will, opined that there was no question of presentations for admission; pupils 'would be selected by interview and audition at which potential pupils must demonstrate an ability in dance, music and drama... . The emphasis will be on contemporary performing arts and the commercial and technological aspects of the entertainment industry.'

As it happened, the press conference saw Rupert busy with his counterparts negotiating the composition of the primary members. The BPI wanted one from the SPA; with the help of George Martin, two were agreed, with the implication that George would be one. He hurried up to me with this news.

I was, at that moment, feeling another mixture of emotions. It was the first press conference where I knew more about the project being promoted than most, if not everyone. So I was naturally excited. In a way, despite these fundamental gaps, it seemed that this event marked the reality; it was now public knowledge, key players were being identified. I felt there was now no going back and was rather struck by Kenneth Baker making the same point, quoting from *The Phantom of the Opera* to anyone who would listen. However, once again, I felt I was looking on.

There was an impromptu reconstruction of the Beatles' familiar walk over the nearby zebra crossing. Matt Goss of the brother band, Bros, was there to provide some industry glitter, but until this moment and every moment afterwards, had nothing to do with the project. As the walkers were being arranged, George realised that I was not going to included and insisted I should be. Kenneth Baker pretended to be a headmaster marshalling his pupils and led Richard Branson, David Puttnam, Matt Goss, George Martin and me across the crossing.

During the press conference itself, the speakers had a hazy idea of what was then being called The London School for Performing Arts and Technology was actually going to do – which was hardly surprising. That taught me a sharp lesson: never enter a press conference without answers.

As it happened, a then journalist, Jerome Johnson was sitting a few seats away from me and, during what was intended to be good news about the BRIT Trust and the BRIT School as its first recipient, persistently asked tricky questions about funding and objectives. Mr Baker's special advisor later described Johnson to the press as 'a failed rock star turned arts correspondent', which, although unfair, was an attempt to underplay the as yet unworked-out issues that Johnson had skilfully drawn attention to. I stepped into the debate when it became apparent that the panel was in difficulty. Kenneth Baker became unstuck trying to emphasise the CTC brief about the technology of the arts. 'So it's not a performing arts school at all,' shouted Johnson; 'it's all about knob twiddling.'

Despite this, the following day showed a triumphant press conference with happy press photographs.

The Liverpool initiative gets its first airing

The shudder for some, not least the government and the CTC Trust who foresaw the rejuvenation of the CTC programme with other similar schools, was the piece in *The Times*. The picture showed the walk across the Abbey Road zebra crossing; the text started with 'The founders of Britain's first school for performing arts, which was announced yesterday, are planning to open a second in Liverpool with the support of Paul McCartney and the city's Labour council'. It was not going to be part of the City Technology College programme, but would be 'paid for by the entertainment industry and the ratepayer'. The piece went on to say that 'Mr Keith Hackett, chairman of the council's finance and strategy committee, said last night that the performing arts school was an integral part of plans for Merseyside's industrial recovery'. He went on in *The Times Education Supplement* to describe the Liverpool school as 'an open college for the theatre and the arts. It would cover, at least, secondary schooling through to adult education and training.'

How had this come about?

Chapter Six

Pete Fulwell, the manager of The Christians and Keith Hackett, the Chair of Finance for Liverpool City Council appear – my first Liverpool visits – early Liverpool activity

Once George Martin had raised potential support for the London school with Paul, I wrote the more detailed letter. His then manager, Stephen Shrimpton had written back informing me that Paul felt Liverpool needed the same 'given the desperate plight of the northern provinces...and he would certainly be more than happy to lend his name and give active support to such an institution'. I suggested an interim Paul McCartney Foundation to support pupils from the northern provinces to study at a SPA school in London. Stephen's response was simple: Paul's interest would only be held by a school in Liverpool, and he would see if there was local interest in the idea.

News of the BRIT School had interested two key people in Liverpool.

Pete Fulwell and Keith Hackett appear

Pete Fulwell, then busy managing The Christians, was also involved with Liverpool City Council in discussions about the musical future of the city. Following the discussions, he had undertaken to write a report, 'Music City' about elements of a possible musical future for the city. He contacted Clive Banks, MD of The Christians' record label (and was initially on the Steering

Committee for the BRIT School), who suggested he contact George, who suggested he contact me. Pete's interest was to describe (and ultimately achieve), in the one section of his report, the creation of a music performing resource for the city, to provide a level of expertise, independent from political dogma.

Close on his heals was Keith Hackett, then the city's chair of finance. He had an intense interest in the capacity of the arts to rejuvenate inner cities and, outside his city council work, was reporting for the embryonic arts and entertainment lead body for national vocational qualifications for the range of activities (and so employment) the sector encompassed.

Opening their copies of the *Liverpool Echo* on the 24th February 1989, they read an open letter from Paul to the people of Liverpool. Essentially the letter linked two items: the disintegration of his old school, empty for some four years, and the possibility of creating a performing arts school in the space. 'If interest in such an idea is low then of course there is no point in carrying on. If, on the other hand, people were interested in something that would give ordinary kids such a great opportunity, then I would be more than happy to give my support to a campaign to establish a "fame"-type school in Liverpool,' said Paul.

The *Echo* invited readers to respond by printing a 'yes' and a 'no' phone line. Four days later the vote was published: 1,748 to 48 in favour of the project. Keith told me later that he'd (along with other like-minded friends) voted a number of times. When the results were announced, he'd spoken warmly of the result as well as my impending first visit to the City. He had also in a later piece in *The Times Educational Supplement* stated that the council had no intention of making its plans fit the CCTA mould.

My first Liverpool visits

As I set eyes on the Liverpool skyline before the train entered Lime Street Station, I was entranced. This was the place where the Beatles began. Their songs had given form to my teenage years, as they had millions of others. Christmases then had been Beatle Christmases; the latest album followed by a dive to the bedroom, which lasted into the New Year and beyond. Up until this moment, Liverpool was simply a name, a name that conjured up images. Here was the solid reality.

I had no idea what a chair of finance might look like and what etiquette he might respect. I anticipated an accountant-type figure and dressed accordingly. I hadn't anticipated Keith; the first impression and word that popped in my mind was 'student'. Not only was he decidedly not an accountant-type figure, but an enthusiastic, round-glassed, heavy-smoking, outgoing man, younger than me.

Keith was not a follower of fashion. I remember being with Keith when he was introduced to the Earl of Wessex after a first night at Liverpool Playhouse. Yes, Keith was wearing a somewhat forlorn mackintosh indoors, but also yes, the royal personage looked at Keith and stiffly commented that he looked like a bookie. There was no ready answer that sprang to the listeners' lips.

We talked about our ideas. Keith was anxious to build upon and expand the work being undertaken by Hope Street, which was a partnership between the Everyman Theatre (where Willy Russell and Alan Bleasdale amongst others had had their work first performed) and Liverpool City Council to provide quality theatre training opportunities for all the communities of Liverpool. This was largely achieved through short course workshops.

Pete was also there, thoughtful and tired, but committed both to Liverpool and the city's musical future. He described the 'Music City' report, which he had agreed to undertake. As we all parted, Keith promised to show me round Paul's old school, The Liverpool Institute for Boys.

On the next visit, a month later, Keith opened the double doors at the front of the Liverpool Institute for

Boys. I stepped into the building for the first time; in fact, the gloomy hallway for the first time. Although the building was busily decaying with its full complement of wet and dry rot (the rotten roof had allowed water to cascade down the interior of the building to the basement where a mini swimming pool was forming), there was a grandeur I had never seen in London. The grandeur partly came from the quality of original workmanship in the Georgian building (parquet flooring, ceramic basins, mahogany throughout for work benches, the height of the rooms) and partly from the location (the expanse of the solid Liverpool Anglican Cathedral from every back window and the neat Georgian houses from the front – it was a visual arrest from both sides). There was also the sheer size – bigger than both parts of the BRIT School, more akin to the empty London secondary school building I'd also set my heart on. There was passageway upon passageway; gloomy, damp, littered with fallen plaster, upturned books, syringes, even a dead cat but potentially grand, once simple partitions had been taken away.

It was a re-run of my experience in Southwark. This time I peopled the building with school pupils shouting as they went from classroom to classroom; in the main hall, I could hear the headmasters, over the decades, holding assembly. The chemistry lab at the top of the building still had experiments out on the benches – it was as if the last bell had sounded just five minutes before, rather than five years ago. Human life had just drained away.

Viewing the line of Honours Boards, I wondered what calibre of school had it been where a former pupil who had achieved the Nobel Prize for Physics was listed on a board headed 'Miscellaneous Honours'.

I felt I was experiencing the childhood of decades, countless stories clamoured in what was now a silent, solemn stage in a glorious two-tier assembly room. I was overwhelmed. The building reverberated in my imagination on the train back to Euston.

Early Liverpool activity

Keith, Pete and I met a variety of arts organisations. Keith had done his work in preparation. The final meeting was with various local councillors who had agreed on a further feasibility study for a performing arts institute.

Just occasionally in the years which followed, I came across bureaucrats who had not learnt how to become human beings through a correspondence course – Mick Farley, then working for Liverpool City Council was one of the first. A quirky and questioning soul with pictures of the mountains he had climbed covering the walls of his office, alongside thoughtful quotations, Mick dispatched a letter to the Training Agency asking for £24,500 from the Work-Related Further Education Development Fund 'to carry out a research project investigating the development of performing arts education and training in the city'. There was a prospect, the application said, 'of a substantial sum coming into the city to establish an education and training facility for the performing arts, but the source appears to wish to operate on a partnership basis with the City Council rather than provide money to any one organisation/agency'.

Much to many people's surprise, the Training Agency agreed to fund the research. The surprise resided in the fact that this was true research; no one had the faintest idea what shape the initiative might take.

The start of a feasibility study wasn't the only activity taking place.

Keith pulled together a day in the town hall to explain to me, with Susan Fey (then chief executive of the CTC Trust) as listener and information-giver what, in broad terms, was happening in the city and what key individuals felt the needs were. There was a wide range of opinions reflecting the breadth of performing arts activity throughout the city, delivered through equally broad outlets and mechanisms. It seemed that he wanted to pull all the activity together in some way within one centre.

Finally, an interview with the *Liverpool Echo* was also thrown in.

I can now recall how the grandeur of the room in the town hall was matched with its coldness and that to counteract this, I smoked throughout the six hours – my own small personal fire.

After returning to London, Susan Fey wrote a report for circulation to Cyril Taylor, the DES, Kenneth Baker's advisor and me. She was judicious (which left me unprepared for her onslaught six weeks later) in her assessment of the potential for a CCTA – 'a very reserved yes. Cllr Hackett's vision of a centre for performing arts is not that of a CCTA. He sees it as a place of "open access" for everyone.' She ended her report: 'As to whether it is worth pursuing the idea of a CCTA in Liverpool: I think it is worth pursuing through the medium of the SPA Trust.'

Shortly afterwards a key suggestion emerged: to tie up the investigation into an emerging institute for performing arts with the 'Music City Report'.

A month later, the brief charged the consultants to look at the feasibility of establishing an institute for performing arts which would need 'to be politically, financially and, above all, educationally acceptable'. A steering committee would oversee the consultants.

Within nine months, there would be a report examining seven major areas: scope, existing provision, demands from the industry, possible educational models, possible organisational models, the physical developments needed and the finance required and possible funding models.

Then had came the London press conference for LSPAT.

A journalist had asked about spreading a SPA-type facility beyond London. I had mentioned Liverpool, alongside other possible locations. Two journalists picked up the Liverpool theme, contacted Liverpool Council and found Keith.

When the piece came out, George counselled me to write to Paul immediately because he feared that the early release of unauthorised information would frighten Paul away. I had imagined that George also talked with Paul or vice versa.

A month later, I was writing to Richard Ogden, Paul's manager, expressing delight that Paul had agreed to my request to be a patron of the SPA Trust, as well as my other request: to contribute towards the Liverpool Feasibility Study.

Chapter Seven

*The eighth BRIT Awards – early
Croydon reaction to the Abbey Road
press conference – the BRIT School
gets underway – a flurry over costings*

Two days after the London press launch came the
eighth consecutive British Record Industry Awards or
the BRITs in the Albert Hall. This was the year when
the best British male artist was Phil Collins and the
best female, Annie Lennox; Bros, being the best
newcomers. I trotted along with Will Whitehorn who
was resplendent in a kilt. We briefly met Mr and Mrs
Baker who seemed pleased, bemused and tired, before
entering the hall. The organisers had placed the
industry and their guests in the seating, while
youngsters stood in the arena – the idea being to inject
some spontaneity into the proceedings. Spontaneity was
just what they achieved.

The moment Mick Fleetwood announced the
proceeding's pleasure at having Kenneth Baker and his
wife present, given the support from government for the
school, part of audience, the spontaneous part, jeered.
Mick did his best to make light of the incident and, in
the process, seemed to lose his place with the autocue
and somehow never quite regained it. (There may have
been technical difficulties as well.) Samantha Fox had
had difficulty with the autocue from the start. The
autocue ended up foxing them both. In the hall, the
mistakes had an element of charm and anyway two
humans were suffering; on TV later, the charm played

differently. There simply seemed to be one cock-up after another.

As the BPI's *Yearbook 1989/90* ruefully noted: 'As a public relations performance, the show failed on the night. From the outset, there were technical and management problems which turned months of careful planning into a disappointment. There were no recriminations in the aftermath but the British press enjoyed a field day in mocking many who took part and adding to the embarrassment of those involved.'

Indeed, the next day, Peter Jamieson, then chairman of the BPI, had the unenviable task of appearing on TV to answer the charge that the previous evening's BRIT Awards were symbolic of the chaos within the industry and, by the way, what's the BRIT School?

Towards the end of the BRITs, Cliff Richard was given a lifetime achievement award or (long version) Special Award For Outstanding Contribution. During his speech, he castigated the arena youngsters for their lack of manners. It was simply not right to treat guests, like the Bakers, as they had done. The youngsters shuffled, thought for a moment and then decided to jeer again. So, for the best motives, Cliff Richard, trying to right a wrong, had reminded the audience about an earlier incident they were doing their best to forget.

Early Croydon reaction to the Abbey Road press conference

The other matter that some of the audience were trying to push out of their minds were the pieces which had started to appear in the *Croydon Advertiser*. It appeared that the Abbey Road press conference had come as a complete surprise to staff and students at Croydon's new Selhurst Centre – the sizeable site visited earlier by Richard Branson and others, at least half green-field and so capable of accommodating a new building or two. It was reported that one of the new converted buildings (the old girls' grammar school), recently converted at a cost of some £250,000, would be leased to LSPAT.

Within a week, an action committee was proposed and created. Two hundred students at the existing centre staged a four-hour sit-in. When interviewed, various Croydon Council officers were at a loss. While it was true that some sort of performing arts school was in the wind, there was uncertainty about the amount of money raised by the music industry, what it was going to be used for or how much the industry was prepared to spend on the buildings it wanted or where existing Selhurst students might go to make way for LSPAT. Croydon Council's deputy leader wondered, out loud, how LSPAT would start up in just fifteen months' time.

I recalled a meeting held at the DES six months earlier, attended by Croydon Council officers, amongst others, where it had been agreed that no announcement would be made by the sponsors until a site was confirmed. What had pushed the key players into a public announcement when such uncertainty about the site existed, let alone the curriculum and a cast list of concerns, which would alight staff and students calmly going about their business on site?

We never knew.

I was also never able to discover quite how the site was chosen in the first place. When, with Tony, I finally met Lyn Agilgat, chair of the Selhurst Action Committee a few months down the line, I found that the powers that were had chosen a site which had been the subject of an eight-year campaign by another committee (Parents Against Cuts in Education – PACE) to save the site as a tertiary college. What both action committees apparently did not know was that Croydon was experiencing a forty per cent drop in further education rolls and had to relocate (if necessary) any courses which could share facilities.

The BRIT School gets underway

All this activity took place without a structure to sustain and co-ordinate the project. This is not unusual, but also not perfect. There comes a moment, often earlier, when a committee structure is put in place with a co-ordinating, strategic committee at the centre.

For 'ShowTech' (as it was next called), it was called a steering committee, which evolved into an executive committee, which was intended to evolve into a governing body.

By the time it first met in April 1989, a start had been made. Maureen Milgram had been appointed project director. I had been appointed senior academic advisor. Bergen was to be one of the education advisors. The first meeting of the steering committee had taken place at the BPI offices and had identified the immediate tasks that both Maureen and I needed to tackle. The countdown indicated a September 1990 opening – some sixteen months away.

All the while, the trustees of the SPA were meeting monthly, Shuttling back and forth between committees and individuals was an essential part of the start-up.

Each committee is a story on its own. Then there was the inter-play between the committees and last but not least, the various personalities to cope with, some easy-going and problem-solving (the dream collaborator) and some almost the exact opposite. But this is not a project handbook, this is about my journey, right now coming to grips with a process I'd never participated in before and hoping all the while the destination would be recognisable.

A flurry over costings

Up until this time, the Selhurst Development Study Group had been meeting at the DES with representatives from the BPI, CTC, DES and consultant architects and builders (these last changed in time to Cassidy Taggart). The problem for this group was how

1 Above—The fantasy in Southwark: what I was looking at.

2 Below—Cyril Taylor, City Technology College Trust executive director, Donald Naismith, Croydon Director of Education and Richard Branson, Virgin Group chairman, emerge from the Selhurst buildings.

3 Opposite—Walking across the Abbey Road during the press launch of the BRIT School were: Kenneth Baker, Secretary of State for Education; Richard Branson, Virgin Group chairman, David Puttnam, film producer; Matt Goss of 'Bros'; George Martin, record producer and Mark Featherstone-Witty.

4 Above—Talking to George Martin during the press launch of the BRIT School – the godfather of both institutions (Tim Rice on the left).

5 Below—Talking to Kenneth Baker during the press launch of the BRIT School (Julia Fordham on the left was not considered well known enough to join the group for the Abbey Road press shot).

THE LONDON SCHOOL FOR PERFORMING ARTS AND TECHNOLOGY

A CONSULTATIVE DOCUMENT

CROYDON

6 The cover of the consultative document, issued by Croydon Council, for what was to become the BRIT School.

7 Above—The BRIT Steering Committee meeting at the BPI with: Sara John (BPI observer), John Deacon (BPI nominee and BPI director general); Rupert Grey (SPA nominee); Anthony Field (SPA nominee); unidentified; Michael Levi (BPI nominee); Clive Banks (BPI nominee and director of Island Records); Susan Fey (CTC Trust) and Maureen Milgram (Project Director). Not visible or not present were Will Whitehorn (BPI nominee and head of Corporate Relations at Virgin); Terry Ellis (BPI nominee and member of SPA Trust), Patrick Isherwood (BPI nominee/BPI legal advisor).

8 Below—The press launch before Paul's 'Let It Be Liverpool' 1990.

9 Above—The photograph for the press from the first meeting.

10 Opposite—Group photograph from the European Union lunch held in Brussels with: (back row) David Walker, Steffen Smidt, Ros Reuter, Etienne Reuter, Richard Odgen, Begona Rodriguez, Peter Coldrick, John Morley, Robert Davies, Geoffrey Brown; (middle row) Steve Bagnell, Jeremy Harrison, Petrus Cornelissen, Lutti, Patricia Rawlings, Sir Jack Stewart-Clark, Ken Stewart, Christine Morley, Jean Flamson, Enrico Boarretto, Keith Hackett; (front row) Dame Jocelyn Barrow, Hywel Ceri Jones, Humphrey Walwyn, Mark Featherstone-Witty, Linda McCartney, Paul McCartney, Vasso Papandreou, John Flamson, Graham Meadows, Will Haire, Mary Banotti. Also attended: Collette Flesch.

11 Group photograph from the first fund-raising lunch held at The Performing Right Society with: (back row) Pete Waterman, Jonathan Simon, Michael Freeguard, Robert Abrahams, Mark Featherstone-Witty, Steve Lindsay, Jon Crawley, Charles Armitage, Peter Cox, Richard Ogden (middle row standing) Ken Berry, John Eastman, Paul Curran, Peter Dadswell, Stewart Slater, Stephen Howard, Steve Lewis, Stuart Hornall, Donald Mitchell, Andrew Potter, Robin Godfrey-Cass, Lucien Grainge, Joanne Cohen, (second middle row) Bob Wise, Vivian Ellis, Linda McCartney, Paul McCartney, Wayne Bickerton, Chris Wright, Jim Fifield (front row) John Axon, David Hockman, Humphrey Walwyn, Tony Silov, Tony Field, Nigel Elderton, John Billingham, Peter Reichard, Marshall Lees.

Also attended: James Little, Steven Norris MP, Adam White

to place the BRIT School on the Selhurst site within the cash limit of £5,000,000 and on time. The favoured option was to rent part of the Selhurst Centre at a peppercorn rent and with minimal upgrading to be used for teaching, administration and some basic technology, including science laboratories to meet the requirements of the national curriculum. The bulk of the spend would be on a 500-square-metre new building (hopefully headlined as 'low cost, high technology') that would house the performing arts part of the enterprise.

The architect was the ever positive Brian Taggart who had come up with the inventive idea that the new building could be built with a central, mainly two-floored, rectangle (that would accommodate the theatre, recording studios, offices, cafeteria and so on), while classrooms would jut out from this main structure with gaps between them. As more money became available, it would be possible (passageways and staircases were designed to make this achievable) to build more classrooms within the gaps.

By the time, Brian had sketched out indicative costings, based on indicative facilities required, the cost was nearer £6.5 million. Given the political trickiness and public scrutiny of the CTC programme, the first DES thought was to reduce the size and use cheaper materials, but the saving would be marginal and, in the end, not cost-effective. Given the forty-sixty gearing that the DES was now insisting upon, the sponsors were now looking at a bill of roughly £2.6 million, rather than £2 million. The £0.9 million in the budget for furniture and equipment would not cover most of the specialist equipment for the theatre, video and radio suite, recording studio and so on. Although it was hoped for donations, it would mean in time that the school would open without some facilities; this also became a moot point: if the sponsors were successful in raising more money than £2.6 million, would the DES gearing simply continue?

John Deacon who was chairing the steering committee afterwards (and who chaired most of these meetings) was at his diplomatic best. He reminded everyone that the BPI was in for £1.1 million as had been agreed. He used the time honoured 'best endeavour' statement for the remaining £1.4 million. I wondered out loud what effect the money thus far expended on the project would have. Could this be counted? At this point, it was agreed this should be put to the DES.

Site acquisition was going to be a further problem: how much would be charged for the rent for the site and for how long? And, given local activists, this could not be a peppercorn rent (and would, in time, be a six-figure sum). And how much would Croydon charge for the land on which to build the school?

Another minefield was local consultation, which had to begin straightaway: the planning permission process, which would enable and attract opposition to the scheme.

Chapter Eight

Meeting Paul (and Linda) for our first talks

May 1989, I met Paul for the first time. Although it was a business meeting, it took most of my self-control not to smile inanely or try to memorise every word. Throughout the discussion, my mind was in two places. The first place was maintaining the conversation I was having. The second place was sheer amazement: I was talking with the man who had largely shaped the soundtrack of my teenage years.

It's taken me a while to realise that, for me, when meeting an icon from my youth, I was also meeting the person I once was (and, in part, still am). It's yourself that rushes back at you.

Paul described his recent visit to the institute and the home movie he'd made. This showed him wandering around the building at night reminiscing about his school days (although he didn't mention the song about Liverpool he had sung during the visit on the stage in the main auditorium). He was anxious to enable access for working-class youngsters and to encourage them to aim high – 'if you are not aiming high, you are not aiming at all'. This was an aspiration from his parents that he treasured. He saw the well-off paying for the less well-off. He could see in particular his well-off American friends paying to send their children to LIPA (The Liverpool Institute for Performing Arts – as he wished it to be called).

I described the ideas that lay behind the London school, how they had come about and how they were being translated into a curriculum. I outlined three alternatives: an independent school; a CCTA and a resource centre; the latter capable of being combined with the first two.

Paul's liked the idea of a number of activities being combined, but was more concerned with a light in-touch shaping of natural ability and instinct. He wanted youngsters to find their own way. He wanted to discuss the whole teaching side much further. Was it to be a SPA clone or a Mark II?

Before the meeting, we had agreed there should be a photo-session to inform Liverpool people that work was going on and that they should 'watch this space'. He wanted me to be his eyes and ears and, when appropriate, mouth too.

I was excited to bits and yet needed to look calm and ambassadorial. When, later, I asked Shelagh Jones, Paul's long-time PA, if I could have some copies, some thirty copies, I noticed Shelagh gently smiling. Although I felt naïve and gauche, I could not resist sending them to my family and friends. She had witnessed yet again the effect of Paul's charm and wondered about the journey I had started with Paul.

There were to be six meetings with Paul before I watched him perform on the Albert Dock in Liverpool. One of the early next meetings was held, not at the converted Sussex mill that housed Paul's recording studio and was essentially his home work base, but in his home.

Still reacting to my excitement, I told the Hastings taxi driver the name of the country lane from which, I imagined, there would be a lengthy drive. My ill-formed, spontaneous idea was to arrive at Paul and Linda's house by foot. As I walked up the drive, I was overcome by the sensation that this was the wrong drive. What had been, however misbegotten, a romantic idea was coming to pieces.

Luckily, there was a man who opened the door of the house at the top of the drive and proceeded to direct me over a few fields, along a bank and beyond a small coppice. I saw myself actually being late. With a quickening heart, I set off, my shoes soon wet with dew. After a while, I was at a gate with a cattle grid. As if from nowhere, two burley men materialised and asked me what I was doing. After I'd finished explaining, the men enquired how I had reached the spot without transport. If it looked fishy, I felt fishy as I explained my naïve idea. They made a telephone call and I was directed to another homely house. This was not the ingle-knooked image I had unthinkingly conjured up. In fact, I wondered if this multi-millionaire lived his life as if he wasn't a multi-millionaire. Facing me was a family house with outhouses and stables beyond.

After Linda had prepared a simple lunch and had washed up afterwards, I was impressed and captivated. We had been like any strangers getting to know enough about each other to work together. There had been no barrier, other than the need for a public couple to maintain a private life.

For most of the remainder of 1989, Paul was taken up with preparations for his world tour – the first after a gap of some thirteen years. One meeting, at Shepperton Studios, fitted in during a band rehearsal break, took place in a pre-fab in the parking lot in November. Attended by Pete Fulwell, his assistant and me, we wanted to hear what he had in mind for the institute.

Sixteen was the starting age for students with a local, national and international intake. He liked the mix of performing and technical skills, but wanted a heavy bias towards popular music, also popular dance and even comedy. He was concerned about the nature of the teaching: the structure of the courses had to be flexible to meet the needs of an individual student. There should be no sense of moulding people. He wanted the teachers (or perhaps facilitators would be the best word) to be professionals in the business, with master classes being held by the world-famous.

Moving on to the revenue side, he foresaw British students attending free and again mentioned fee-paying students from abroad. He wanted students to be selected, since the aim was to develop highly talented and motivated students.

He asked us to keep him briefed so that he could maximise the media attention on the tour by developing an international profile for the institute. Thinking about the future, he was prepared to paint the old school himself: 'I'll get a load of kids together and we'll paint the place ourselves with paint donated by the paint companies.'

Finally, he asked about the finance needed to get the project up and running. I realised at that point that I had nothing for him to react to, whereupon Paul asked me what were the harsh realities of the building and was there a financial plan? I could only agree these were needed. This didn't stop Paul ruminating on local Liverpool businesses helping out by supplying material at or below cost, 'a bunch of us at Downing Street to get the government to chip in', using the old boys of the institute to take part by contributing their skills (architects, lawyers). He wanted to play an active part in fund-raising but be part of a crowd rather than being the crowd. In summary, he wanted, in terms of planning, 'a clean machine' which he reminded me was a line from 'Penny Lane'.

Chapter Nine

*Terry Ellis becomes the BPI Chairman –
confusion over ownership of the BRIT School –
the CTC Trust tell the SPA Trust to keep out of
Liverpool – the CTC movement – the first
principal and the first artistic director – Croydon
Council's internal divisions – the Selhurst Action
Committee swings into action*

The BPI's council had decided in May to nominate
Terry Ellis as BPI chairman. This was a landmark for
two reasons: the first was he would be the first non-
BPI council member to chair the BPI; the second was
the impetus we felt this appointment would herald for
'ShowTech' , since Terry was a SPA trustee. Here, at
last, was the opportunity for the SPA and the BPI to
work hand-in-glove to achieve the objectives.

Confusion over ownership of the BRIT School

Flushed with enthusiasm and frustration, I decided to
write to Terry outlining key concerns. The overriding
concern was who exactly was in charge of the creation
of LSPAT? Was it the government, the CTC Trust, the
BPI or the SPA?

This point was raised again at our next SPA trustees'
meeting. No one was certain. Terry felt there was
accumulating evidence that government appeared to be
attracting sponsors from industry merely to run CTCs
themselves. It seemed as if the DES and the CTC Trust
were filling a power vacuum. Terry went on to say that

the BPI had muddled reasons for backing the project, but would stand by their decision since it was beneficial from a PR standpoint. The discussion again reverted to the Articles of Association for the school, which no one had seen, it seemed. Why didn't Terry, with his new powers, act?

Here was the central dilemma the SPA found itself in. We were motivated by nothing more or less than a specific training philosophy. Tony, around this time, was becoming frustrated by the evidence he had seen from the DES relating to an admission policy. The DES was either ignoring or failed to understand what we were on about. He wrote and told them that 'it is absolutely essential that we do *not* attempt to produce great artists in their own media as Margot Fonteyn, Maria Callas or Sir John Gielgud. Unless the importance of our *integrated* training is properly understood, fully appreciated and totally accepted, our London school is a dead duck.'

As it happened, one of the SPA patrons, Gillian Lynne (the choreographer), writing in *The Stage* at this very time wrote: 'After *Cats* the emphasis in the job market was on technical achievement and versatility. If it had long been important for dancers to be able to sing, now it became vital that they should sing stylishly.' She went on: 'Initially, to find the cream for the first cast, I had to scour the country, and, when contracts ended, it became a regular battle to find fresh cream. For casting, despite all the hype, it was still a matter of sometimes ploughing through mediocre ground to reap a handful of blooms. It can be pulverisingly hard and depressing to find actors with a performing talent. And every choreographer I talk to says the same.'

To achieve the vision, we needed the support of the BPI. The BPI however were busy with a myriad of other industry concerns and could really only devote minimal time to an activity which, they would admit, they knew little about. Terry and others frequently reminded everyone that the BPI did not want to run a school.

To balance the influence of the DES, Terry had spoken with David Puttnam who had suggested we should go through our patron list and find eight or ten patrons prepared, once or twice a year, to attend a lunch which would also be attended by three or four journalists and three or four trustees. The patrons would be briefed by the trustees before the lunch and the purpose would be to give a view on how the activities surrounding the first school were developing. This would influence everyone, since the last thing that was wanted was highly visible people being negative. Terry thought this was an excellent idea and the trustees approved it. (During the next meeting, Terry argued against the idea and it was dropped.)

The CTC Trust tell the SPA Trust to keep out of Liverpool

We were also, as it happened, alienating the CTC Trust, through our Liverpool activity. Evidence of this began with a telephone call from Susan Fey to me. She was annoyed. Why hadn't the Liverpool Feasibility Study been cleared with the BRIT Steering Committee? This was a clear case of conflict of interest and she should, henceforward, be kept in touch with any Liverpool development.

This was all a bit strange. After all, she had been present in Liverpool just six weeks before and knew as much as I did.

Drawing breath, I wrote to her the next day pointing out that there was no conflict of interest; LSPAT was my time priority, my role in Liverpool was supervisory and advisory. I apologised for inadvertently placing her in any difficult position, but also pointed out that she had told Keith Hackett, amongst others, that I was wholly paid by the CTC Trust (which wasn't the case).

I decided it was time to clarify the SPA's role. Some of my irritation with the press seeped through. Shortly after the glimmering of the London school had been seen, *The Sunday Times* published a piece in which it was said that the SPA patrons were lining up behind Kenneth Baker for a performing arts school. I reminded Susan this was rubbish. When the SPA's patrons were being gathered by me, Mr Baker had no connection with the project. The patrons were lining up behind a concept, which they wished to see widely adopted. It could include CCTAs, but it could also include schools in Europe or, for instance, a magnet school along American lines, which Wandsworth Borough Council was then considering.

I also felt it was time to clarify the standing of the Liverpool Feasibility Study, which had to be independent if it was going to carry weight with Liverpool councillors. I reminded her that a CTC-inspired document was not the requirement. What was needed was an independent report, driven wholly by educational rationales with no political colouring.

I went on to say that the shortly-to-be-appointed project director to further CTCs in Liverpool announced in her report to the CTC Council, was premature. It would be sensible to see what our report recommended and, yes, the CCTA option would be examined.

What I did not know was that the CTC had achieved the agreement of the DES to purchase a property in Liverpool for transfer to a suitable CTC sponsor. I did know that Cyril had written to George asking him to approach Paul to support a Liverpool CTC. In response, George had recommended two things: one, that the appropriate avenue was Apple Corps (the company jointly owned by Paul, George Harrison, Ringo Starr and Yoko Ono – he had already spoken with Yoko Ono about the proposal and she was welcoming towards CTC ideals) and two, that it was too early; a convincing start to Selhurst would enhance the chance of an *Apple* approach.

At a lunch meeting with Tony and Rupert, convened shortly after the second Liverpool meeting, Cyril Taylor fumed about me 'parachuting into Liverpool'. When our role in Liverpool was pointed out, it cut no ice. Cyril

Taylor told us in no uncertain terms to keep out. Our involvement was little more than a nuisance. The possibility that our stated role of propagating other schools might be useful was discounted. Tony decided, with the trustees' agreement, that he would write to Cyril Taylor, reassuring him of our commitment to making Croydon work, but that the trustees felt they were bound to assist in the setting up of as many schools as were required and that their advice and expertise, when sought (as has happened in Liverpool) should not be unreasonably withheld. Mr Taylor did not reply.

A week earlier (which was why the lunch took place) I had been summoned to Cyril Taylor's office, who proceeded to berate me roundly for being involved in Liverpool. Plans were already afoot with the Moores family and the Royal Insurance Company; he mentioned the interest of religious denominations in the city and the highlighting of Liverpool in the original Secretary of State for Education's CTC brochure. When I reminded him that I wasn't, as yet, employed by anyone to undertake CTC-related work, Cyril swore, told me that was irrelevant and to get on with the Croydon project or he would see to it that I would find things very difficult in the future.

For Susan and Cyril, the SPA had overstepped its rightful place. For the SPA, Susan and Cyril had misunderstood the impetus that was taking Liverpool plans forward.

Meanwhile, every issue for LSPAT seemed to pivot around a lack of precision about leadership, be it sole or joint. At this point, the pressing business of appointing a principal became the next issue: who would be making the choice? We were was anxious that the appointee would endorse and foster the philosophy as we, rather than the government, saw it. It seemed likely that the DES and the CTC Trust would be anxious to secure an appointee whose credentials were more likely to suit the government's approach to the curriculum. As it happened, I dearly hoped I might be chosen, but, even if I wasn't, my prime concern was the translation of the philosophy into practice.

The CTC movement

To make matters somewhat worse, we were becoming alarmed by the profile, and so attendant emotions towards the CTC movement.

A piece had appeared in the *Independent* that began: 'The government is spending more on each City Technology College than it has allowed for the entire stock of schools in the local authority areas where the new colleges are planned.' The piece quoted the announcement brochure which said that: 'The principle of funding will be that the promoters will meet all or a substantial part of the capital costs', and went on to note 'but the Government has later forced to admit costs have been grossly underestimated and is now funding up to 80 per cent of capital costs as well as running costs... . A survey carried out by the *Independent* reveals that in all but two (Conservative controlled) of the 10 local authorities where CTCs are planned, and where capital costs are viable, the Government is investing up to 10 times more cash in one CTC than it allows the council to spend on hundreds of primary and secondary schools.'

In 1993, a study was published by the Association of Teachers and Lecturers showing that the fifteen existing CTCs raised £30,000,000 from sponsors towards the costs of £150,000,000 between 1987 to 1993, which meant total capital spending met by the taxpayer was £120,000,000 for 15,150 pupils.

From this distance and without the clamour of rhetoric and advocacy, it is worth just pausing to think about what the CTC enterprise was facing. This is not a résumé of the initiative (although a history and assessment is overdue). This is just a side view from one person, working on one unique project.

At the Council of the CTC Trust I attended on 10th July 1989 (as Richard's alternate), there was one CTC open, two due to open in September, ten due to open the following September and six the next September, in addition to three with no dates. It was akin to starting up this number of new businesses and, at the time, there were just seven full-time employees of the CTC Trust.

The reaction to CTCs could be sharp. I recall being invited to address a teachers' conference about LIPA. Two days before I was set to go on, an organising official rang me to enquire if I had had any hand in the creation of the BRIT School. When I told her I did, she told me that she and other union members would feel contaminated if I attended the conference, let alone speak. The invitation was withdrawn there and then.

Putting to one side the public rows about cost, CTCs became a home, sometimes permanent, sometimes temporary, for a plethora of individuals attracted for a plethora of reasons. For some, it was the chance to start again outside local authority control; for others, it was a chance to pioneer new curricula; for others, a chance to activate cost-effective management; for others, a chance to close the gap between education and employers; for others, a chance to bring in private-sector management techniques – and this was just the few I met. The DES was concerned with the cost of the whole enterprise, recognising on the one hand that new approaches required flexibility, while, on the other, the need for accountability within existing structures.

One example: as CTCs developed, Susan Fey was asked to see if there were points of common agreement between CTCs. In particular, she was asked to see if there was a common agreement over contracts of employment and appraisal procedures that might determine salary increases. She found it impossible to determine commonality. The 'escape to freedom' which motivated CTC supporters and employees could not contemplate external interference – even from within the same cause.

So, while everyone agreed that there needed to be proper contracts of employment, no agreement could be reached over a 'no strike' clause or that CTCs might or might not negotiate with unions. While everyone agreed that appraisal procedures were needed, no agreement could be reached linking appraisal with salary increases. The secretary of state had said that these matters were the responsibility of trustees and governors, although he did have a bottom line – there would be no pre- or post-entry closed shop.

The first principal and the first artistic director

By September 1989, the first principal of the BRIT School had been appointed, Anne Rumney, the former head teacher of Sydenham School. John Deacon told the steering committee that, because of her lack of performing arts experience, I had been offered the post of artistic director (a permanent part-time post, three days a week) with responsibility for the performing arts curriculum, forming alliances with the industry and performers and reporting directly to the governors. Everyone was delighted.

Although I was deeply disappointed not to have been the first principal, I reflected I would enjoy and be good at the alternative.

But my mind was also elsewhere. I was wondering how we were going to step through the minefield of local consultation.

Croydon Council's internal divisions

Approval for the BRIT School by Croydon Council had not been a serene affair. An education sub-committee of the council had decided to stop the BRIT School on the Selhurst site. This was a surprise for the leadership, not to say the sponsors; however, this Labour motion had been passed in the absence of Conservative councillors. A full council meeting took place soon afterwards where the item was again on the agenda. A demonstration met councillors as they entered their building, including a double-decker bus complete with students, teachers and parents urging passers-by to sign a petition.

The council meeting itself had been stormy. Once the Conservative majority councillors voted in favour of the project, so winning the strongly fought battle, the public gallery erupted. Shouting 'Shame on Fame' and 'sell out', the Selhurst Action Committee (SAC) and its supporters were removed by security guards from the chambers.

When news of this reached me, I was appalled to be involved with a place where the dream wasn't welcome. Despite the progress to date, I emotionally rang Tony to see what he felt and to suggest that, if this was the reality, we'd better pull out. Tony advised caution.

The Selhurst Action Committee swings into action

Frustrated by the final decision of Croydon Council, SAC considered their next move. They decided to write to all the SPA Patrons (and so patrons of the BRIT School) presenting LSPAT as the death knell on their highly popular, over-subscribed tertiary centre. LSPAT would take the adjoining playing fields, remove a third of the existing classrooms from Selhurst Tertiary Centre use and introduce teenagers on the site. 'It is our belief that robbed of its adult ethos, cramped into a corner of the site and offering fewer courses next year will deal a death blow to our college.'

We had no idea about this manoeuvre until one of the patrons, the actor, film director/producer and writer, Bryan Forbes, rang me up asking what was going on. Bryan fell short of withdrawing his name, but complained that he had known nothing about local opposition and had no wish to become publicly embroiled in something he knew nothing about. Some other patrons resigned on the strength of the SAC letter. Sir Kenneth Macmillan explained, 'When I agreed to become a patron, I had no idea that the students of LSPAT would be taking precedence over local Croydon residents.' Through the press, I learnt that Jonathan

Miller was 'incensed'; Melvyn Bragg had signed a letter supporting SAC, Paul Scofield described LSPAT as a 'tragedy' for local students and said 'as an organisation sponsored by a commercial company, LSPAT must have the ability and the means to find a vacant site' (as it happened, Joy, his wife, graciously offered to meet me in London to explain the dismay Paul and others were feeling); Victoria Wood, George Melly and John Mortimer asked for their names to be removed.

An earlier meeting of the LSPAT Steering Committee had decided that it was important not to over-react to SAC's activities in general, and this particular manoeuvre in particular. By keeping quiet, they surmised, SAC would lose heart. I was incensed; it was easy for the Steering Committee to be relaxed; first, it wasn't their work at risk and secondly, they seemed to misunderstand the significance of the Patrons (and so the significance of the SPA) – unlike the SAC, who spotted their significance and were running with it.

At the SPA's Trustees' October meeting, Robert Davies pointed out that the patrons would be concerned about their reputations and that anything which challenged their credibility would destabilise their relationship with the project. Unusually for him, he went on: 'CTCs and their promotion has been politically abrasive and we are in bed with a bunch of political hustlers who care little, if anything, for people who stand in their way. By tackling us, SAC has its teeth into the soft underbelly of the enterprise. There is no merit in doing nothing. We have to meet SAC face-to-face; start an active campaign, which includes rebuttals in the press, includes a press statement. This must be started now and Mark must re-establish trust with the patrons outlining where the SAC had got it wrong.' We agreed. As it happened, CTCs were having other press problems, so much so that the CTC Trust were thinking about engaging a PR company to help out.

Tony and I finally met Lynda Agilgat shortly afterwards. The meeting was delicate to fix up, since Lynda told Tony that unless Richard Branson and

George Martin were present and 'the meeting was to be of this calibre, we would not be interested in attending'.

The meeting itself went through the familiar strained start to shared talk. However, the SAC was grateful that someone had taken the trouble to meet them. Both parties found much in common, including the need for a school such as the one the SPA had been pioneering and the value of having LSPAT in Croydon. The problem was the site. When the interplay between LSPAT and Croydon College on the Selhurst site was explained to the group, they were not convinced and wondered why the school could not be accommodated elsewhere in the borough. Tony and I looked at each, realising we had the same thought in our heads. We asked if an alternative site really did exist (later SAC suggested Queen's Hospital). Lynda accepted that Maureen and I had done our best towards local consultation with the consultation flyer and the open office near Croydon Station to discuss issues of concern. Tony asked the SAC not to go to the media again until they had had a chance to review the detailed response that was being made. Both groups agreed that their interests were similar and that they didn't want Croydon youngsters to miss out on opportunities.

The only publicity machine that felt it couldn't relax was Virgin's. Students throughout Croydon were deciding to boycott Virgin products. In London's *Evening Standard*, a Virgin spokesman stated 'If we saw evidence of massive local opposition, we'd withdraw. But we've had letters from 17,000 kids who want to come to the college. We don't want to force through something which local people don't want to happen.' The figure was fictional.

In fact, the SAC itself had made a number of claims and assumptions that were simply wrong, ranging from statements about the Selhurst Centre, the site and the ethos of other institutions. Once corrections were published and sent to patrons and press (which did not print them) and the principal of Croydon College also publicly counted the claims made, the dust settled. Aside from Sir Kenneth MacMillan, George Melly and John Mortimer, who resigned, the patrons remained intact.

By October 1989, the curriculum had finally reached the crossroads that had been self-evident from the beginning.

Chapter Ten

The Curriculum Committee creates a new curriculum – the DES object – the principal-designate and the SPA's vocational emphasis – the Admissions Committee produces an admissions process – opening delayed

The first curriculum committee had met auspiciously to create a curriculum that would meet my original aspirations. Bergen was assigned research into syllabuses which might allow the highest amount of performance (so French, for instance, should include acting French plays); Alan Stephenson was assigned to investigate the link between vocational courses and the needs of the various industries being served; Nigel Morgan was assigned the technology and performing arts interface. IT and the technology bias for the National Curriculum was not assigned to anyone and became a matter for the whole team, while the link with Selhurst Sixth Form Centre fell to Bergen. So it was that we education advisors found ourselves struggling to marry our aspirations with the needs of others.

The first meeting of the curriculum sub-committee went swimmingly with common agreement over the philosophy underlying the school. However, it was apparent, without our detailed curriculum work, there would have been no chance of meeting the planned opening date. Because of the link between the building programme and what went in it (i.e. the curriculum), draft detail would have to be available within four weeks. This would result in an integrated curriculum for both the lower school (thirteen-to-sixteen year olds) and the upper school (sixteen-to-eighteen-year-olds), with the major difference that, within the lower school, there would no specialisation. The equal division was reinstated, again within the lower school, between vocational and academic study.

The two main mechanisms to deliver the breadth of experience was a project afternoon where all pupils would devote themselves to projects which would cross not just ages but vocational interest and a project term where cross-age-range performances (with the attendant technology) would take place.

The Upper School curriculum was facing a variety of validated alternatives: GCE 'A' & 'AS' levels, BTEC, City and Guilds and the emerging National Vocational Qualification framework. Alan pointed out that an attractive option, BTEC qualifications, were missing engineering courses related to the performing arts; industry influence here would be essential. (He was to find this input was not forthcoming – even from the record industry which was supporting the school.) There was also talk of an exclusive diploma issued by the school and achieving the acceptance of both the industry and the world of higher and further education.

By the next meeting, Maureen had proposed that there should be a monthly bulletin to Croydon residents and other interested parties that would update everyone about what was going on, as well as sharing what the school was about. The first issue introduced the concept of the school.

You can read this in Appendix One on page 241.

The building programme was being driven by the curriculum, which itself was undergoing refinement at this stage, so the Design and Building Sub-Committee began joint meetings with the Curriculum Sub-Committee.

The education advisors were becoming frantic, since the DES at these meetings was unwilling even to consider the needs of the proposed curriculum. One evening we settled down to an hour's meeting, which lasted three. We realised that it was again time to put our worries on paper.

Aside from modest compromises that had to be made to bring the building in on cost, we still felt that the sixteen+ curriculum was as the founders had hoped. The problem lay with the thirteen-to-sixteen curriculum.

The DES object

The CTC Unit at the DES was sticking to a number of guns – in essence an instance of the detail, not the spirit, of the National Curriculum. Bergen, in particular, had done all he could to redefine names so that performing arts and technology received attention: for instance, dance was called PE; design/technology became art, but he couldn't achieve much more. The education team was beginning to realise that the school might not deliver what it claimed.

Bergen had estimated that, as things stood, out of 200 leaving students (180 at 18 and 20 leaving at 16), no more than 20 would have any real hope of performing careers, even after further specialist training; up to 80 would have a real amateur interest in the performing arts, but their job prospects would be outside this field and half (100) would have a real prospect of careers in the arts – all within the technological side and only after further specialist training. He recognised that these technicians would be better equipped that competitors from other schools, but not to a depth previously anticipated.

I realised all this ran counter to the arguments put forward to Croydon residents when the Selhurst Action Committee was campaigning and where BPI spokespeople were saying that: 'A show such as *Cats* requires a cast which can dance, sing, act and operate electronic equipment. A BRIT School graduate could handle this assignment with ease.' The philosophy was embraced, but not the means of achieving it.

Before this could be addressed, there was also the need to ensure that the curriculum fitted into the cost plan. The DES CTC Unit lost no time in reminding everyone that £5.9 million was the cash limit and was the standard for the 720 pupils specified. Although increases in area and a delayed on-site start had already lifted this total by £700,000, Brian, (the architect) had cut costs by a variety of means, including shaving items in the specification (including a plant room above the theatre – which would come back and haunt the project) to bring the building back within the cash limit. It was also clear that the BRIT School would have to subcontract some sixteen+ BTEC courses to Croydon College to achieve economies of scale. Without this manoeuvre, the school would need to drop one complete BTEC course.

The fundamental issue remained: with the DES sticking to its guns, it was not possible for us to achieve our aims within the thirteen-to-sixteen curriculum (the sixteen-to-eighteen curriculum fell outside the embrace of the National Curriculum).

We were in a familiar quandary. After years of work, there was this opportunity and yet it seemed as if our primary aim could not be achieved. After a long discussion, Bergen and I were mandated to inform the DES that an ordinary secondary school from thirteen-to-sixteen, with an appendix of performing arts was unacceptable. The SPA Trustees went further. If the BPI were persuaded to go along with the DES, it was likely that the SPA would itself withdraw. A serious diminution of the concept that had gained such industry support was not an option. As it happened, the BPI was feeling the same way. Whatever the SPA felt, they were inclined to drop out if a workable compromise could not be reached and demanded a meeting with the secretary of state.

For the DES, this was a situation approaching meltdown and they agreed to hold a meeting to resolve the balance of the curriculum.

Terry chaired it and aside from Maureen, myself and Bergen, attendees were Susan Fey (CTC Trust); Alex

Stewart (DES), Neil Flint (DES) and Alan Callender (HMI). The purpose of the meeting was to achieve unanimity in the aims and objectives of the school.

The meeting began with a skirmish over letters: letters from Richard Branson to Kenneth Baker and vice versa. Terry Ellis went into bat for the sponsors, while Alex Stewart went into bat for the government. Although I was delighted that, at last, key issues where being addressed, I felt bound to ask the meeting to consider two alternatives: that the school went ahead in a form that everyone felt moderately comfortable with or the project was stopped. I saw, from people's faces, the ramifications that were crossing their minds over the second option. From political to public relations, the abyss was too awful.

Terry told the meeting that the school was designed to provide performers with a sound technological background and technicians with an understanding of the performance background with a sound academic background. The development of ability in performing arts and the technology of the performing arts were the vocational missions of the school. Everyone agreed.

Then one of points raised by the education advisers was also voiced by Terry: that the present curriculum would not deliver performers with a significant capability. The CTC/DES model would deliver technicians.

The outcome was a modification of the curriculum to create more opportunities for performing arts training at the expense of GCSE studies. Eight GCSEs were reduced to seven. Of the seven, one would be a performing arts subject. The remainder would be English, Maths and Science together with foundation subjects of Technology, Humanities and a Modern Language. Double science would not be mandatory. This took the average of time spent purely on the performing arts, as a minimum bias, to thirty-seven and a half per cent There was also agreement of slanting the academic curriculum towards the performing arts, and using the performing arts as exemplars.

This was fine as an idea, but in practice we believed to achieve its potential it would mean that teachers of regular school subjects needed a working understanding of the industry to adapt existing school materials confidently.

Anyway, everyone was reasonably happy and relieved, and agreed that strong counselling support should underpin the choices that pupils made. They were even happier when Bergen confirmed the building would accommodate the newly agreed curriculum model. The DES representatives left were charged to obtain approval from the secretary of state. I was charged to amend admissions and selection documents.

The principal designate and the SPA's vocational emphasis

It seemed the fog had lifted and the skies had cleared, but the advisors had not reckoned with the Principal-designate, Anne Rumney.

She had her own ideas, her own personality and her own way of achieving goals. What she did not have was an appreciation of the founder's aims, the expertise which had been devoted to the project or (and it would be impossible for one person to encompass the breadth of knowledge) the breadth of knowledge to reach the conclusions she claimed were hers alone.

This was alarmingly apparent at the first meeting she had with the education advisers. She advised the team that she would 'chew up and spit out' anyone who disagreed with the way she saw the school being run and what the school would do. I tried my best not to rise, saying that I'd like to help the school achieve its potential, particularly in relationship with the industry. She retorted that the school was not going to provide cannon fodder for the industry: 'This is not a cheap way for them to find new employees.' At that point, the team fell silent; she seemed to see the sponsors as a threat with ulterior motives rather than as a partner.

The same sentiments were echoed a year later by one of the school's vice-principals, at the opening when she told a *Times* reporter that: 'A few have been taken on (by the industry) but we are careful to make sure that they are not exploited. We don't want the industry to think this is an easy pool. We can advise the pupils whether it would be a good idea to go ahead.'

It seemed that the weary visionaries were going to have to canter round the circuit once again.

The Admissions Committee produces an admissions process

Aside from the demands that would be placed on facilities and the need to settle the building, there was the admissions process, which inevitably rested on a fundamental question: admission to what? While 'the what' in the education advisors' minds was clear, progress was made. It was going to be difficult to reconcile the admissions process for the curriculum experience we had in mind (and so what the industry the school was serving wanted) and the process the government had outlined in parliament – to deliver Section 205 of the Education Reform Act 1988, which would counter the oft-stated suggestion that CTCs were elitist schools.

Although it was not known how many might actually apply to LSPAT (the rough guess was 5000 applicants for 300 places; the actual initial reality was 1000 applicants for 300 places), the Performing Arts High School in New York had 16,000 applications for 600 places; 12,000 of which were auditioned. Even if the school could admit performers, even if the CTC movement could accept auditioning, the committee began looking at a screening process that involved an application form, containing some diagnostic questions/ tests (which ideally it would be impossible for parents/ others to guess the 'correct' answers); verbal reasoning tests and psychometric testing of attributes that could be deemed desirable (creativity, resilience, perseverance and a test that could place applicants along the team player/leader continuum.) It was hoped that the school would develop its own form of psychometric testing in due course, rather than rely on existing tests – in other words, apply quite novel screening techniques.

We also had to consider the requirements of the CTC movement.

CTCs were supposed to:

1   have a pupil intake that was 'representative of the community they serve'

2   admit 'pupils spanning the full range of ability represented in the catchment area'

3   select pupils on

       general aptitude

       the commitment of parents to full-time education/training to eighteen and to CTCs

4   have as prime selection consideration 'whether pupils are likely to benefit from what the CTC offers'

5   to balance provision for boys and girls.

The difficulty here was interpretation. One definition, in the opinion of the project director for the Middlesborough CTC, was useless. 'Where was the child who would not benefit from a CTC?'

One central problem was that the DES did not wish there to be an audition; instead there would be a 'presentation'. During early meetings with the DES, Will Whitehorn from Virgin consistently insisted: 'OK call them presentations, but we know they are auditions.' The DES would have none of it; indeed, they went even further: best performers could not be identified. When I wondered out loud if this was, in the unlikely event, agreed by sponsors, how would you compare a poetry recitation with a talk about computer graphics? 'That's your problem,' was the DES response.

Putting these difficulties to one side, the committee debated: the application form, the use of a non-verbal reasoning test (which on balance the committee approved), psychometric tests (which needed more analysis), teachers' reports (which were questioned) and parental involvement (which was also questioned).

Concerns over teachers' reports were that teachers had difficulty, from time to time, in making a realistic assessment about the ability of a pupil; that a problem pupil in the eyes of a teacher could be offloaded or, conversely, that a star pupil could be handicapped into staying; that teachers could confuse loud and vivacious pupils with potential performers. Parents could be problematic in that they could be disinterested in their children's education and so jeopardise a talented applicant or be too involved, so preventing their children from expressing their own aims and the direction they felt their education should take.

Gender balance, it was felt, would be achieved through the range of curriculum on offer. Patsy Rodenburg pointed out, drawing from her Guildhall School of Music and Drama experience, that for music and drama there was one male applicant for every six female applicants. The DES reminded the committee that applicants had to reflect the community from which applications were being drawn; the exact make-up of the community in question had not been defined. The other CTC criterion was the 'disadvantaged urban youngster' banner. The question here again being: what exactly did this mean?

Because of time constraints, the committee had to produce an application form, alongside a guidance sheet. The form was straightforward with seven sections. After 'Personal Information', 'Your Present School Information', 'School Subjects and Health', there were two open-ended questions: 'What have you done or seen recently that has excited you? Tell us about it.'

And 'What would you like to achieve at the BRIT School and what would you like to do, when you leave?' and two questions about what a candidate had done already, experience and training and 'What would you like to know more about?' There was a form for parents/guardians and a form for head teachers.

The LIPA application form was to be similar in structure.

Opening delayed

By February 1990, it was clear that the school would not achieve its 1990 opening – for one thing, there wouldn't be a new building up in time; for another, it had proved impossible to click into the required admissions recruitment period so the number of potential pupils, judging from returned application forms, was tiny; for another still, the lease of the East Wing was still unsigned, and, finally, Croydon Council had only just approved planning so that the contractors could start on site.

Discussions with the secretary of state and Croydon Council had shown ready appreciation; it was now a matter of making the decision to delay, which was made, and then arranging the press release. There was a cost implication with the delay for a further £0.25 million. As time went on, the start on site was delayed a month or so more, while the total cost rose to £10.5 million; this was to be partly met from the 1990 Silver Clef Knebworth Concert.

One incident showed me how politics could take precedence over cost containment. During one Design and Building Sub-Committee, it was spotted that the theatre space in the centre of the new building had no air-handling plant. The committee considered where it should be placed. The obvious spot was on the roof. The problem with this was that planning regulations would demand a further planning application, which could mean further SAC activity and negative local press interest. The committee considered other locations, but they proved logistically impossible. The upshot was that the whole building was sunk into the ground at an additional cost of £350,000, so not altering the height of the building above ground to necessitate a further planning hearing. The PR officers for the BPI and the BRIT School placed a story that confirmed that sinking the building had been the original intention. Even Tony told the press that this had stemmed from the sponsor's concerns about the outbreak of noise.

Chapter Eleven

The education advisors are no longer required –
the DES renege over the curriculum agreement –
the SPA again consider withdrawing – the
Principal makes up her mind

The time had come to tackle the curriculum once more, although the employment landscape had changed. It so happened that the non-existent contracts for the education advisors meant the consultancies could be easily stopped – and they were. So the education advisors were no longer advising. Despite the danger that the advisors would be seen as intransigent trouble-makers and that both the BPI, the DES and the CTC Trust would lose patience, now with no jobs to protect, we felt we had little to lose and just our aspirations to achieve.

Tony too was becoming exasperated. Writing to Rupert, he wrote: 'I am astonished, perplexed and annoyed that I now find myself thinking that I am wasting valuable professional time on the whole Selhurst project. This is illustrated by a number of fundamental matters which continue to go by default.'

I, who had been sent a copy, wrote to Tony, in despair about 'the almost fraudulent gap that now exists between the school which was launched last February and the school we now have before us', and returned, once again, to the curriculum: 'There are 25 hours in maintained secondary schools in any one week. Through the National Curriculum, the DES are insisting that a full complement of academic studies are undertaken. These leave 3 hours (out of the 25) to be given to the performing arts *and* their technologies. Clearly the school could not be described as a specialist school.

'To improve the ratio, the BRIT School has a longer day, which effectively adds a further five hours a week. So, eight hours out of a 30-hour week are being devoted to the areas we pioneered. So, 14 to 15 year olds are spending 1.6 hours a day on all three performing arts and their technologies. Clearly, this also prevents the school being described as a specialist school. If all students take a GCSE in performing arts, as part of their 25 hours' DES time, then their total exposure goes up to 10.5 hours a week for performing arts and technology or 32% of their time. The DES has rescinded the removal of a double science. The "Showcase" term, which would have added 150 hours more performing arts provision and experience for the below 16s, has not been favoured by Anne who prefers simply longer terms with the DES diet... . To finish it off, the 16-18 curriculum will now in the main be delivered by Croydon College, which raises questions about control of staff, staff expertise, staff experience and so on.'

I went on: 'I feel that integrity guides us into withdrawal. This is an unparalleled sadness. I really cannot continue to work in this unhappy climate where I am so consistently isolated. The DES does not support our vision. The Principal may dislike it or not understand it. Which leaves the BPI, which cannot spend more time than it has on the project, certainly does not want any more controversy or headaches and cannot care as much as we do about what is going on in the school.' I ended up hoping 'that, with the lessons learnt, Liverpool will be a happier environment for us all'.

Tony had had enough. He wrote to Terry Ellis informing him that at the next BPI Steering Committee meeting, the SPA would be withdrawing from the Selhurst Project only because its provision for pupils was so radically different from the patron's wishes and, indeed, by sponsors lined up. He was aware of the awkwardness this might create once this withdrawal became public knowledge, and suggested that a carefully worded statement would need to be tackled, placing the blame upon the DES for moving the goalposts on the curriculum.

The DES renege over the curriculum agreement

But there was worse to come. The progress the advisors felt they had achieved with the DES during the emergency curriculum meeting was a chimera.

Three days later, Terry wrote back to Tony specifically stressing that he was 'astonished and horrified to hear that further discussions had taken place at which it was implied that the DES were reneging on their agreement'. It appeared that the DES was not prepared to confirm the agreement of seven GCSEs. He could not understand why the SPA had not been confirmed as a primary member, except that other matters had become more pressing. He understood why SPA Trustees were worried and demoralised and would come to the next meeting to meet the concerns. He ended: 'We don't want you to pull out of the Selhurst nightmare. On the contrary we desperately want to share the pain and frustration.... . For the SPA to pull out of the school at this time is unthinkable.'

The SPA Trust again considers withdrawing

The February 1990 meeting of the SPA Trustees was notable for its atmosphere of suppressed frustration. There were the usual greetings, but we quickly sat down and waited for the discussion to begin.

Tony went straight to the main points – the dismay the educational advisors were experiencing over the curriculum; the fact that some advisors were still working without payment; the fact there was no sign of my appointment and finally, despite all the brouhaha and, indeed confirmations, we had still not been recognised as a primary member.

Although Tony had written to Terry intimating that, without change, we wanted to reconsider our support for the BRIT School, he turned to him and said, 'As far as I am concerned and for many here, it seems as if neither the Steering Committee or the Principal, take us seriously. If we leave now, there will be a hell of a stink, but it may be the only option open to us.'

Terry told the meeting that he was now in charge of the BRIT School, which hadn't been heard before and had arranged for a meeting with the advisors and Anne Rumney, which he would chair.

This wasn't quite enough for us. Why was it that we were not a primary member? Why wasn't there an artistic director? Why had the advisors been virtually sacked? What did Anne actually know about the subject areas being tackled in the school, if she was so confident about dispensing with the advisors? Why had I been treated so badly? Had the steering committee made the concept of the school clear to Anne?

Terry looked thoughtful, nodded and stressed that the BPI's goals were the same as ours and asked for a month to put things right. He went on: 'It is essential that the reality is the same as the dream. All the work that has gone into this, particularly Mark's, must be achieved.'

On our behalf, Tony agreed but added that it was not possible to hold the SPA's trustees together unless there was decisive action.

A month later we convened again.

Terry reported that, a few days earlier, a meeting had confirmed that the primary members were: Terry (BPI), John Deacon (BPI), George Martin (in his personal capacity) and Tony Field (SPA). Although this did not fulfil the undertaking made at the Abbey Road press conference, we felt our concern about this had now largely been met.

By this time, Terry had chaired two meetings: the first with the four advisors and the second with the advisors, Anne and Tony. Without resolving the main issue (the balance between the performing arts and the regular school curriculum), his conclusion was that there was a lot to be done but that things were moving in the right direction. One of Anne's central beliefs was that this was a school first and foremost and that must be created first; the depth of performing arts provision would come later. I blanched at the implication of auditing the school for years to come and keenly felt that the school should start as it meant to go on. What might be described as temporary would inevitably become hard to change and, in fact, permanent.

Tony wasn't so sure, feeling there were conflicting purposes, but in reality, the key group was the steering committee where we were well represented and the principal was working to that committee. Everyone agreed that the committee should inform Anne that it was behind the implementation of the SPA/BPI requirements.

Terry reported that he had spoken with John Deacon to appoint a chief executive for the school who would be a formidable advocate for the school externally (and so raise funds) and for the vision internally. He felt that within two months he could report on positive progress. As far as my contract was concerned, he promised he would sit down with Anne and work out the terms.

On balance, we could feel again there had been progress. The legal objectives had been achieved, curriculum discussions were encouraging; there was common ground with the BPI over the appointment of a chief executive; some payments for advisory work was underway.

There had also been a letter from the DES confirming it would pay for the work the advisors had done for the BRIT School, but there was a question mark remaining over when the advisors began their work. A compromise was finally reached.

The principal makes up her mind

The key lay in the curriculum and, following the meetings between Anne and the advisors with Terry in the chair, she prepared a document on the curriculum stating that her concern (and that of the two senior staff appointed) was to 'reassure members of the (Steering) committee regarding the time and emphasis on performing arts and its technology, giving some indication of percentages of time, as the pattern takes shape'.

Despite the professional reservations between her and the advisors (she had initially advised the three appointed BRIT staff not to talk with the advisors), we sat down one Thursday afternoon to digest the contents.

There were of course detailed curriculum issues, but, fundamentally and in summary, we were aghast to discover the maximum time devoted to performing arts and technology for thirteen-to-sixteen-year-olds had been reduced to 23.4 per cent, with some pupils being allowed to spend a mere 15 per cent in these areas. Far from being reassuring, the document confirmed our worst fears. The final heave had changed nothing.

In retrospect, and some ten years on, the struggle the founders of the BRIT School were engaged in would simply not have taken place, given what the national curriculum has now become: insistence upon English, a much scaled-down emphasis on mathematics, religious education, science and physical education. This is all that is left, but at that time...

She presented the paper to the steering committee, although it had not been circulated beforehand. Rupert, although a lawyer, wrote to Tony reporting Anne's answers to specific questions about the time devoted to the performing arts. Aside from curriculum time, there would be 'periodic performances' but 'not too often'. While the whole curriculum was geared towards the performing arts, pupils would be 'working up to it in stages'.

It was difficult to know quite what to do next. I was exhausted, hurt and angry. The curriculum was still hopelessly flawed. Eight months had passed since I was offered the artistic director post and still nothing had transpired, except reassurances that the formal offer was about to be made.

During this period, I had sold my companies to an American educational conglomerate who wanted me to remain, heading up their European operations. I was also putting serious time into LIPA; Paul had asked me to work further on it, taking the lead, and be in regular consultation. George had told me that this personal rapport was an achievement and should not, if possible, be adjusted at this moment. I was clearly nearing a deadline of choice.

Tony was beginning to feel that, since the SPA was now legally an intrinsic part of the BRIT School at the highest level, it was growing increasingly impossible to consider extricating us without incurring the charge that we were letting everyone down at a very late stage.

Despite this, two months later, we felt misguided, both by others and by our own, perhaps hopeful, interpretation of events — the clincher being Anne's curriculum paper. We considered four options: pulling out and resigning; slowly sliding out; stay in passively or stay in actively. The facts were that, despite Terry's statements, only the appointment of primary members had been achieved. Tony still felt that everyone was capable of moving in the right direction and that all our concerns would be met, but was still dismayed. The fourth option was chosen. The first action was to write to all primary members requesting an emergency meeting.

Tony wrote to Terry: 'I am simply not accustomed to being associated with such a badly run enterprise and I am fast losing confidence that the programme can move forward properly as we envisage without some overall control which does not appear to be achieved under the present Steering Committee arrangements. It is not my style to have to threaten to resign in order to achieve our original objects. When I tabled the draft SPA press release of our proposed withdrawal some months ago, everyone did their utmost to reassure me about the importance of the SPA's participation. George Martin and you wrote me thoughtful letters; the CTC Unit, DES and BPI representatives all gave reassurances that the matters which concerned us would be dealt with and that the administrative and financial machinery would work better in future. Yet our trustees want to know why I am so ineffective when I am now one of the primary members.'

But no one enlightened him.

At the next steering committee meeting, Tony was surprised to learn that the entry age had been raised from thirteen to fourteen. Will Whitehorn assured him that this was in my original plan. Tony was experiencing a curious sensation; whenever I wasn't there, Terry, John, Maureen and even Anne justified changes with this sort of imprimatur – even though he knew better than anyone present what I had in mind.

The June 1990 Knebworth dawned. Since Paul was amongst those playing, Richard Ogden, his then manager, had suggested to the BPI that LIPA also benefit from Knebworth; unsurprisingly this was not going to be favoured.

Chapter Twelve

A potential further / higher education model emerges in Liverpool – the press launch before Paul's 'Let It Be Liverpool' 1990 Tour performance – 'Talking Chinese'

Two days before Knebworth saw the launch of the campaign to create a performing arts institute in Liverpool.

A potential further/higher education model emerges in Liverpool

It was almost a year since work had begun on the first feasibility study in Liverpool. Despite the measured style of Susan Fey's initial report, the CTC Trust had put some pressure on the city for the approval of a CCTA. Meanwhile and unbeknownst to me, Pete Fulwell was called to attend late night sessions, where sections of elected members, often Militant, were in favour of allowing a CCTA to start which they would then, they thought, turn into the institution they preferred – which would not be a CCTA.

Pete had become concerned enough to write to Mick Farley in July 1989: 'In view of the vigorous attempts by the CTC Trust to secure approval in principle of a CCTA model for LIPA within the next two weeks, could you please confirm the following: any application for the use of the Liverpool Institute building must have the approval of the City Council and the City Council would not approve any application for use of the building until it has considered the results of the LIPA Feasibility Study'. Mick reassured Pete, reminding him that the charity commissioners needed to give their approval as well.

The first Liverpool Steering Committee meeting took place on the 5th September 1989. By the time Paul's Liverpool concert took place, the *Music City* report had been completed with a substantial section about LIPA. Before the final version appeared, Paul's desire for a centre of excellence had to be married with a broader-based resource facility. Quite quickly, the steering committee had spotted a possible split between one element and the other and agreed there would be no separation. Provision for both should come from the same source.

Essentially, the team working on the LIPA model had been trying to marry Paul's vision for LIPA (post-sixteen focusing on popular music, with other performing arts feeding into musicians' needs, while technical skills were also acquired) with the Training Agency's vision (it was paying for the study and wanted an new further education initiative in the city) and Liverpool Council's own views (community involvement, inner city economic and social regeneration through the development of the music industry in Liverpool and the rationalisation of further education provision).

The model that emerged satisfied everyone (although it wasn't quite the LIPA that began later). There were four components of what was to be a new national and international training centre for popular music; each serviced by a central resource centre. In summary, there was 'An International Centre for Popular Musics of the World', where musicians world-wide would come and teach, record, give concerts and use the latest technologies. The second strand was essentially a model for a full-time college. The third was an area resource centre for part-time, weekend, and evening activities, which would include the production and use of distance learning materials and, finally, a full-time certificated course in community music-making. This became known as 'the mixed model'.

As the meetings had progressed, the building was touched upon: not only its poor state but also the cost of refurbishment. There was no saying what Paul's financial contribution might be in terms of capital; revenue he clearly saw coming from commercial activities.

I met Paul five weeks before the Liverpool concert. Basically, he felt that the mixed model was an admirable response in that it made educational, artistic and commercial good sense. He liked the way in which those without financial resources could benefit. On the money side, he wanted to raise funds in this country and America, as well as making his own contribution. He wanted to be on the Council of Management for the Institute, however it was going to be constituted (although, in the end, his work demands prevented this).

The press launch before Paul's 'Let It Be Liverpool' 1990 Tour performance

The venue was Liverpool's Albert Dock area, where Paul was playing one of the last dates of his 1990 World Tour. For a variety of reasons, but mainly because of the absence of a suitable venue, an entire stadium, with seating on three sides and the stage occupying the fourth, was built from scratch. Behind the stage were tents, one of them designated for the launch.

For me, this was deep immersion – with help from Geoff Baker, Paul's loyal publicist. I was about to talk to a tent full of journalists, film-makers, possible supporters, Liobians (as the old boys of the Liverpool Institute for Boys were called), members of the SPA Trust who could make the journey, some local members of Paul's family, local councillors and a few of Paul's old teachers. Against a backdrop of five huge blow-ups of pictures I had taken of the present day institute, I launched, bungee-like, out into the experience.

After George Martin reminded everyone what had emerged musically from Liverpool and urged the city to 'do it again', Paul bounced in (as it happened, without wearing an old school cap, which had been one of Geoff's many ideas). As his talk progressed, he repeated that there were 'no guarantees' that LIPA would happen. My heart fluttered. I was looking for unalloyed enthusiasm, a 'we can make it happen' message, feeling that anything less would shake confidence in what was, yet again, a fragile dream. I realised later that Paul wanted to balance giving his name to the scheme with his name being the only name on the cheque that would make it happen.

A local man, Gabriel Muies, who had been a parent-governor when the school existed, had been waging his campaign for the restoration of those institute artefacts that he claimed had been purloined by the city. Somehow he had managed to infiltrate the press conference, stood up during the question-and-answer session and challenged Paul to do something about it whilst declaring the whole business a national scandal. Deftly, Paul responded by inviting the assembled press to take note of what might be a story. That wasn't enough for Gabriel. He shouted that since Paul was now getting involved with the institute building, he was now part of the scandal. 'Just a moment, mate,' responded Paul, 'I've just arrived and you are pulling me into this.' 'You're part of it,' responded Gabriel. 'Now there *is* a story here,' Paul motioned to Gabriel; 'he's your man,' and took another question. I was impressed by Paul's public skill, by the mixture of charm and firmness that had recognised the point and yet taken it no further.

But Gabriel Muies was no flash in the pan. He was to dog the project from then on.

As Paul was introduced to strangers and friends, the air around the individual meetings became charged. Whatever was said, and it was often inconsequential, there was a sense of occasion. My first experience in London was being duplicated.

The launch was also a way of thanking everyone for the effort they had put in to date. At one point I sat with the two male representatives from The Training Agency and was touched and delighted that the younger male had decided to turn up in full make-up. Pete Fulwell, meanwhile, was gloomy; the people in the tent were not those he recognised as being key to making LIPA happen. He felt LIPA had not yet been properly born and here were people about to muck around with the embryo. I tried to cheer him up, but it was hopeless. Pete moped. Seeing Pete as the local music world amongst the world of local worthies and business people made me wonder how I was going to marry up the differing elements.

'Talking Chinese'

Some years later Pete told me about the concept of 'Talking Chinese' which explained how he had been feeling. The concept went like this: ideologies from outside China fantasise about taking it over. China is so big and the culture so solid that the only way of doing it involves learning to think and speak Chinese (hence 'Talking Chinese'), so, paradoxically, as the invaders reach their goal, they are transformed into Chinese. As they 'win', reaching the heart of power, they 'lose' because they have turned into the very people they were trying to defeat. There is no way that China can be taken over. So when Pete watched what he felt were strange white middle-class people coming along to shake Paul's hand, he felt that for LIPA to become a reality, it would so fundamentally change in concept that it could not reach its potential.

The memories of that day are snapshots in my mind now. Although you live life in motion, it seems you often recall it in single images – a moment that encapsulates a series of moments. This moment contained a setting sun, over the stage – the outline of the cathedral, around one – the sea of faces, three seas of faces, and the bright stage with the Brian Clarke backdrops and the music thundering out from diminutive figures. And then you add to the photographic picture the essential ingredient, the spirit of the experience shown on the faces around you – pride, enjoyment, memory of youth, enthusiasm, recognition and gratitude. This was the pride of a city in one of its greatest natives.

Chapter Thirteen

Lord Michael Birkett becomes the BRIT School president – the artistic director post vanishes – I visit the BRIT School – the primary members remove the SPA Trust

Ten months later, the BPI had appointed a chief executive for the school, except he wasn't a chief executive, he was the president. He was Lord Michael Birkett. Tony knew Michael, promoted his candidature and felt heartened by the appointment. I had been invited to the Institute of Contemporary Arts in London to hear the announcement of his appointment. When I realised that I wasn't going to be introduced, I introduced myself and asked if I might brief him on the history of the project. Michael agreed. We met a few weeks later at the school.

Michael was affable and talkative, usually about himself. Once I started speaking, I gained the impression that Michael was just partially listening, so I petered out. Birkett didn't prompt, so the meeting drew to a close.

The artistic director post vanishes

Tony meanwhile was also talking to Michael about the resolution of the past and a fair framework for the future, which included reminding him about the artistic director post.

Four months later, Michael wrote to me. He was rolling together two issues: the non-payment for work while the BRIT project was in formation and the non-actioned post of artistic director.

He argued that my role had been seen as voluntary, despite attending some forty-five meetings and working on behalf of the project and that this was also how the role of artistic director was seen. 'I can find no indication that the role of artistic director, and which was to be the subject of a contract, was ever accepted as a salaried, school post... . The agreed structure of staffing (for the school) never allowed for a position of artistic director. It is clear that such a structure evolved gradually, as the Project Director and Principal were appointed and subsequently of course various other members of staff...so I conclude that no contract for your employment, full or part-time, was drawn up simply because no post agreed by all the parties concerned (i.e. the DES, the CTC Trust, the BPI, and eventually the school itself) was ever established.'

As I read the letter, I realised that the door on my creation was being shut in my face – so, when I had been offered the post a year earlier, it hadn't been a post at all; in fact, it hadn't existed. The fact that the then chairman of the BPI, one Terry Ellis had spoken the words 'artistic director' (and had later confirmed this in writing) was immaterial. The lack of a contract, far from being evidence of slovenly management, was now evidence that the post didn't exist.

I didn't have the energy to do battle about the artistic director post. Even if I was to take the now voluntary post up, who were my allies going to be and how could Anne and I work alongside each other now the curriculum was so far adrift from the original aspirations? The proposed admissions process too had effectively gone. There were no auditions. The format was an interview with parents present; participation in a discussion group which involved potential pupil presentations, a timed half-hour test to check intellectual ability and an informal chat – effectively indistinguishable from other CTCs.

This didn't stop me feeling crushed. My investment of vision and energy had been dismantled. This didn't stop me longing to see the school and sense the atmosphere.

I visit the BRIT School

It was August 1991 that I first visited the BRIT School after the dismissal in February 1990. I took one of the SPA patrons, Monica Parker of the Benesh Institute, who also wanted to see the school.

After the visit, I was thrilled and amazed to see the physical reality, but dismayed and depressed by the marginalisation of the SPA in general and myself in particular. Anne had introduced me to staff as 'an early worker on the project'. When told of this remark, Humphrey Walwyn of Mainstream Records (who had succeeded Tony as Chair of the SPA) described this as 'the understatement of the year'.

The visit was highly structured. My meeting with Anne was formal. She agreed with the need to achieve the initial vision. The meeting with senior staff was informative in that none had performing arts experience other than the activities they had experienced through teaching in secondary schools. This reinforced my feeling that this was first and foremost, in ethos, a school.

Although the prospectus indicated a minimum thirty-three per cent weighting for the performing arts, the timetable showed that this would in fact be twenty-seven per cent. The key 'Showcase' Term had disappeared, it seemed, for good.

The informal meeting with staff in a pub later was full of rumblings, but commonplace for educational institutions, let alone for a yet-to-be-started school under pressure. The rumblings essentially surrounded the personality and professionalism of Anne (two at the meeting had handed in their resignations and one was about to do so). There was full enthusiasm for the concept, but dismay about the school ethos. The industry had not been encouraged, beyond sponsorship.

I was conscious that even my questions might have affected the responses, but this didn't stop me feeling gloomy.

Then the bombshell.

The primary members remove the SPA Trust

In October 1991, John Deacon wrote to Tony Field. After noting how delighted the BPI was with the progress of the school, he went on to describe the appointment of governors and then he unveiled the reason for writing:

> Since it has become apparent that the SPA's main focus will, quite understandably, be on the Liverpool school, the BPI Council believes we should acknowledge this situation. As the financing for the school has come entirely from the BPI and the DES, the Council recognises that the management and financial responsibility for the school lies squarely with it, and that they, in consultation with the CTC Trust, should be responsible for constructing the Board of Governors. I am pleased to say that Michael Birkett has agreed to be the Chairman of the Board of Governors.
>
> We are, of course, extremely grateful to you in particular and the SPA for its assistance in connection with the school and I know Michael will want to maintain close contact with you.
>
> However, we have reached the stage where the Board of Governors will be taking over the responsibility for the governing of the school, the Primary members acknowledge that realistically the time has come when the BPI and the SPA should pursue their

respective projects. Whilst the SPA will no
longer be an ordinary member of the
company, I am sure that BPI members will
give Mark every assistance with LIPA and I
very much hope that we will keep you as
valuable friends of the school.

Tony noticed that John had not written to him as
chair of the SPA or to the SPA's address. He felt able
to express his feelings by writing:

'I am profoundly saddened and somewhat
shocked that it should be considered that the
Board of Governors at Selhurst selected solely
by the BPI and DES, as those bodies
financially responsible... . I am sure that no
one who provided the entire conception of the
school expected to count for nothing alongside
financiers... . I find the suggestion that the
BPI and the SPA should pursue their
respective projects reflects a wholly mistaken
understanding of the work of SPA since we
expected to retain some contact formally with
the first school in Selhurst, the next in
Liverpool, the third hopefully on the
continent of Europe.

For Tony, the BRIT School had died. His involvement
was over. He neither spoke or wrote to any of the
participants again.

I was stunned and wondered who was behind it, in the
sense that 'the who' might identify the reasoning. I also
wondered what George Martin might think, or, indeed,
Richard Branson or Terry Ellis or Michael Birkett.

I also wondered how this could come about legally.
As a primary member, after all those reminders, was
it not the case that primary members had not just the
responsibility, but a right to participate in and agree
to decision of this kind? Did this mean that, aside from
not being on the board of governors, that our primary

membership was also being rescinded? I wrote to John asking him.

John responded by enclosing 'a formal notice in accordance with the company's Articles of Association' as well as a copy of the Articles. The formal notice, signed by Cyril Taylor and John, confirmed that 'The School for Performing Arts had been removed as a member of the company'.

George Martin wrote to me: 'I am surprised Deacon has done this, but I think he probably had no alternative and is being driven from behind by Maurice Oberstein [then chair of the BPI].'

I wrote back: 'It seems extraordinary that the people who not only had the idea, but worked so long and hard to see it developed now have no representation whatsoever within their creation, particularly when the BPI are so concerned that originators are not usurped.'

This irony was spotted by my supportive stepfather, Gordon Newbury. He reminded me that the reason why the BPI became involved in the school's creation was its concern, on behalf of the industry, with copyright – the right to own and protect and so benefit from your creation. Here then was the industry perpetrating precisely what it was trying to reduce, even eradicate, and using one of the strategies against the people who had provided strategy.

Humphrey, having spoken with Michael Burkett, was pragmatic. Michael wanted a case to argue with Oberstein, the BPI and the government. Humphrey felt whatever the SPA felt about the past, this would not encourage an adjustment; the SPA had to promote the active usefulness and influence that continued involvement would bring. He acknowledged this was scrabbling for a seat when outrageous treatment had already been meted out.

I then spoke with George who harped on about the size of the BPI's contribution and that, without it, the SPA's idea would have never risen from the ground. This was the only time that George and I disagreed – this alone upset me.

I told him that the SPA was never about money and would be unlikely to ever have the financial resources to fund a school, but its people could devote time, energy and expertise. This could be translated into expenditure. In relation to the BRIT School, it was close to £200,000. George responded that this was work not money. I responded that unpaid work could be recalculated in financial terms. George promised to do what he could by asking to become a governor himself and by seeking the SPA's place on the curriculum committee.

The strongest feeling I had was George's dismay at the SPA's reaction. Writing to me a week later, George achieved governorship of the school, two places for Tony and me on the curriculum committee and clearly wanted and expected the issue to be kicked into touch. 'I do hope that we can forget the slight (which I am certain was unintended) and work together for the common good.'

Humphrey had meanwhile written to John describing the removal as 'irrational, counterproductive and immoral; irrational because it was denying the source of the original idea and labour and in any case the SPA would have no power other than to advise, rather than control; counterproductive because it was unnecessary and needlessly stirred up ill-feeling; immoral because of this treatment to the originators'. He wrote '...there is no such thing as a fait accompli in the music business. It is still not too late to reconsider. I want to do what I can to defuse the situation and hope that you do too.'

As John was digesting this letter, two pieces appeared in *The Times Educational Supplement* one on LIPA, the other on the SPA's exit from the BRIT School. The LIPA piece had been set up two months earlier when I met the reporter, and it proved impossible not to talk about the BRIT School, since the piece was about LIPA being 'the big sister' of the earlier school.

The piece itself was factual, although the headline was odd – 'CTC board ousts Branson charity' with the subhead as 'snub for celebrities who helped launch "Fame" school'. In the next issue, Will Whitehorn for Virgin, Michael Birkett for the BRIT School and I had letters published; Will to say that Richard didn't feel snubbed by anybody (but mentioned the SPA in the creation of the school not once); Michael, a study in diplomacy, gave the SPA credit but noted it was the BPI that made it happen and described the SPA's response (to what, he chose not to elaborate) as 'bruised amour propre'; I to correct one small inaccuracy in the original piece and to add that 'the SPA's £200,000 sweat equity was well and truly spent before the BPI came on board'.

The publicity officer for the BPI, rang me to forestall any further articles by trying to make me feel guilty for the bad vibes which must now be surrounding the new BRIT pupils and which they had done nothing to deserve.

Justice was on Rupert's mind when he spoke to John Deacon a day later. 'Listen, John, stripped to the bare essentials and shorn of all the quasi-rational explanations, this story is of a man with an idea and two men with money, and, once the men with the money have the idea, they get rid of the first chap. This happens all the time. It's essentially lawful theft.'

John told him that, aside from George, Terry was also on the board and he went on to add that Terry had become disillusioned with the SPA when there had been that disagreement over the curriculum. Rupert recalled a lift Terry had given him from a SPA meeting. As an owner of a vintage Rolls Royce himself, Rupert was temperamentally inclined to enjoy lifts from others with Rolls Royces. In the course of the journey, Terry had turned to Rupert and asked him how significant he felt the SPA really was, beyond a bunch of do-gooders meeting in a small college in Holborn.

Rupert told John that the offer of a place on the curriculum committee was not unlike knocking a child to the ground and then offering him a bar of chocolate.

Letters and telephone calls passed back and forth a bit more, George making it clear to me that he disagreed with the SPA's wish to be on the board of the BRIT School.

It was the end. Yes, I had been too trusting, probably too irritating to the DES and the BPI, too insignificant and so easily trod upon and certainly politically naïve. My reward was nothing; I was walking off with nothing. There are not too many good ideas that a not-so-prolific person has in a lifetime. One of my early entrepreneurial heroes, Tony Elliott, had just one: *Time Out*, the London listing magazine. This had been mine and now I had no connection with it. I was airbrushed out.

A year later I wrote to Michael suggesting a link between the BRIT School and the SPA/LIPA, wondering if the idea of a curriculum committee, mentioned to him so many months before by George Martin, might be the thing. Michael wrote back promptly saying that 'the Curriculum Committee didn't exist but might do so around summer time'. That was the last I heard about it.

The next time I saw the school was the invitation to the official opening in July 1992 by David Mellor, then the Secretary of State for National Heritage. I watched three or four short performances and listened to Maurice Oberstein declare how the record industry felt impelled, for the good of the nation, to invest in training. Mellor was asked if he felt the school was elitist and shot back, 'There is no point in wallowing in mediocrity. We have to pick out the achievers [so sweeping away many of the carefully crafted concepts of his bureaucrats].' How was this going to be achieved, I wondered, without some of the innovative testing that we had in mind?

The next time I saw the school was the summer of 1998, when I asked the then principal if I might come down. LIPA was about to admit its first two ex-BRIT School students and it seemed a propitious moment to kick-start a link. Naturally I was a part of history, but I couldn't resist finding out how the current curriculum lined up with the blueprint we had developed. I was told that thirty-three per cent of the fourteen-to-sixteen curriculum was devoted to the performing arts; although there were instances of cross-curricular work, this didn't seem to be a policy; auditions did not take place, neither did IQ tests – the guideline seemed to be aptitude for the fourteen-year-olds with the addition of skill for the sixteen-year-olds. One senior staff member said that, pre-16, 'we do not see ourselves as a performing arts school'– the starkest divergence between the original dream and the reality.

Time has moved on and just recently, nine years on, a new principal – the third – has been appointed. Schools are constantly evolving. What was true in 1998 is probably not so true now. In any case, the new incumbent will have his own ideas.

Chapter Fourteen

*Liverpool City Council endorses
the LIPA model in principle – company structure
and first employees – a series of meetings with
Paul – the fund-raising video – the City
Challenge initiative and others – Michael
Portillo and Paul in the building – LIPA
Steering Committee gets underway – working
and living in Liverpool – earmarking of
£4,000,000 City Challenge money – the first
fund-raising lunch at the Performing Right
Society – Pete Waterman – the funding bodies
and their differing agendas*

One Sunday in July 1990, I sat inside on a blazingly
hot day, typing away on a reclaimed manual typewriter
to Liverpool City Council. The BRIT School experience
brought me echoing sadness. Whenever my mind
entered the chasm of that experience, I heard Carly
Simon singing 'I'm looking forward to looking back'.
I reflected on the future, the imagined future which
might see the dream taking place some two hundred
and fifty miles from where I was sitting, linked – in
some way – with one of, maybe the, most prolific
songwriters born in this country. It seemed
extraordinary, but there was nothing else to do but to
try to progress it. Despite my weariness about stepping
into the ring once more, I hadn't given up.
I was writing to describe what had been achieved
and what was being planned since the Albert Dock

launch. One topic was a better idea about the content of LIPA, what would it actually do. The second topic was the strategy for attracting funding and resourcing. Finally, there was a need for a business plan. I wanted to place this with Paul's London tax advisors in the hope that their Liverpool office might donate time to its creation.

Quite by chance, I came across Keith Hackett once again, this time as a consultant for Practical Arts, a local arts consultancy. Although still a Liverpool councillor, his role as chair of finance and strategy was now someone else's. Keith and I were going to work more closely than either of us had imagined.

In the end, the business plan was a task which would take me and my old colleague, Bergen, nearly a year to complete. The £40,000 cost was paid for by a subset of the Merseyside Task Force, the city's City Action Team, then headed by another unusually human bureaucrat, James Warnock.

I noted that the Training Agency had not yet paid for the initial study and that the donation of £30,000 from the Albert Dock concert had not come through. Funding every activity myself was difficult, but I was still doing it.

Liverpool City Council endorses the LIPA model in principle

By December, a meeting was called in Liverpool by the city council to see where exactly things were. The city had, at council, endorsed the 'mixed model' and had also, in May, agreed, in principle, to the transfer of the trusteeship of the building subject to both its education committee and the Charity Commissioners being happy about the future plans for the site. Nigel Morgan explained how his process of consultation locally was to include experience for locals as well through three small-scale educational projects. The city representatives found this admirable, but were more concerned about energy being put into developing a model that might never see the light of day because the institute would not be in a fit state to accommodate it, nor would the requisite finance be in place.

On this front, Rupert had again been active, liaising with the Charity Commissioners and the city solicitor, the ever generally-exhausted Paul Taylor. The Charity Commissioners were, on the basis of the feasibility study and assurances given by Rupert, prepared to agree the transfer of trusteeship, subject to the project being 'feasible and viable'. The city was trustee of a crumbling building, a building that had grossly deteriorated in contravention of the trusteeship. However, it would be impossible for the council, even if it could, to invest money in the building. If LIPA was not in a ready state to go forward, then the building would be left to deteriorate.

Effectively, no one could move either forwards or backwards on the building.

Shortly after the Albert Dock concert, the SPA had set up a new company limited by guarantee to develop the Liverpool Institute project. After a six-month gap, it would apply for charitable status. The city wanted to be on the LIPA's board. Then the meeting fell to wondering who exactly was LIPA? Informed by a history of good intentions coming to naught in the city, they had seen just me and Nigel at that point. There was a sense in which confirmation was needed that the SPA was a credible body.

Two months later, Humphrey Walwyn with five of the SPA's trustees travelled to Liverpool and restored the officers' confidence. The SPA's confidence was raised by the finances which Paul, with help of Richard Ogden, were getting together. Paul had managed to achieve a donation of £40,000 from Apple, although Yoko Ono had added the condition that a further £40,000 had to be raised before the Apple donation was released (which would be achieved through the Merseyside Task Force business plan support). Richard Ogden was busy tackling BMI, ASCAP, the Knebworth artists (Paul pledged his part of these proceeds to LIPA) and the MPA.

Back at base in London we had to consider how best to maintain the momentum. Nigel's work had piloted a practical dry run of how one element of LIPA might work locally. He had also discussed the proposal with ninety-three people in forty-two organisations.

Company structure and the first employees

The emphasis had to be on shifting to the logistics of creating a new business with, once again, the committee and management structure to guide activities. The board of directors, the SPA decided, could and should have equal representation from itself (with Humphrey, now SPA Chair, as a member), Liverpool and other locally based arts/education bodies.

At the back of the SPA's collective mind and in the front of some, was the fear that LIPA might be hijacked as the BRIT School had been.

Bergen had been increasingly involved in LIPA administration and could work as a part-time co-ordinator; I felt there was a fair chance of the £100,000 needed to fund a year of development activities so decided to leap and work full-time on LIPA.

We would be the first LIPA employees for a year and a half, working from a small converted chemistry laboratory (eleven square metres) and store (nine square metres). This was in The Hahnemann Building (Britain's first homeopathic hospital) on Hope Street (round the corner from the Institute) owned by Liverpool Polytechnic. The rent was a modest £1,000 a year. These then were the first LIPA offices.

A series of meetings with Paul

A series of meetings were taking place in the converted mill that housed Paul's office and recording studio. The mill looked out over the English Channel and achieved ten out of ten for allowing mere mortals spectacular perspectives, both in land and, since it was about forty miles from the coastline, along the coast too. However, the house wasn't grand, none of the rooms were grand. In fact, it was workaday and the kitchen, where you usually waited, could be a squeeze.

The objective was to become more and more familiar with the philosophy and proposed content of LIPA as well as getting to know the people involved and seeing where the conversation led. Each of the four elements was unpicked. Other areas were covered in additional meetings; how the enterprise side might work (Humphrey led); how the company might be legally set up (Rupert led); how courses might be accredited (Roger Breakwell, Head of Liverpool Polytechnic's School of Art and Design led).

Although the meetings achieved their purpose, many took place just between just Paul and me. We were engaged in a project without blueprints to follow. I experienced some sharp shifts in Paul's mood and, indeed, attitude towards the project. At the start of the series of meetings, I travelled down to Hastings station in a naïve state of excitement; as time went on, I began to realise this was not wholly appropriate since I couldn't be sure what mood he'd be in. The thrill of talking with an icon needed to give way to hard debate.

I found it sometimes difficult not to give way when I should have stood firm. I have a natural temptation to achieve consensual agreement; to make a team work – even a team of two. This can collide with a desire to achieve a particular end. There's a tension between these two that I'm not sure I've resolved. Part of the solution I think I've recently found in an engaging book, *Hello He Lied*, written by the American film producer, Lynda Obst, about film-producing but which includes wise business dicta.

Her advice is: 'Ride the horse in the direction it's going.' There's an enjoyable mileage in considering these eight words, but in production terms this translates into 'What you do when you can't do what you planned to do, but achieve roughly the same result in changed circumstances'.

One of Paul's concerns was that LIPA might turn into some cosy middle-class do-gooding activity. Illustrating the point, he told me that it would be ballsy if a student made up a song whose lyrics were all swear words.

At one extreme, Paul was uncertain if the project was going to be at all useful. During one of his visits to Liverpool, he'd met The Christians in a studio. One of them bluntly asked Paul why he was getting involved with the LIPA. Before he could answer, one of the Christian brothers reminded Paul that they, like him, had taken no classes along the road to achievement – 'So what are they going to teach and who are "they" going to be anyway?' Paul didn't have an immediate answer but brooded on the conversation for years, adding it to his worry about middle-class do-gooding. He was even worried about my double-barrelled name. He told me, 'With a name like that, you're going to have to be good to survive and convince people in a place like Liverpool.'

He was to return to this theme time and again.

Paul knew, if the project was going to stand any chance of success, some fund-raising was needed. He also realised that he would have to start it off. The question was how to prime-pump the funding needed to show other potential funders that he was serious, without undue financial exposure or actually spending all the money until it looked as if all the other funders were in place.

Later, during the fund-raising work, someone wrote asking me what would happen to his donation if the project failed to take off. I answered by telling him that it would go into a special fund that would not get spent until all the money was in place, but this missed the essential truth. How can any project get off the ground without spending money to achieve one of the first goals: raising the money needed?

Paul's answer was to pledge £1,000,000. Wait to see how successful the fund-raising would be and in the meantime pass over quite small amounts, which had to be accounted for. This focussed particular attention on me – not just my ability, but on my personality. I was, even in a tangential way, representing Paul in the effort to raise the finance; what if I had some unforeseen and awkward habit which, if it hit the light of day, might be tricky? Richard Ogden rang Pete Fulwell in Liverpool a few times to find out about the locals' reaction to me.

One of the June meetings addressed the mechanics of fund-raising. Paul told me that he would attend three fund-raising events – that was it.

The fund raising video

Then there was the issue of a fund-raising document – and this too was tricky: how did you achieve the balance between attracting people, without producing a lavish fund-raising document? One solution Paul came up with was to print on recycled paper. But something else was needed, something visually exciting, something which visualised the dream. Although I was keen on audio-visual presentations with slides (this was how I'd used to publicise my own colleges), so had been someone selling Linda's idea of vegetarianism to meat-eaters to a supermarket chain – only he'd managed to place a couple of slides in the carousel upside down. As soon as I heard this, I realised the slide idea was dead. Wayne Bickerton (to be Chief Executive of The Performing Right Society), who was at the meeting, suggested a video; everyone swiftly agreed. Paul added, 'You must imagine making the film without me, cutting to Paul is the easy way out. You must look on me as a bonus.'

The moment I left the Mill with Humphrey, I pestered him on the way back to London. I'd never done a fund-raising video before. What were we going to put in it? Who was going to produce it? What sort of budget did he think Paul might be willing to accept? Humphrey was relaxed, suggesting the Beatles' songs 'Hard Day's Night' and 'We Can Work It Out', (both made it to the final version).

As it happened, I had met one of Paul's old schoolmates, Don Andrew, who was working in public relations and knew a keen young video-maker, Terry Zoakipny. I would create and polish a commentary. It wasn't long before a screening of the first section took place at the Mill. It seemed easy-going from the start. The film began with an elegiac vision of the past. With the music from the school section of Paul's soon-to-be-released *Liverpool Oratorio*, ghostly figures wandered down the old school corridors, tipped chemicals through test tubes and sat for assembly in the horseshoe-shaped auditorium...and ended with an uplifting vision of the future.

I had imagined that Paul, with his financial resources, would have gone for the security of an established film-maker. As it happened, the keen young video-maker was paid modestly in the knowledge that the four-minute video would take pride of place in his show reel (which indeed it did).

Richard, I assumed on Paul's behalf, tackled me at this time over the emphasis being placed on Paul to make the finance a reality. While Paul was willing to ask his friends to help him achieve the dream, why wasn't the SPA, with all its resources and patrons, not participating financially? I pointed out that the SPA, at base, was an ideas body which had the experience of creating and founding the BRIT School. The patrons were chosen to reflect the broad sweep of the performing and technical arts; they weren't necessarily people with large disposable incomes, but they were people who would want to contribute their skills and experience once the place was up and running. Then there was Bergen and I, prepared to work all the hours it needed.

While I understood how Paul and Richard could become irritated by my constant requests, what was the alternative? I was wholly willing to solicit Michael Jackson but realised my letter would never be seen by the addressee.

This was graphically demonstrated when I read that

Pete Waterman (of Stock, Aitken and Waterman production fame, which launched Kylie Minogue, Rick Ashley and Jason Donovan amongst others) was enamoured of Paul and Liverpool. I wrote to him, including the appeal document. The letter wasn't answered. When Paul wrote asking him to attend LIPA's first fund-raising lunch at the Performing Right Society, he received an acceptance by return of post.

City Challenge initiative and others

Meanwhile, within government, an initiative was being born which would critically affect LIPA's chance of life in a curiously capricious way. It enabled LIPA to get off the ground, but it was also the mechanism that provided the possibility of a crash landing.

The City Challenge Initiative was sparked off by Michael Heseltine (then Secretary of State for the Environment), who decided to top-slice a small percentage of urban grant through the country to create a fund of £350,000,000. Urban authorities could apply to this fund, but, to succeed, they would need to compete with imaginative urban regeneration schemes. There would be ten winners, each being allotted £35,000,000 a piece.

The positive element was that, in time, Liverpool's bid would succeed. The negative element was the all-too-familiar interface between public and private-sector cultures. Also financially critical, was the Treasury's insistence upon timetables to achieve draw-down of grant – timetables which were designed to meet funding regimes and so often resulted in unachievable project target dates and no space for the unexpected.

All this was to come.

Around this time, there was a visit to the Institute by Michael Portillo, then a minister with responsibility for Merseyside. Merseyside Task Force (and the sub-set City Action Team) agreed to join in the funding of LIPA's business plan. The Liverpool premier of Paul's

Liverpool Oratorio meant Paul would be in Liverpool, so there was a natural opportunity for a photograph.

Paul and I had already discussed the possibility of a blown-up cheque being handed across; Paul felt this would not be appropriate, given the size of the donation and the uses to which the photograph might be put.

Michael Portillo and Paul in the building

The day dawned and I found myself with Paul and Michael Portillo in Paul's old classroom, where he had been taught Spanish by Miss Inkly – a woman who had worn heavy make-up (it was rumoured amongst the schoolboys at the time that this was covering up wounds she'd received during the war, as Paul told Michael) and who'd announced to pupils that they could call her 'sir'. Paul spoke a few words of Spanish to which Michael Portillo responded with full Spanish fluency – both men smiled at each other; it was one of those moments. An engine, which could have misfired, had sprung into life. Michael appeared pleased to be there and to listen to Paul telling him about his schooldays. It fell to me to explain what we were hoping would happen next. I felt proud.

I could also sense the pride in the air when Paul took his bow in the cathedral that evening after the first oratorio performance with Neil Kinnock (the then leader of the Labour Party) in the audience. It was close to the 'Let It Be Liverpool' gig. It was also the first time that money was solicited for LIPA by way of a page in the programme.

I had encouraged Paul to participate in the city's campaign for the additional City Challenge funding, which he did by signing the bid document. When the five-year action plan for regenerating City Centre East was successful, officers felt LIPA deserved a head start, aside from the potential of substantial private investment in a listed building in the city's care.

The LIPA steering committee gets underway

Three days later, the first LIPA steering committee meeting took place with Humphrey in the chair, eighteen appointed members and six observers. The first meeting was designed to get everyone up to speed. The 'everyone' were those people, both in and outside the city, who would be needed to give the project a chance of success.

So, there were prominent Liobians (who later became board members – Stuart Christie and Roger Morris), the Charity Commission (represented by Neil Mackenzie), Liverpool City Council (represented by Jean Maskell and Aelwyn Pugh), Liverpool Polytechnic (represented by Peter Toyne), the School for Performing Arts Trust (represented by Joanna Moriarty, Humphrey Walwyn and, a meeting later, by Rupert Grey), the industry (represented by Wayne Bickerton of the Performing Right Society) and national politics (represented by Steven Norris MP, also a Liobian).

There were also people who represented agencies and advisors; Positive Solutions, Merseyside Task Force, City Challenge and the accountants, Pannell Kerr Forster (their representative, Jim Dimmock, was to play the key role in the creation of LIPA's corporate structure as well as becoming LIPA's financial advisor, while his wife, Katharine, was the first part-time employee – as LIPA's accountant).

Three months later, the meeting discussed the draft business plan during a three-hour meeting. The benefit of such a range of expertise led to the key editing of sections, as well as a sense of involvement. Inevitably, the funding section led to a lively debate, not only about the amount needed, but the familiar conundrum – which comes first: the private or the public sector? Both required evidence that the other was committed, but that commitment was only achievable, from either, if the other was committed.

Working and living in Liverpool

Looking back, once Bergen and I started working in Liverpool, I began one of the most focussed and yet almost imprisoned phases of my working life.

There was the sudden switch from being in colleges surrounded by staff and some 500 students to being in a small room with one other person. The texture of a day would be determined by the quality of the relationship. Although not bosom pals, we got on well enough, which was just as well since there would be little respite from each other. This wouldn't have been so emphasised if we were going to real homes at night. We weren't. At night, we stayed in a cheap hotel within walking distance. Bergen was working part-time and so was away a lot. At night, there were the simple prospects of working (which we did – probably too much) or entertainment (cinema, bowling or TV). We had no real local friends as the people we were getting to know tended to be people who worked as consultants on the project.

Because the possibility of LIPA was risky, I hadn't felt confident about selling the house I owned with Alison in Bishops Stortford. This became a touch irritating when it transpired that working in Liverpool corresponded with a rise in house prices; thereafter, they sank – so sale became unattractive and we became landlords for eight years. Every weekend, I drove the two hundred or so miles back home and tried to stoke up on enough emotional closeness to carry me through the week.

Aside from a day-time working week which was exhilarating and frightening, it was a withdrawn two years, until I was able to feel confident enough to buy what was for me a huge house at a small price – £52,000 for six bedrooms, four living rooms and all the original plaster work you could ask for – in sunny Toxteth, and Alison was able to shift branches within The John Lewis Partnership to work for George Henry Lee, Liverpool.

I am often asked an impossible-to-answer question: as an outsider, what do I think about living in Liverpool? Just concentrating on the physical environment, it is easy for me to say that I have rarely experienced such a variety of environments in one city (the recently released film, *Hilary and Jackie,* which included scenes – amongst others – in The Cotswolds, Russia, Germany, Spain, Italy, France, Israel and the USA, was all shot in Liverpool) and that I live in a style I couldn't afford anywhere else.

Back to the story: around November time, Paul was becoming demoralised for another reason: the financial progress of the project both to get it going and to continue it once it was up and running. Richard urged me to provide some good news.

The earmarking of £4,000,000 City Challenge money

As it happened, there was good news to give. The first was that the business plan had revealed that LIPA would, once full students numbers had been reached, have a year-on-year surplus of between £400,000 to £500,000. The second was that Liverpool City Challenge had confirmed that LIPA was one of their flagship projects, with the rider that projects were thin on the ground in the first year so a first-year application by LIPA was favoured. Allied with this were the funds that were attached to the Institute itself by way of scholarships, which could form the basis of the student endowment fund.

There was a difficulty here that we had encountered in spades in Liverpool and would encounter outside: why couldn't Paul donate more? One City of Liverpool report suggested that Paul should underwrite the whole venture so that if the cash were not raised, he'd be down to fund the project. City Council officers would go on and on about Paul's wealth and I felt increasingly targeted – as if I had anything to do with a personal decision that was someone else's. During one meeting, I pointed out that if this is what happened to wealthy people who were prepared to sink £1,000,000 of their own money, taxed at that, into a project, how on earth did they propose to promote giving to other worthy causes? The wealthy would hardly be encouraged to give when word got around about this sort of treatment.

Time and again, I faced the same conundrum: both Paul and the public sector wanted to be the icing on the cake. In a positive report written by a city economic planning officer in March 1992 and when the project cost had risen to £18.2 million (including VAT), these words conveyed the public-sector feeling: 'The business plan identifies three principal courses of capital funding: UK/EC public resources (35%); UK private resources (50%), international resources (15%)... . The vast majority of finance will need to come from the private sector. Public-sector investment can only be seen as the last cog in the funding of the project.'

Three days later, Bergen and I emerged from a meeting with Liverpool City Council officers, which also included Merseyside Task Force and City Challenge people hardly daring to believe our luck. Council officers, recognising that the building needed to be secured from further decay to enable a potential user to move into the building would be recommending to elected members that £18,000 should be spent on a structural survey, including emergency works to the roof; £40,000 for a new roof design and £600,000 for a new roof. This was in additional to the £4,000,000 in principle from Liverpool City Challenge, which itself was increased to £5,000,000.

Paul was delighted but was concerned that some sort of futuristic hat might be popped over the building. I explained it was a listed building. There needed to be consultation with LIPA as the only existing potential user and the immediate need was to supplement the two down pipes which were coping with rain-water landing upon a 14,000 square foot roof.

Seven days later, this did indeed turn out to be too good to be true and, somewhat shamefacedly, I had to tell Paul that the total sum was in fact just over

£4,000,000 which also had to meet the cost of a new roof – but still, I had been told it was the largest grant from Urban Grant given in this country and was 26.7 per cent of the total cost.

By the time the third and last steering committee meeting took place during January 1992, Liverpool Polytechnic had become Liverpool John Moores University. Peter Toyne, now vice-chancellor as well as chief executive, advised the meeting that LIPA's status as associate college would be key to its future. I hadn't at the time really twigged how critical this could be. I simply perceived the relationship as a mechanism for delivering student fees from the public purse.

Liverpool City Council outlined the next stage: a business plan presentation to the council's Liverpool Institute Working Group, then to relevant committees, a full project appraisal of nine months, and a report to full council to be followed by submission to the Department of the Environment. This met the Department of Environment requirements. When Rupert pointed out that the building could collapse in the meantime, there was nothing that could be done to alter the process, except speed it up.

At the back of everyone's mind was the financial capital mountain that had to be climbed.

While it could be said that City Challenge was backing LIPA in principle by £4,000,000 and Paul was prepared to donate £1,000,000, there was still £7,000,000 to obtain, to meet the estimated £12,000,000 cost – a cost that covered, not simply the building renovation, but the cost of all the activities needed before the first student walked through the door and, on top of that, to meet the student-access element.

As Bergen and I had done, Steve Norris wondered whether in-house fund-raising was the best solution; professional fund-raisers could be held to account. Aside from the cost, I raised the personal relationship this would need if the process would meet Paul's requirements. It would be perfectly possible for Paul to raise major sums, simply, for instance, by endorsements, but it seemed unlikely he would be prepared to do these. A professional fund-raiser would need to appreciate a variety of sensitivities and yet make the fund-raising successful.

Winding up, Humphrey told everyone that the next meeting would be the first meeting of the board of directors.

The first fund raising lunch at The Performing Right Society

The first outing for the fund-raising video was the first fund-raising lunch, held in February at the Performing Right Society. The suggestion had been Humphrey's. Of all the performing arts, music was still the wealthiest and, once again, like the BRIT School before it, LIPA had to return to this sector for support. Although it was in one sense a nicety, music publishers had not supported the BRIT School in the way that record companies had, so a lunch for music publishers at the PRS, particularly since Wayne Bickerton was on board, seemed a natural choice for one of the three lunches Paul undertook to attend.

One of the many discussions would be the menu for the lunch, as later on would the nature of the canteen within LIPA. Vegetarianism was not a passing phase for either Linda or Paul (which would later mean initial negotiations with Macdonalds never moved past the initial stage). At this time, it wasn't easy to find a caterer prepared to provide a visual and delicate vegetarian lunch.

The other keen area for debate was the seating arrangements – partly the protocol and partly the effectiveness.

While guests and leaders of the music publishing industry started their pre-lunch drinks upstairs (together with Humphrey and Tony), Paul and Linda began a floor-by-floor ascent, meeting the PRS staff who undertook the painstaking task of collecting royalties from around the world. Pausing at work-stations as they walked through the open-plan offices, they posed for pictures with happy staff. Vivian Ellis, then president of the PRS, met them as they finally stepped out of the top floor lift.

By this time, I was having a friendly chat with John Eastman, Linda's brother. Linda spotted us and came over. I wondered if this kind of experience was new to all of them; turning up to a fund-raising event was not so novel, but turning up and making your own possibly was. I had met John a couple of times in New York and found him confiding, bright, easy to be honest with and supportive. Quite shortly, I came to realise that John was one of the relatively few people Paul wholly respected and would listen to, aside from being a treasured relative.

I had wondered quite which message would appeal. I'd decided that it had to be an appeal to opportunity: the opportunity of ensuring that some of the planned fifteen per cent increase in students entering higher education would experience the best vocational training for the performing arts on offer; the opportunity for building upon the new status being given to national vocational qualifications; the opportunity for an industry lead institution; the opportunity for taking advantage of the £4,000,000 pledged by the public sector; the opportunity to build upon the £250,000 pledged by Paul as a music publisher; the opportunity to invest in the future; the opportunity to look for support from the other industries which benefit from a thriving entertainment sector; the opportunity to have their institution.

Paul's speech came in two parts, sharing the way in which he had become involved. The first part was a conversation he had had with a man from Toxteth who had told him, shortly after the riots, that what Liverpool needed was a fame school. He'd been wondering what he could do, aside from taking up one hair-brained scheme suggested to him – starting up a car factory which would possibly go bust after a couple of years. The second part was a nostalgic return to make a film in the building and so witnessing its disgraceful state, although he didn't really see it as it was – he had simply reverted to the youngster he once was.

He also told the story of meeting Derek Hatton (a notorious left-wing leader of Liverpool City Council, whose spending of money it didn't have finally spurred the national government of the day to remove Derek and his like from office) when he had received the freedom of the city; Derek telling Paul that he remembered him from Stan Reed's art class in the building. When Paul wondered aloud whether Derek had been interested in art, he told Paul that he'd been the lad in detention. Although Paul wasn't planning for the campaign to be in anyway political, it could be, he mused, that Derek closed the school as an act of revenge.

This probably wasn't the case in reality. The school had closed partly due to the severe population decrease Liverpool had experienced since its heyday (in excess of 900,000 people now down to 410,000), and partly due to a move away from city-living to the Wirral and other nearby areas.

Then came, as it did at each fund-raising lunch, the group photograph which was a way of recording the event, as well as helping everyone realise they were part of the new venture. Everyone received a copy.

In fund-raising terms, the lunch was a success with virtually all contributing something – the largest, being EMI, the company which had largely made itself the size it was with the Beatles. Chris Wright and Pete Waterman did not donate.

Pete Waterman

Pete Waterman was going to be even more surprising. Two years later, Granada filmed an extended news piece on the launch of LIPA's first prospectus at a local theatre, complete with a rock band that had taken part in one of LIPA's first pilot courses. After a positive summary, the programme cut to Pete who was standing in front of his train collection (real trains) at Crewe Station for what was perhaps originally designed to be a ringing endorsement of the idea.

Not a bit of it. Pete thought LIPA was a terrible idea. After touching upon the elitist angle, he went on to opine: 'You can't teach anyone to be a pop star. It's the most amateur activity; if you're not an amateur, it can't work. We are all enthusiastic amateurs. We are not professionals. The minute we become professional, the accountant in us takes over and we lose the creativity of the music.'

When the newscaster suggested that there must be something useful from experience that people like Paul and him could pass on, this was swiftly dismissed: 'There's nothing we can teach young kids. They won't want to listen to people like us; they'll want to do it themselves, The only way to do it is to put people on the ground and make them do it.'

I thought all this was rather odd; odd because I had a small group picture with Pete, Paul and Linda, amongst others, at the PRS lunch when Pete had his own thumbs up, at the time declaring how great the idea was and odd because here was a multi-millionaire claiming that expertise had had nothing to do with his success, while learning from scratch did.

The funding bodies and their differing agendas

Regardless of how successful it really was, all the main players who had a potential stake in the creation of LIPA wanted significance to be attached to the first fund-raising lunch. The public sector wanted and needed to feel that the private sector was getting behind the project; Paul wanted and needed to feel he was amongst others, while I wanted and needed to be able to inspire everyone with a dream.

A month later I was addressing Liverpool councillors. Two-thirds of the way through my presentation, I referred to the lunch: 'Perhaps I can give you an example of the kind of event we can mount. Three weeks ago, Paul hosted a lunch at the Performing Right Society. Twenty representatives from seventeen of the largest and most prominent companies attended. The director general of the PRS told me that he had never seen so many movers and shakers on their doorstep. You will be aware that company decisions involve a number of people and so are not immediate. However, I can tell you that we have already received a six-figure pledge from one of the majors.' (This was the £100,000 pledge from EMI, Paul's record company.)

At the time, I was writing to Humphrey about the 'remarkably lacklustre' responses; I had assumed EMI would chip in and, aside from Warner Chappell, which had pledged £45,000, there was little sense of enthusiasm. I was impatient; it took a while. In the end, the first lunch achieved an excellent £275,375.

Two weeks later the first City Council LIPA Working Group met. The report that was presented recommended that 'in principle' support be given to the project. However, there were many concerns. The responses from senior Liverpool City Council officers were mixed, sometimes idealistic in terms of required information, but underlying their remarks was concern about the size of project, the sheer risk.

At this point, the total cost of the project was £15.4 million (possibly as much as £18.2, depending how VAT might be handled). The costs were: building £9.1 million; project development £1.6 million; student endowment fund £3 million; and £1.7 million of contingency. This meant, if £4 million was coming from the public sector, £8.4 million had to be raised from the private sector over two years, during a recession.

The embryonic LIPA had to climb through the hoops of compatibility with existing local institutions; comply with the physical, people, enterprise and growth and management visions of Liverpool City Challenge; meet the City's Arts and Cultural Industries Strategy and meet the Tourism Strategy. Then officers wanted certainty about employment destinations for students, which took account of the needs of the industry; the achievement of a specific fund-raising strategy within agreed time limits; reassurance about Paul McCartney's commitment and support for the project; the creation of a contingency plan should LIPA fail to meet revenue targets; costings that would accurately reflect the cost of renovation and the strengthening of the current LIPA team by a partnership arrangement with JMU to ensure long-term use of the building, should LIPA fail.

The possibility of failure exercised so many minds to the point that I wondered whether emotional and intellectual energy was being invested simply in risk reduction or even project failure, rather than suggesting mechanisms for success. There was still the over-riding need for money, which, if achieved, would alter the landscape, not only on Mount Street (where the Institute was), but within people's minds.

The appeal document had allowed for small donations (£50 for the naming of a seat in the main auditorium; £100 for the naming of a stair-tread outside the auditorium). Donors largely from Japan, Germany and the United States (largely Beatles fans) were steady from the start. In the US, Charles Rosenay!!!, the editor and founder of *Good Day Sunshine*, the most respected US Beatles fan magazine, helped attract donors, while Tetsuo Hamada, for the Beatles Cine Club in Japan, did the same.

Just before the first meeting of LIPA's board of directors, at the end of January 1992, I had had a severe shock. Arthur Johnson, a journalist from *The Liverpool Echo*, rang me, asking how I felt about LIPA being demoted to Liverpool City Challenge's reserve list. How did I feel? Words like 'lift descending too rapidly' were close.

The ramifications, given the profile Paul had embued the project, meant my next call had to be to Richard, who, on his boss's behalf, shifted into outrage mode. 'Paul is not going to put on a branch which is sawn off,' he fumed. 'If they want a fight, they can have one and we'll win. We'll give them a week to turn it around, otherwise we are going national,' and went on to make a number of unflattering comments about Liverpool and its treatment of the ex-Beatles in general.

That morning we devised a letter to Peter Bounds, chief executive of Liverpool City Council and, at the time, Chair of Liverpool City Challenge. Within six days there had been two meetings and a letter to me. In it, John Flamson, the project director of Liverpool City Challenge, stated that the exclusion of LIPA from the current to a reserve list was 'in no way, any reflection of its importance'. I read on to find out what it was precisely. 'The Department of the Environment are insisting that no over-programming of the Action Plan above £37.5 million for the five years is permissible.' John then went on to write that 'the content of the Action Plan will be subject to continuous change' and ended 'the LIPA project, as far as the Executive Group is concerned, *will* be implemented as part of the five year Action Plan, with the appropriate commitment of public funding to make sure it happens'.

I was confused by events, but relieved by the outcome. The lift was rising. It was clear though that too many key people were jittery. Large contributors were needed.

A note that Keith Hackett wrote to me one Saturday morning was to be more pivotal than either of us could have imagined.

Chapter Fifteen

*EU meetings in Brussels – the Brussels
fund-raising lunch – additionality – Liverpool
fund-raising activities – The LIPA Group scheme
– the LIPA office moves onto the site – Grundig
AG – the London fund-raising lunch – LIPA's
provision refined – Grundig, LIPA and MPL –
the signing*

Ever-inventive, Keith had been galvanised by the
metaphor of the Parthenon – the way in which the EEC
directorate, aside from all its huge subcategories of
funding, had created a special fund for the Parthenon,
because it represented the birthplace of European
civilisation. The link he had made between this and a
new institution for performing arts in Liverpool was
that Liverpool represented (and could develop further
with the right support) the European birthplace of
contemporary popular music. The 'further' was LIPA –
anticipating changes in training, cultural exchanges
and industry developments and building on one popular
strength of a city in an EEC priority area.

At a stroke, the map to meet the capital cost could
be redrawn into thirds: one third, UK public sector; one
third, EEC and one third, private.

EU meetings in Brussels

Within weeks, I was collecting Keith at five-thirty a.m.
for the first of many visits to Brussels. Flying was not
a mixed blessing for him. The only way he could cope

was to sit at the back and smoke heavily. I joined him, weighed down with appeal brochures and videos.

The first visit lasted three days and took in eleven meetings. As ever, I'd imagined a formality that never materialised. I was struck not only by the youth, but by the informality of the civil servants I met and, stupidly, I had not realised quite how many would be British. Keith had coached me extensively for each meeting – 'be inspirational and concise for this one and stress the involvement of industry figures' and 'aside from the vision of LIPA, you need to stress the ability of Merseyside to hold on to the individuals trained at LIPA when they come out'.

The first meeting turned out to be the gloomiest and showed how immense the task some European agencies were facing. One European department was embarking on a journey that was aiming to achieve European comparability of vocational qualifications. The cultural industries were regarded as being 'too soft' to be a major priority so data was not collected. How different things are now; it is almost true that you can't read an EU directive without reference to the cultural sector. I've been told that LIPA had been one of the drivers.

A few meetings on and we met Graham Meadows – the third key human bureaucrat in a short, but exhilarating, line of like bureaucrats. Graham Meadows, with his tongue-in-cheek bluntness, reminded me of a movie star, although I couldn't recall quite which one, an actor in a Western perhaps. Graham was the desk officer for the all-important DG XVI in Brussels, which handled structural funds and had the all-important task of promoting particular schemes to EU politicians and higher level bureaucrats. In particular, he was a key to the huge European Regional Development Fund and the way it was to be applied to Merseyside. He was positive about LIPA from the first meeting. In later meetings, when LIPA began to be bogged down in the tensions between Brussels and the UK government, Graham was so breezily confident that he advised me to take six weeks' holiday.

There was a potential second track for a new budget line in the EC Budget, which was not activated. The first and most promising track however was liable to be troubled by the UK government's habit of substituting European funds for its own. The EU was about to insist on 'additionality' – a new topic about to become appallingly familiar to the LIPA team.

The Brussels fund raising lunch

One of the aims of the first visit was to find out if a political European launch event would cement European Union support. Within a week of arriving back from Brussels, I was pitching the idea to Paul. For the project, it was reasonably high risk, given that this left just one further lunch I could pitch for and three months to pull the event together.

The mechanics of pulling the lunch together, given the politicians' diaries, was severe. Accurately judged letters of support from prime British political figures were required; a setting which struck the right note of prudence with good taste; the identification and clarification of appropriate support to inform responding speeches; a European Parliament and Commission guest list which would cover all bases and eventualities; a judiciously worded letter of invitation, let alone a date which most could manage and a menu that met with Linda and Paul's approval – and more: a political host (which turned out to be the urbane Sir Jack Stewart-Clark, the MEP for Paul's local constituency); audio-visual arrangements; police liaison; press coverage; as it happened, a lunch sponsor (Volkswagen); a seating arrangement which would satisfy most of the guests (both for the lunch and for the group photograph); and precise timings from the technical run-through to arrivals, to the start of the lunch, the serving and clearing of each course, the team photograph and guest departures.

Once the speakers were identified (Sir Jack Stewart-Clark for the European Parliament; me for LIPA and its European dimensions, John Flamson for Liverpool and the City Challenge initiative there, Paul, and a final response from the most senior Commission representative – Commissioner Vasso Papandreou, merely responsible for employment, industrial relations and social affairs, human resources and education and training!), there was also the business of dovetailing speeches – attempting to balance what people wanted to say, against repeating what another speaker might say and hitting all the European funding policy fundamentals.

In the course of their five pre-launch Brussels visits, Keith and I met two men who became firm friends of the project: John Morley (Head of Division DGV) and Jeremy Harrison (then a director of a technical assistance unit), whose friendship was quickly tested by the pressure placed upon them to make the lunch work.

No less pressure was placed upon Sir Jack: a month before the lunch, I was writing and ringing every other day when I realised that out of twelve EC parliamentarians, only three had accepted, three were maybes and three unlikelies.

Paul was also asking how things were progressing. Perhaps, unlike the PRS lunch, this was the moment when I reflected upon the stakes involved and how, with relatively little adjustment, a dream lunch could tip into a nightmare.

Inevitably, David Mellor swung back into view again. Unable to come to the lunch, he provided a ringing statement of endorsement from the British government. John Major responded by adding his weight behind what his minister had written.

For Geoff Baker, this was enough for a press release, casting the City Challenge 'in principle' matching, as 'an amazing pound-for-pound wager' between the prime minister and Paul McCartney ('the government has promised to donate £4,000,000 – if Paul can raise another £4,000,000 by the end of the year'). Moving swiftly on, he cast John Major's response for a message to be read at the lunch, as 'his first move in charge of the presidency of the EC'.

This creative upbeat release offered a journalist or two a chance to review the government's economic policies. Charles Moore of the *Daily Telegraph* was one. 'Mr McCartney is a very rich man,' he observed. Taking into account the tax advantages for the well-off since the Conservative victory at the last election, 'a rough calculation suggests that the return of the Tories has therefore saved Mr McCartney much more than the required £4,000,000 this year alone. Does he need any further assistance for his projects, however worthy?'

He also wondered why it was that 'the Fab Four never got an Arts Council grant. Why should their successors be treated differently?' He went on to wonder what had happened to the quite impressive subsidies which had been 'poured into Merseyside'.

As I was continuing to learn, the twinning of Paul and fund-raising had a downside, as well as the upside.

The night before the lunch I was in a hotel, briefing Humphrey (who represented the SPA), tidying up loose ends and reflecting upon the performance aspect of the whole thing: it was like a production, everyone was supposed to play a part, the spoken lines were written (aside from Paul's) and the event had a time limit.

When Paul and Linda arrived at the lunch venue, I fractionally wondered about the lives lived by those others who made events like this happen, the people behind the people we all saw in the press. As Paul and Linda posed for photographs outside the building, Richard sharply asked if there was a room for Paul and Linda to rest in, which luckily, had been arranged.

After the meal, the speeches. In a wave of emotion towards the end of my speech (tiredness played a part), I said, 'The European Community itself was a dream and that's becoming real, so you are used to making dreams come true. This project could be part of your dream. I hope you agree it should be,' and became quite overcome.

John Flamson, measured and eloquent, ended his speech by saying, 'I have confidence in the LIPA team – their professionalism, sincerity and commitment. I do not apologise for stressing this human resource, because contrary to received wisdom, it is not money which makes the world go round, but people. We have the right people, but a little money would help.'

Paul's speech was similar to his earlier PRS speech, although he added a ringing statement: 'As far as I am concerned, this is going to be the very best performing arts school in the world. I'm sure of that and I'll do everything I can to make that come true.' The reticence of statements in Britain seemed far away. 'I'll do everything I can' sounded good.

The key speech though was the response given by Commissioner Vasso Papandreou in English, with a strong Greek accent, which gave her delivery a gentle informality. 'It seems that we support the young people to have qualifications they cannot use or jobs they find very boring sometimes. I can see, through your institute, the young people will receive the training they will admire and welcome, which will benefit them and Europe. This is a worthwhile project; we wish you all the best and we shall do the most we can do.'

Senior Europeans were child-like and enchanted with Paul in their midst. After the group photograph at the end, real children did emerged, it seemed from behind pillars, the children of many present, only too eager for autographs and photographs. By then, everyone had relaxed into enjoyment. Mary Banotti, the MEP for Dublin, summarised this element in a post-lunch letter: '...it was really a delicious lunch and I certainly enjoyed seeing my fellow ex-groupies from the sixties fluttering around the Beatle flame'.

Additionality

There were other brimmingly enthusiastic post-lunch letters. I was lulled into thinking that it was just a matter of time before substantial financial support was on its way to the project; it was a matter of time and the financial support was substantial, but there was more, much more to be done before it materialised, caught up as it was about to be, in the UK government's interpretation of 'additionality'.

Four months later, time had become essential. I drafted a letter for Paul to send to Michael Portillo. Mid-November and there was tense conversation between Richard and me about lack of progress. Aside from Paul's letter, I decided to write to everyone he could think of: Department of National Heritage, Department of the Environment, European MEPs, and Geoff Hoon MP, who was convening an all-party committee on the music industry for the House of Commons.

The problem was indeed additionality. Consideration of ERDF grants in Liverpool had been deferred three times in the absence of a government statement. It appeared that the old problem of additionality had been resolved, but that a new one (private-sector funds being used to reduce public-sector contribution) had emerged.

Liverpool fund raising activities

It was difficult to know quite where to pitch the fund-raising effort: high level? low level? everything in between? everything? Occasionally, needle in a burning haystack were the words that came to my mind when thinking about the target dates set by funders.

A chance visitor to the Beatles Story (a local Beatles exhibition created by Mike Burne and his wife on Albert Dock) might be well off and see LIPA as an immortal link, so I set up a lectern with the image of Paul in a cap and gown (achieved while receiving an honorary degree at Sussex University) with flyers. A chance visitor at the annual Liverpool Beatles Convention might stand a good chance of achieving the same trick.

So August found me selling the original Cavern bricks at the 1992 Beatles Convention. With three of the blow-up pictures of the institute behind me (last seen at Paul's Albert Dock concert), I stood behind a table laden with whole and half-bricks (donated by Bill Heckle and David Jones of Cavern City Tours), along with some copies of the fund-raising video. The evening before I'd been trying to ensure that the plastic notices on the front of each brick were stuck on, as well as signing letters attesting to authenticity, interspersed with fund-raising letters to national figures. Is this the richness of the whole experience or a measure of desperation I'd wondered?

It was the first time I met Cathy Skelly, who had come along to help and, in time, was LIPA's first new full-time employee. Her rise from general secretary to communications manager reflected her alert, outgoing personality, replete with Liverpool expressions ('I wouldn't have your job for a big clock,' she once told Geoff Baker). In time, this was a trait I associated with Liverpool. You could rely on a scouser for a pithy quote.

Wandering around the convention was an eye-opener. There, sitting behind tables and displays, were people whose knowledge of the Beatles had grown up with them and was volumetric – as was the variety of memorabilia displayed and for sale. I was dimly aware this sort of thing went on, but nothing prepared me for the attention to detail shown by exhibitors; it would have been a brave bet to place: who knew the most about the Beatles?

Were they sad unfilled souls? Not a bit of it, these were people who felt at home, wherever they had journeyed from and this was not the first visit. They met friends, wandered down to the open-air festival in Matthew Street, took the ferry across the Mersey, had a drink in the Cavern, caught one of the many bands and generally reminded themselves what it had been like nearly thirty years earlier.

I was due to speak on the opening day for forty-five minutes, but as I spoke about LIPA –what it wanted to do and how it hoped to get there – I had a sense that audience attention was slipping away. What people wanted to know about was every moment I had spent with Paul. I realised how little material I had on this subject since the focus had been on LIPA. Luckily, no one asked me for what I would have considered was gossip and tat. Thirty minutes was as much as I could manage.

Which meant that I rarely returned to subsequent conventions. Brave, enthusiastic and, often delightful, fans bought bricks, which often meant transporting them back to home countries, more often than not – the States and Japan.

The LIPA group scheme

Meanwhile, the solution Jim and his accounting colleagues devised for the LIPA Group, which obviated VAT on renovation (but also meant VAT would slowly be recouped at a lower level from rental) went like this:

The Liverpool Institute for Performing Arts Limited (the charitable company) which owned the building and would grant a lease to LIPA Holdings Limited (a company limited by shares and a wholly owned subsidiary) which would undertake the refurbishment. Once the building was refurbished, LIPA Limited would pay rent to LIPA Holdings Limited, while LIPA Holdings would in turn repay interest on the grant monies which only the charity could receive. The idea was that the flow of money between the two companies would achieve an equilibrium.

The LIPA office moves on site

The first meeting of the LIPA Board took place at the start of 1992. Bergen and I had applied to the city to move from their tiny office to a set of empty laboratories that were set along one wall of the institute's playground.

I was gripped by the idea: it would be first time after a seven-year gap that people would be working on the Liverpool Institute site. I would just need to look up from my desk and, out of the laboratory windows, see the building that could house the dream.

Time and again, I had wandered through the empty building when the need to imagine what might be overtook me. I'd jokingly described the feeling to others as 'endless foreplay' – the sensation that something wonderful was around the corner and yet turning the corner was just the hardest task, however minimal it might seem.

Although scary, it was also pleasurable; risk and excitement were linked. I came to realise that at one end of a scale, total comfort was totally boring and, at the other, total excitement was exhausting. Yet, both were part of life and difficult to live without; risk made you feel alive...and both had the potential, at their extremes, to kill you...

Grundig AG

There was a major unexpected outcome from the Brussels lunch.

I first heard, from an officer of Liverpool City Council, that a Mr Schneider from Grundig had called, wanting to get in touch with LIPA. As it happened, my optimism about raising private-sector finance was starting to plummet, so I was glad that, for the first time, someone had contacted us.

'We are interested,' Dieter Schneider began, 'in supporting your planned rock university; I would like to meet you.' I described the Brussels lunch. Dieter told me he already knew about the lunch; a news report in the *Frankfurter Allgemeine Zeitung* had caught an employee's (Gerhard Seiferth) attention, which was the reason he was ringing. Grundig were the largest supplier of consumer electronics in Germany and second largest after Philips in Europe, who had a significant stake in Grundig.

Within the month, I drove to Manchester airport to meet him. I had decided that my little Japanese runabout was not quite the image and hired a midrange car, which added to the unreality I felt. Dieter was a large, bulky and talkative man. Indeed, we were so busy talking and I so anxious to make a positive impressive that I missed a key turning. Although I'd been in Liverpool for a short while, nothing outside the car window seemed remotely familiar. It dawned on me that I'd driven mistakenly into Manchester. Struggling to maintain the flow of conversation, I searched for a turning that would help me travel west – without drawing attention to the mistake I'd made.

With as much urbanity as I could muster, I attempted to impress Dieter. The tour of the institute was not the problem.

The problem was the tiny office that Bergen and I occupied. This was, I felt, unlikely to give Dieter much confidence, so, without actually lying, I gave Dieter the impression that the remainder of the Hahnemann Building was in some unspecified way connected with the project; this was just the executive office. Luckily, since there wasn't any, Dieter did not enquire about secretarial assistance.

Within a further month, the return match took place with me flying to Grundig's headquarters in Furth, the first of many, many journeys, to present LIPA to Hans Bartel (Grundig's executive sales director) and Johan van Splunter (a Grundig board member). I tried not to think too long about the importance of each meeting.

Fortunately, there were joint interests. I ran through the LIPA philosophy and its practical expression: what would be taught and how it would be taught, stressing the pan-European perspective.

Johan responded by acknowledging that Grundig was a respected brand, but, for survival, needed rejuvenating, needed to appeal to the existing youth market. The new associations made with youth sport (mountain bike racing, free style ski-ing) had bought the brand youth credibility; they now wished to address the cultural side.

As the exchange continued, I became aware that Grundig was considering sponsorship and not short-term either – between three to five years, most likely five. I knew enough about sponsorship at this point to realise that LIPA would have to give something in return. Just as I was wondering what that might be or could even be, Johan wondered aloud how realistically they could sponsor a project which was planned, rather than existing and so which was not one hundred per cent certain. (This was an unwelcome reminder of the man who wanted to donate £50, but wanted reassurance while doing so.)

This problem was left hanging as Hans went on to describe the main idea they had in mind: musical competence, linking future music industry employees and leaders, often as performers, with hi-fi equipment; it was, after all, the mechanism through which music was heard. This was an idea that would take time to consider, cost and activate. The first step would be a presentation to the board.

Johan returned to what the deal might be, the way in which LIPA might deliver, aside from not using any other supplier for consumer electronics, a benefit that they could exploit. Clearly PR was the key: gaining LIPA students in mainland Europe, promoting LIPA in company product brochures, competitions and a European benefit concert.

As I waited in the clean, neat Nuremberg air terminal, I couldn't fail to wonder if this was the needle in the now burning haystack. After the BRIT School disappointments, was the philosophy really going to see the light of day? Were the dreams really going to become a reality? Was I, in short, within striking distance of orgasm?

The London fund raising lunch

The *Liverpool Echo* talked up the October 1992 London lunch: 'Paul McCartney today addressed leaders of the arts and business worlds at a free lunch expected to raise thousands of pounds for his Fame-style school in Liverpool'; the truth fell far short. In fact, the only positive result was a unique encounter with George Walker as he left.

Government officials had felt chary about George Walker sharing a table with Robert Key, the then National Heritage under-secretary. I had pointed out that George was a brother to the brother who had admittedly a few business problems. As he was leaving the lunch, George pressed £100 in £10 notes into my hands saying, 'Very nice, I hope it works.'

When we had supper a few weeks later, I discovered that George was also supporting the development of the Globe Theatre in Southwark and was wondering if there might be a tie-up between the Globe and LIPA. I found George a man of quiet dignity, who could call up a member of his extended family for a ride at two in the morning and yet another to take me to an airport hotel so that I could catch an aeroplane early in the morning.

Aside from George, not a single person (outside Dieter who attended on Grundig's behalf) affected the project – despite the diligent research that had led to their presence. The research was partly the result of reference to all the handbooks on corporate giving and partly through an acquaintance of George Martin's, who had heard about LIPA while talking with him during a garden party in Wiltshire. The acquaintance was, she impressed me, clicked into private donors – this seemed a familiarly unfamiliar scene, hello Susan Davenport again. 'The ladies who lunch' was still an alien world so I was only too glad to have an ally, one who was agreeable to being paid expenses only.

As it turned out, she was unable to encourage one to attend, by which time it was too late to do much else except to go ahead. The corporate guest list was strong and included Bill Kenwright, a Liobian, who had been a near contemporary of Paul's.

After lunch, Christian Simon, a German journalist and a hard-working LIPA supporter, had had the idea for providing a book for sale throughout Europe, as part of a series about the dream of a united Europe through interviews with leading artists, which would help publicise LIPA's dream as well. The series editor interviewed Paul in English and then asked him to read a German message for a radio promotion of the book. I was seated at the other end of the table and heard Paul speak with idiomatic fluency – he sounded pretty much like a German speaker.

I returned to Liverpool low in spirits; the third lunch had been a waste of time; the last lunch Paul had promised he would attend. I gazed miserably at Runcorn Bridge, which had before rarely failed to lift my spirits.

A month later I drafted my 'End of 1992 Term Fund-raising Report'. On reading it, Richard told me that he and Paul had felt I'd been depressed when writing it. I simply wanted to log the work done, identify what had been achieved, what could be learnt and how could this be turned into positive action.

Most had potentially been achieved within the public sector. Liverpool City Challenge seemed likely to contribute £3.4 million, aside from the £0.6 million they would be putting towards a water-tight building, so long as their money could be matched from the private sector. The European Regional Development Fund was likely to contribute around £4.5 million, as long as the money would be treated as truly 'additional'; there was support as well from other European funds enabling the development of cross-Europe training materials, ideally through open and distance learning.

For the amount of work devoted, the return from the private sector was slimmer. Aside from Paul's £1,000,000 donation, I reported £275,375 from the lunch held at the PRS; £75,375 stemming from letters Paul had written soliciting support from friends, £70,628 from his work, alongside friends he'd drafted in to help; £40,000 from the Merseyside Task Force for the business plan; £40,000 from Apple Corps and £1,000 from a friend of Richard's.

There had also been a donation from HM the Queen. It had been Paul's idea to write to her, while I concocted the letter. It had reminded me of one of the exercises I used to set as a Scale 1 English teacher; 'Write to…in the style of...'. Life had now offered me the task of writing to the Queen in the style of Paul McCartney – for real. The benefit of the donation really resided in the publicity.

The spark was Grundig which was considering DM1,000,000 a year for five years – effectively £2,000,000 – by way of donation, with a further possible DM30,000,000 to DM57,000,000 for activities to support the relationship between the two organisations.

I noted the certainty needed by Liverpool City Challenge that the financial targets would be met; the political to-ing and fro-ing between the European Union and the UK and, here was where weariness crept in, an assessment of private-sector work. 570 approaches had been made: 143 to music publishing companies; 12 to local business organisations and 414 to major national or international companies, trusts or prominent individuals.

The research into the 414 alone had been substantial and had included extensive use of 'The Richest' listings, particularly those from Liverpool. I'd tried, for instance, Paul Raymond's daughter, an old student of the Guildhall School of Music and Drama. Her father began life in Liverpool. I'd wondered at the time how I'd handle the press, let alone Paul, if the approach to a publisher of soft pornographic magazines (amongst other allied activities) had worked.

I felt five areas were worth pursuing within the private sector. The first was the continuation of Paul's approaches, and finding another partner of Paul's stature to supplement this work.

Cameron Mackintosh was identified and, through Tony, met Paul just before a pre-1993 World Tour try-out in Docklands. Paul asked Cameron how Stephen Sondheim, one of the recipients of Cameron's Oxford visiting professorial scheme, had taught. Beyond that, nothing practical had come of the meeting.

Picking firmly up on what I understood was a Richard Ogden idea, the second was selling a special ticket for Paul's 1993 World Tour. This was to become known as the LIPA Ticket; it began life as a corporate hospitality opportunity (although, as time went on, the time and work to sell the corporate aspect across the world became unachievable and tickets were largely brought by private individuals).

The third was to do whatever could be done to support the Japanese fund-raising effort. The fourth was to achieve Steve Lewis's (then head of music publishing at Virgin Records) and Music Publishers' Association's idea of a record where famous artists chose songwriters to write a song for them which would be heard on a charitable album to raise money for LIPA and the fifth was to achieve the Grundig sponsorship in a way which would not affect other possible sponsors.

One fund-raising approach came from an Alan 'Taz' Meinzinger, a concert promoter who offered to donate the profits from concert tours featuring Long John Baldry. Since I had no idea what level of revenue this might mean, I contacted Richard who advised me to keep well away from any involvement at any level. I was puzzled. In the fight for support, this seemed as innocuous an idea as any...perhaps up until the moment I asked Alan why he called his company 'FEA Productions'. 'What does FEA stand for?' I innocently asked. 'Fuck 'em all. I've been fucked over so many times by so many people, that I was fucking going to show them and then shove FEA in their faces.'

This tale, alongside detailed fund-raising, education and building reports were topics for the first executive committee meeting in May 1992. By the end of the year, five more meetings had taken place.

LIPA's provision refined

The education committee (all volunteers to begin with) was trying to get to grips with the teaching framework. The link with JMU meant inevitable involvement with the Integrated Credit Scheme – an almost straight lift from the USA; this enabled students to exercise a degree of choice about the elements that would make up their three years of study. There was an international version (the Credit Accumulation and Transfer Scheme), which would allow students to draw elements from institutions across the globe: one year in Liverpool, one semester in Nashville, another semester elsewhere. The pragmatic US solution to enable degree acquisition alongside a fair amount of mobility (credits could be clocked up anywhere until ninety were earned and a degree gained) was being adopted in the UK.

The idea now was that this would take in a variety of provision from other local providers – a network of providers, so that students had a *smorgasbord* of choice (this carried with it the obvious danger: a little bit of this and that, possibly without rational thought, resulting in a meal of sorts, however incoherent).

This was the latest reincarnation of embedding LIPA at a variety of levels within the local area. The purely higher education element was going to be much smaller than the main bulk of students: part-time students who would be coming to LIPA for vocational training, delivered through the National Vocational Qualification structure. In fact, there was a hope for dual qualification.

To gauge how well this would work, a series of short courses would be run during the development period by Denise Stanley.

As the year progressed, some work would be done on an outline curriculum and some work on the details of each module (a self-contained learning programme, where thirty a year made up the ninety needed for a degree), but it wasn't until the appointment of David Price (one of the initial volunteers) that the degree programme came fully into focus and until the appointment of six subject heads that the detail did as well.

By this time, the government (in response to the enthusiastic take-up of additional student numbers by universities) had needed to close a five-year expansion programme early. This was to mean that LIPA would find itself recruiting students without certainty of fee support and the planned ethos of part-timers was affected. This was to be a major headache.

Towards the end of 1992, Liverpool City Challenge was interested in little else other than LIPA's ability to meet its funding target. Nor were too many other people either – not least the people who were working or volunteering their time to make LIPA possible.

The £12.2 million was now divided up: £4.6 million from the private sector, £4.2 million from Europe and £3.4 million from City Challenge. The report noted that LIPA was likely to be (as indeed it turned out to be) the test case to determine that European funding, if agreed by the European Commission, would be truly additional to other UK private- and public-sector support. The work that Keith and I had done in Brussels was bearing fruit: the European Commission was insisting upon LIPA because of its potential effect on regeneration, its European training dimension, student placement and cultural development and also insisting upon true additionality.

The Liverpool City Challenge Executive Group decided to force the additionality issue by agreeing to support LIPA in principle by allocating £1.5 million in 93/94; £1.5 million in 94/95 and £0.4 million in 95/96. The green light was dependent upon a detailed project appraisal in the spring of 1993.

Grundig, LIPA and MPL

The key to achieving the private-sector target was Grundig. Key for Grundig was the involvement of Paul and, to this end, they wanted to view the VISA TV spot from a previous tour. Key for Paul was non-endorsement of product and a suspicion (shared by Richard) that he needed to be extra vigilant. Key for me was to find a solution.

Sponsorship of rock and pop tours was a vexed subject, especially, I imagined, for Paul. Here was an artist who felt creative artefacts should not be used for anything else other than for what they were originally intended but who had, however, allowed his tours to be sponsored, since, presumably, he could not resist the revenue. (He was not alone in this; all major acts had sponsored tours.) The upcoming 1993 tour was to be sponsored by VW. A VW promotional executive was working on the re-launch of the Beetle car and it had crossed his mind that a Beatle to re-launch a Beetle was a gift idea from God in a promotional mood.

The integration of Paul, Grundig and LIPA was a task that took up the last three months of 1992. Paul's 1993 upcoming World Tour was an added ingredient that Grundig found attractive for dealer incentives, amongst other benefits.

There were four prerequisites that were needed to secure Grundig's commitment: a guarantee the project would be carried out; Grundig would be the exclusive main sponsor; Paul McCartney's endorsement and commitment to LIPA and the achievement of its European dimension.

It seemed to me that fund-raising foreplay was nearly over. I'd known that if I could get everyone to the point where each was saying 'I will, if you will' and the sums stacked up, there would be no going back.

One of the elements that would loom large was the TV spot. Faxes went back and forth between Richard and Dieter (on behalf of Grundig) and me. It seemed as if we three, at least, could reach a workable solution: a TV spot with a statement about LIPA by Paul, no endorsement of product, no mention of Grundig except a 'sponsored by Grundig' at the end, which would then change into an advertisement for Grundig product. The product Grundig had in mind was a range of hi-fi equipment they were to name 'Performing Arts'.

Richard and Paul were, in the meantime, having serious misgivings. Paul saw the potential Grundig sponsorship as a commercial move too far and pointing towards the kind of institution it might become: an advertising vehicle, rather than providing quality education with an appropriate level of gravitas.

He rang me over a number of weekends, worrying about the link between commerce and education. 'I'm expecting LIPA to be on the level of Oxford and Cambridge; you wouldn't expect them to link with a commercial product in this way, would you?' I pointed out that traditional universities did already have colleges named after their founders and benefactors. 'But not like this!' countered Paul. 'I haven't named it the Paul McCartney College, why should Grundig get their name up there?'

'Because that's what they are paying for,' I responded.

'It's all too commercial, you've got to do this another way,' Paul continued.

When I protested that I had done my best to raise money and time was running short, Paul told me, returning to an earlier theme, to get the other patrons involved. 'It's only me,' Paul complained, 'even Grundig's only me.' Thinking as fast as I could (which was rarely one of my strong points), I asked whether he'd feel better if Joan Armatrading joined in the TV spot. (As it happened, Joan later agreed but was not taken up on her agreement.)

As I had become used to do, I went into my garden after the call was over, brooding and smoking. I felt I'd tried everything. Here was a sum which could make the dream come true and what's more, on Grundig's side, a sensitivity that would also try to manage commercial benefit alongside a quality product and yet, it seemed, in some minor way, unacceptable.

Whatever I felt, I had to keep my composure and try my best to make the Grundig sponsorship acceptable...somehow. My mother adapted a famous quote, which I pinned up 'If you decide to ride a tiger, you cannot dismount or looked pissed off.'

Richard followed up Paul's call along similar lines. I pointed out (again) that the patrons were neither individually or collectively wealthy. One person was – Cameron – and it was tough, even for John Eastman, to encourage him to donate. I was unsure about what

Paul expected me to do, but I would do whatever he asked and pointed out that, once again, Paul was likely to have the best response from the wealthy.

Then a surprise.

Linda, it was rumoured, became concerned about VW tour sponsorship – to be sponsored by a product that polluted the planet. All of a sudden, Richard had to find a new European sponsor and fast. His instant solution was to ask Grundig. In the McCartney camp, if Grundig were about to support the tour, it was more acceptable for them to support LIPA too.

Once I found out, I pleaded with Richard not to let this affect the embryonic Grundig/LIPA five-year sponsorship agreement undergoing legal preparation. It was no use. The Grundig/LIPA agreement was reduced by a year and the funds applied to the European leg of Paul's 1993 tour. Since this would affect what I had told City Challenge and others, I had one last try. I asked Grundig if they would be prepared to provide equipment to the value of one year's sponsorship, which would not cost them as much as pure money. Grundig felt enough was enough. I thought of a third option: counting the amount Grundig was prepared to apply to publicising LIPA through the TV spot as matching funding – which I did.

As 1992 ended, intensive negotiations were underway between Grundig, MPL and LIPA. This wasn't easy. The New Year began with Paul and Richard still concerned about the linkage between LIPA and Grundig; the fundamental point being the definition of title sponsor. The visual attachment of Grundig to the LIPA name/logo was to be a major issue – Paul still felt uncomfortable about the image this created and felt it was inappropriate to the quality he hoped LIPA would achieve – despite the level of financial support.

As drafts of the agreement between LIPA and Grundig began to exist and, with the strictest confidence, began to circulate within the public sector, the reaction there was diametrically opposite – here was the commercial sponsor they wanted and, indeed, needed – and could boast about to the mandarins in Whitehall – to demonstrate the success of public-sector support in encouraging private-sector support; the truth in LIPA's case was that this was a sponsorship, not a donation and that without Paul's connection with LIPA, this interest would not have been forthcoming.

The Grundig signing

The intensity of faxes between LIPA, Grundig and MPL reached a crescendo in February 1993, because on the 23rd, in the Festhalle in Frankfurt, the agreements were going to be signed, before the second of Paul's New World Tour concerts.

Among the many points needing to be agreed was the Grundig insistence that the LIPA/Grundig agreement would last for an initial year, and could only be extended by Grundig if it was satisfied that LIPA was likely to achieve its goals, particularly the European goals and that LIPA would deliver 'the performer' (Paul McCartney) at a variety of events. Neither were possibilities for LIPA, the second point needing a detailed statement in the MPL/Grundig agreement.

Part too of the faxing intensity was Grundig's own cost-cutting activities, which had necessitated the closing of a German factory and subsequent trade union activity. The press conference that had been planned following the agreement signing, and which had been subject of prolonged negotiation, abruptly needed to go. To close a factory and then hand over £1.4 million of sponsorship was unlikely to be understood by workers who had suddenly found themselves out of work.

In contrast to the sparky activity before, the actual agreements were signed in a small dressing room, complete with shower, beneath the stage, with me signing on behalf of LIPA, Alison, my wife, as witness and Johan van Splunter, signing for Grundig.

The next event was a photograph and handshake with Paul. The Grundig people, with me and photographer in tow, waited in a narrow corridor backstage. At this point, the show was thirty minutes away. With twenty minutes to go, we were moved to the main corridor leading past Paul's dressing room. By the time it was approaching ten minutes to show time, we had been edged further down the corridor. We politely waited. The seconds ticked away. No one knew what to say. Paul emerged four minutes later and started walking down the corridor. He approached us (the photographer sprang into action), telling us he was about to go on stage. Quick handshakes, thumbs up, flash, flash and off he went to sing.

It took me a moment or two to drag myself away from the immediacy of what had just taken place to realise that this was a major moment: LIPA now had the private-sector finance it needed.

I thought I had achieved all the finance needed. I wasn't to know that the public sector was still to remain unconvinced LIPA was a viable project; nor that a year or so on, I would need to raise further sums as the building cost spiralled upwards.

Chapter Sixteen

*Managing the Liverpool end of EU grants –
design team – the roof – the LIPA Tour Ticket
and the fans – the public sector ask for
safeguards LIPA can't accept – Grundig's London
press conference – the playground – Japanese
activities – the pilot courses are delivered –
Paul's concerns erupt – the building contract is
signed – Thomas arrives*

The spinning plates in 1993 coalesced around three major activities: fund-raising (most of it involving the LIPA Ticket for 'The New World Tour'), the building and what LIPA would provide for its students. The three activities took place pretty well simultaneously, with shadows heralding the major moments and enduring when the moments passed.

One shadow over LIPA's potential provision occurred shortly after Paul's 1992 staff Christmas party, which was generally held in a hotel near his home in Sussex, when I was asked to meet Richard in MPL's London office the next day.

But before the shadow, a prologue – the long-lasting concern over me, as a person, emerged.

Shortly after I walked in, Richard exploded. 'What do you mean by bringing someone who was so obviously gay to Paul's Christmas party? Have you any idea about the responsibility you carry in this project?'

I was bewildered. 'Who are you talking about? The person I brought to the party was the SPA's accountant who had worked for years without pay and I knew that, since he was a great Beatles fan, meeting Paul would be a moment he would never forget.'

Richard shouted, 'But he was gay, you stupid fucker!'

'No, he isn't. He's rabidly heterosexual and is currently divorced and dating another woman.'

Richard sighed. 'You've got to be careful. You can't do anything that would embarrass Paul. As far as most of the people you meet are concerned, you are him.'

Then the shadow: the problem was the pilot courses, which Richard flatly asked me to cancel 'to show your solidarity with Paul'. The content and the personnel were a worry. I hoped the perceived difficulty could be dealt with rationally and, following this meeting, wrote a six-page letter to Paul outlining the rationale, which, I was later to discover, was not an appreciated move – but then, occasionally, nothing was going to be.

While I was writing it, I was wondering how best to marry the intensely personal and practical nature of popular music-making with the world of accountable state-funded provision. Despite this, I had to point out the time-scale which had emerged: for courses to start in 1995, admissions had to begin in 1994 and for admissions, there needed to be an outline of LIPA's provision which would appear in a handbook in January 1994. Provision was also closely linked with validation. Since, at the time, LIPA was due to deliver courses in partnership with other Liverpool institutions, the partnerships needed testing in practice. There was also a degree of confusion about what LIPA would be doing. Finally, there was the balance that needed to be achieved between uniqueness and risk. Why not test, at our own expense, the viability of a course or two, away from the glare of the spotlights?

The recent European support meant that the courses would also be run in Spain, Dublin and Germany.

Aside from suggesting a meeting with Denise, the course leader, I sent Paul her résumé and explained, since local venues could be seen as second-rate, why they were being used.

A meeting with Paul went well enough, although Paul had wondered if the building could be saved without an end-user. I tried not to be winded. He was also concerned that the total funding should be in place before any activities, such as discussion with the design team and the short courses, were underway. After a bit, he decided that the short courses were an excellent mechanism to keep the public sector on track because if they fancied withdrawing, it would be seen to be too late – LIPA was underway.

I now see that things were happening too fast from the vantage-point of Paul's natural caution. Ideally, there should have been a step-by-step approach that was invisible, but this was impossible.

Paul approved the tour brochure two months before, which included this quote: 'People ask, am I going to teach there? Teach, I don't know about that, but I'd be very glad to sit and talk to the kids there. We mustn't be too strict in our approach, though. Probably my role in the thing is keeping it away from being too establishment, which isn't rock'n' roll. We know music isn't like Latin – a dead language, it's over, you can learn it all. With what we're teaching there is no limit. If a kid wrote a song full of swear words, for instance, we mustn't be saying, "No, you can't!" What the teachers have to do is encourage the love for it, get kids making their own music. That's what I'm passionate about.'

Although a tricky discussion was nine months off, the issue was fundamental: how was LIPA going to address the requirements of popular musicians? Public revenue money, which was needed to enable students to attend regardless of family income, could only be achieved by fitting into the teaching world; but here was Britain's most prolific songwriter saying that teaching was on the margins of rock 'n' roll.

The tour left Europe for Australia and New Zealand in March, for America the month afterwards for three months, returning to Europe in July.

Managing the Liverpool end of EU grants

Seven days before the Grundig signing in Frankfurt, Bergen, Keith and I were in Birkenhead Town Hall presenting LIPA to the public representatives of the Merseyside Integrated Development Organisation (the Merseyside end of the European Regional Development Fund).

At the time, concern was flowing from Paul's office that should support from ERDF not be forthcoming, then LIPA was finished. Although I tried to argue that with the £4,000,000 in sight from the private sector, this matched the City Challenge support and that many avenues for fund-raising were open, including significant later fit-out costs being met through equipment donations and gifts in kind, in my heart I too was concerned.

Within three days, we knew that the MIDO Steering Group had supported LIPA's application, although the size meant it had to be referred to the MIDO Directing Group. Since this body was not due to meet for over two months, we were told that the application would be dealt with under 'Written Procedures' so that a final decision could be taken by the end of March.

A month later, I discovered that this decision, which was a formality, had to be preceded by a successful appraisal by Liverpool City Challenge, which would only begin at the start of April and be completed by July.

With the need to meet the timetable for planning consents, another problem was emerging.

There had to be a moment when what LIPA was going to do had to be translated into bricks and mortar and, inevitably, facilities. Because it was not possible (as with the BRIT School) to have senior full-time subject heads on board and so the detail of the curriculum, there had to be a fair element of latitude, which was largely absorbed by rooms with multi-use.

This basic information was to be conveyed on room data sheets. The services and facilities required for each room had to be decided. The detail included room usage with potential variations; the number of occupants; its relationship with other rooms; heating/cooling; ventilation; small power requirements, likely client fitting/equipment and in-built fittings/equipment; lighting requirements, data outlet requirements; security requirements, CCTV; piped services (water, communications); fire requirements; loading, access, daylight and glazing requirements and, finally, the finishes (wall, ceiling and floor). This activity took Bergen out of circulation for a month or two.

The design team

The next stage was for architects (Brock Carmichael) to adapt and add to the existing building, the mechanical and electrical engineers (Ernest Griffiths & Sons) to work out the services provision and for the structural engineers (Roy Billington Associates) to work out the loading and so structure needed to support the facilities, before the quantity surveyors (Walfords) costed the whole scheme. If this turned out to be exceeding the amount of money available, then adjustments needed to be made to bring the scheme within budget.

The point was that this needed doing forthwith to meet the September 1995 opening date. A timetable showed that tender information needed to be available by May 1993 when listed building and planning submissions had to be achieved; the contract awarded by October 1993; the start on site by November 1993 with practical completion by May 1995. This allowed for fit-out completion in July 1995, in readiness for staff training in August to meet the September deadline.

The present difficulty was this: who was going to pay the design team for this work and when? If City Challenge paid before April 1993, then there would be less available for matching funding from ERDF. If LIPA paid before April (or when the building was transferred), then it would be paying for work on a building it did not legally own.

This was aside from the fact that the private sector was becoming fed up with funding the project in its entirety. When was the famous private/public-sector partnership going to start?

The roof

Then there had been a curious manoeuvre by the Department for the Environment just before the roof replacement work began. For some reason, which I and other LIPA directors were never able to fathom, it was judged politically expedient to begin work on the institute building – if not for LIPA, then another user. (Maybe there were spending targets that had to be met.) The objective was to replace the rotting roof to prevent further damage to the interior of the building. When we later discovered there was no possible further interior damage that could have been done during their renovation work, the mystery deepened.

It became quite an issue: partly because the DoE asked LIPA to guarantee private-sector support up to the level of the roof-replacement cost and that the sum had to be available by April 1993 (even though the building was not LIPA's); partly because the sum used, £600,000 was deducted from City Challenge's match funding; partly because it was unclear at what point we could have a say in the roof we wanted and so we had to spend more money later on to this end.

I met John Flamson for the first time to see if there could be a solution. When I'd invited John for lunch, he'd started quoting T S Elliot. I'd realised the project was fortunate to be in the hands of yet another human bureaucrat. The solution he came up with involved the design team deferring fee payment until April 1993 to avoid prejudicing ERDF match-funding. If the project was aborted after April, I had to confirm that LIPA directors could not guarantee fee payment to the design team, since the private sector was awaiting commitment from the public sector.

John suggested that an approved appraisal of the

LIPA project would be reported to his board in March. This would mean that City Challenge could guarantee fee payments to the design team in April if the project could not proceed because of public-sector withdrawal. The *quid pro quo* was that John reserved the right to ask LIPA for the guaranteed fee payments, if the project could not proceed because of private-sector withdrawal.

Since private-sector finance was in place, the loss to the public sector would be minimal, since all the issues relating to fire, building regulations, planning and listed building consents would have been determined and could be used for the realisation of another project.

In the meantime, the tour had completed the Australian leg and the LIPA Ticket was in jeopardy.

The LIPA Tour Ticket and the fans

Richard had brought Fiona Cohen on board to manage the LIPA Ticket. In a way, this was one of those splendid ideas that needed adequate pre-planning and the personnel to make it work – it really had neither. This was more than one person, however good (and Fe was good) could manage. By the time it was evident that one person was needed for managing the arrangements and another was needed for the promotion and sale of tickets, the cost and so income generation of the exercise was being seriously questioned and from time to time the LIPA Ticket seemed doomed.

Fe had visited the site to see the project for herself. Her enthusiasm matched ours.

The time problem and the need to bring this initiative within a significant surplus meant a significant change – offering the LIPA Ticket to anyone who wanted to buy one.

Even this change had not managed to turn the LIPA Ticket's Australian leg into a real surplus. It seemed as if it was heading for a loss. Aside from the smallness of promotional time, part of the problem was the level of accommodation and service being given to attendees, which had been geared around the corporate, rather than private, sector.

Another difficulty emerged. Although the brochure made no mention of a meeting with Paul, some LIPA Ticket-purchasers felt this was implicit. This was about to bedevil the first leg of the US Tour.

The previous August, out of the blue, John Rago, an American lawyer, rang MPL to see if there was anything he could do to help. He turned out to be the kind of man who was prepared to write 'I am delighted to be a small part of your team contributing to this project' out of a simple wish to see LIPA succeed.

Marcy Oldham, a New Yorker, also began fund-raising on her own initiative. The work which was needed to make the LIPA Ticket work on the US leg turned out to be a major task. The solicitation work was a task all of its own. Then there was the management of concerts where the LIPA Ticket, due to small take-ups, was cancelled or where, due to concern about its viability in general, it was put on hold (I was urging Richard not to do this, since the LIPA Ticket-receipts were the balancing figure needed for the private-sector match). What John, and no one else for that matter, could have foreseen, was the work that stemmed from the mistaken unauthorised assurances given to enquirers by the promoters. Four significant undertakings were given to encourage Americans to hand over their money and included the chance of shaking Paul's hand.

Some of the others, like not receiving a personal signed photograph, annoyed LIPA Ticket-holders and then turned into rage when they saw Paul on a TV show signing photographs and meeting fans. Rhetorically, John and I were asked whether if these people had also paid $1000.

Other problems also emerged – what pictorial record could LIPA Ticket-holders keep of the sound-check? It was decided that still cameras would be OK for a few minutes at the beginning of the sound-check. Then there were complaints that seating was too far back to take a decent picture – a need, it was said, that was dictated by the requirements of security.

Every slight, real or imagined, could result in a publicity fall-out. Then, in the midst of far weightier matters on Paul's mind, let alone carrying the tour, one fan had decided to hold up a placard at one of the concerts claiming '$1,000 LIPA Scam'. There were certainly positive letters, praising Fe's work and the experience generally, but the placard-holding fan took another tack. Her letter to me started; 'Paul did see it. I will never forget the look of shock on this face when he realised what it said. He recovered, like the professional he is, and communicated a message to me. Throughout the show I had been holding signs of love to him, so Paul should know that I love him unconditionally and that I am deeply hurt by the LIPA Scam. I had to know that Paul knew how I felt as I didn't know how insulated he is from criticism.'

One letter concluded: 'You blew it, LIPA, big time. You don't screw around with Beatle fans. We have a network. We don't deserve to be treated this way. Without us, Paul McCartney and his LIPA dream are nothing. We have been fans since the beginning – February 9, 1964. Without us, his career would have been over years ago. Who do you think is buying *Off the Ground*? It isn't selling, but everyone who had a LIPA Ticket knew all the words to all the songs.'

The abandonment of the corporate package brought its own woes; another letter: 'Since I was 13 my dream has been to meet Paul. This ticket seemed to be my dream come true. When I looked at it that way, $1000 wasn't much to pay for a lifetime's dream, although all-at-once it *is* hardship as my husband was laid off work and has been unemployed for two months and my car's in the shop and taxes are due, etc. etc. My husband knew how much it meant – Paul's the only guy I've loved longer than him! – so he said go for it...then there was the bold-faced statement that meeting Paul was not part of the deal...then there was the part about

Corporate America getting processed first... . What! Why are we being treated as second class citizens? Corporate America did not put Paul where he is today. It was the *fans*...now in an instant, my whole view of Paul as a fellow human being has come crashing down – he's only in it for the bucks after all? What a fool I've been! After 29 years of supporting him, this is how I'm treated? I'm too embarrassed to seek therapy on this one – but it's a heavy one!'

Each time misinformation entered the public bloodstream, statements had to be issued with agreement from five camps in two continents. The change of policy needed a carefully worded statement from me. Then came the question of responsibility and blame. John and I had decided early on, whatever the rights or wrongs, that the tour, MPL and Paul should be insulated, with LIPA's US Foundation taking the heat. More letters, more statements.

At the time, we faithfully and graciously answered each letter, hoping that the recognition we gave would satisfy the disappointment each sender was experiencing. From this distance, the intensity of reaction is curious; it's as if the success of an artist is solely dependent upon the response of the recipient of the artist's work. It paralleled some Liverpool conversations where it was alleged that the success of the Beatles was down to their local fans; simply put 'we made them', followed, often swiftly, by 'they deserted us' – not the kind of requirement placed upon successful Liverpool-born engineers or architects. The perceived personal stake carried acute feelings of loyalty and so dismay when disloyalty was perceived.

When Jane, my half-sister, picked up a cab from Lime Street to attend our inauguration and shared with the driver the good news of the many inevitable fares due that day, the driver moaned about what good had the Beatles ever done for Liverpool. He had apparently forgotten that she would not have been in his cab, but for Paul.

None of this was helped by the disappointing

financial returns on the tour itself and the apparent returns on the LIPA Ticket: 'apparent' because there seemed to be different interpretations of the existing financial figures. Humphrey, who had met with Richard and Fe in Las Vegas, had itemised what he felt were the correct costings. A suspicion was emerging that audience numbers were being manipulated to make up tour deficits.

It was also becoming apparent that Richard's time with Paul was coming to an end. At one point, he was told to return home and everyone was enjoined, for a short period, essentially while severance was being worked out, not to contact him. Part of the reconstruction involved extending the US stay for a further leg.

With Grundig and Dieter throwing their weight behind the second European leg, the LIPA Ticket finally achieved both complete customer satisfaction and the solid financial return that had been hoped for from the start.

The public sector ask for safeguards that LIPA can't accept

Back in Liverpool, the various upsets on the earlier legs need to be fitted around the all-important task of receiving an endorsement through the report KPMP Management Consulting was preparing for the Liverpool City Challenge Executive and negotiating, where possible, the terms under which a grant would be given.

After the human drama of the US LIPA Ticket, this may seem prosaic, but it is worth telling, because it will give you an insight into public- and private-sector partnerships, the way two different cultures, who are encouraged by government to work together, have different accountabilities and, so, approach to risk. For the private sector, risk, managed and assessed risk, is the very stuff of business, for the public sector, the KPMG experience showed me that a new business venture needed, if possible, to be one hundred per cent risk-free.

Hence, the clash.

(If you want, you can also skip this part and move to the London press launch announcing Grundig's sponsorship.)

KPMG Management Consulting was given just seven weeks to review LIPA, which included proving a draft report for discussion and the amendment of fact.

The review was 'the feasibility and viability of the proposals to develop LIPA' to be followed by 'an inter-related series of events involving the appraisal of the project by all of its public-sector partners for grant funding purposes. It will also be considered by the Charity Commission in order to commence the process for the transfer of the legal estate in the Liverpool Institute building to LIPA.'

The recommendations, which covered some thirteen pages and under a section titled 'The Way Forward', concluded that 'at best an overall analysis of the LIPA project at this stage would lead to the view that it has the *potential* to be feasible and viable'.

Although Tim Johnston, who was the author, was known by LIPA to be generally supportive and keen for the project to proceed, this was considerably less than the ringing endorsement we'd hoped for (and even expected). The conclusion seemed to be a tautology: that LIPA was possibly possible. Ah, not so. LIPA was possible, provided that a number of hurdles were cleared. The feasibility and viability of the hurdles were what the LIPA board had to consider. During a meeting years later, Tim outlined a variety of local and national governmental forces which were dubious about the project and willing to pull the plug. 'You had no idea what you were up against, which was just as well.'

If KPMG had time restraints, so had LIPA's board – four-and-a-half working days to respond to five key issues and various 'solid and enforceable safeguards' suggested by the report.

There were five key issues Liverpool City Challenge wanted to hear about from LIPA's board. The first was resolution of the uncertainty over long-term revenue support. 'The long-term viability of the project has not yet been fully demonstrated.' What did LIPA's board have in mind should applications for either the Higher Education Funding Council (HEFC) or the Further Education Funding Council (FEFC) support be unsuccessful? The question then went on to ask how would LIPA achieve agreed outputs and deliver the project in a form acceptable to the public funders?

As usual, here was the chicken and here was the egg. Without an institution and validated programmes, no application could be made to HEFC or anyone else.

Our response countered thus: 'If we are not successful, we would be in exactly the same situation as (and no worse than) existing institutions of performing arts, such as The Royal Academy of Dramatic Art and the London Academy of Music and Dramatic Art (the list goes on), whose students seeks discretionary awards. We trust that no one is suggesting that these prestigious institutions, and others like them, are on the verge of bankruptcy. Indeed our Business Plan makes it plain that demand for places at performing arts institutions outstrips supply by a factor of 20:1. We therefore find it difficult to understand why KPMG should feel that LIPA will be the only exception.'

The 'agreed outputs' (which had not in fact been agreed) referred to the profile of the student body – a healthy gender, racial and Merseyside balance. This was to be an issue that remained tricky.

The second key issue was the need for more, substantially more, private-sector money to complete and run the project.

Our response was to agree to a written undertaking that, should the ceiling on refurbishment and rebuilding costs be breached, the additional costs would be met by the private sector.

The endowment fund proved to be a long-running issue. At this point, we pointed out that raising an endowment fund for a non-existent institution was a non-starter and that the endowment fund, should it be raised, was not a replacement for HEFC funding. It was also unclear for whom the endowment fund would be applied. (I wondered if the thinking was – and so it turned out to be – that this would just be available for Merseysiders. If so, this was going to be an impossible task.)

The third and fifth key issues stressed the need to progress the education and training proposals and to appoint staff to achieve this. We agreed, but wanted confirmation that we had a project to progress.

The fourth issue stressed the need to strengthen the LIPA board and for the board to review the issues in the KPMG report. This was also accepted, but we couldn't resist pointing out that we had invited Liverpool City Council to participate at board level a year and a half earlier and this invitation had not been taken up.

It was the public-sector safeguards suggested by KMPG that startled.

There were six options presented; all were designed to protect the public sector's interest and financial support. The last three concentrated on the building and its transfer; whether through a mortgage, a deferment of building transfer or a long leasehold transfer, the idea was to defer transfer until a variety of yet-to-be-defined conditions/targets had been met. Legally, this was not possible; neither could building be developed in two stages (a shell and other works) without substantial additional costs.

We pointed out that the Liverpool Institute Educational Foundation, which owned the building, existed in perpetuity. The new scheme that the Charity Commissioners were in the process of drawing up would give LIPA a freehold interest in the building as long as the new scheme met its educational purposes. In the event of failure, the building would revert to the original objectives. In this sense, no public-sector money would be lost, because the building would remain within the public sector; it would be the private sector that would experience loss.

The first two recommendations were the real eye-openers, putting aside their legal feasibility.

The first recommendation was that Liverpool City Council would obtain 'a temporary controlling voting interest in LIPA...until certain targets or milestones...had been satisfactorily met in the development phase'. It was recommended this would be achieved by giving a Liverpool City Council representative 'enough of a weighted vote to outvote the rest of the Board'. In the longer term, it was also recommended that a city council nominee should take up the existing directorship on offer to the council and that LIPA's memorandum and articles of association 'would be amended to ensure that the City Council nominee could outvote all members of the company in a company meeting'.

The report noted that the Charity Commission might object, however. It was also noted that this would make LIPA a controlled company under Section 67 of the Local Government and Housing Act 1989 and that the city might wish to seek 'an exemption order from the secretary of state as permitted by the Act'.

If this recommendation wasn't workable (the report noted that 'such a control could be interpreted as the acceptance of full responsibility for the success or failure of LIPA – a risk that the City Council may not wish to take'), then an alternative was suggested: the right of veto or a 'golden' vote at both board and membership levels to be exercised for the same reasons as defined in the first recommendation.

Taken together, these two recommendations appeared to pay scant regard to the essential nature of partnership. We wrote back:

> What depresses us most about these
> suggestions is the negation of partnership
> which is said to be at the heart of Liverpool

City Challenge. For one partner to have the right to veto all other partners (indeed, possibly remove them) seems to us a long way away from partnership... . Nor it is fair... . We also foresee that these suggestions will lead to protracted debates with our private-sector partners who might wish to secure their position in a similar fashion... . The SPA Trust and its existing partners wishes to repeat the achievement of the BRIT School, but this time in Liverpool; to create, through the mechanism of private/public partnership, the finest performing arts school in the world, based in the city where the British music industry effectively began thirty years ago. The private sector can bring money, expertise, prestige and profile; the partnership can deliver economic activity, educational infrastructure and a brilliant example of how private/public partnerships can work – and work in Liverpool. Each partner needs the others. Without all of them, LIPA could not be created...for one partner to be able to pull the plug on the others is therefore inappropriate.

We are tempted to remind you that all the financial support which LIPA has gained is money which the city could access in no other way. And further, that our Grundig Agreement has been described by a representative of the Business Sponsorship Incentive Scheme as the largest sponsorship agreement in living memory.

Let's have the partnership, but let it be real.

We would have liked to end on that clarion note, however there is one further issue which must be introduced, namely the time scale, which is wholly determined by the need to open in 1995. For this reason, LIPA has to have the trusteeship of the building by early August 1993. We understand that Liverpool City Council's LIPA Working Group will be meeting just prior to a full Council Meeting on 26th May, which will decide whether to proceed with the Charitable scheme to transfer trusteeship. We urge Liverpool City Challenge to make an announcement in time for this transfer to begin.

We understand that the publication of the new scheme may have to be twin tracked with Ministerial approval for LIPA, in which case we urge Liverpool City Challenge Executive Group to address their minds to ensuring this late manoeuvre is undertaken. Please be in no doubt about the inflexibility of the timetable: if the building is not transferred by early August 1993, LIPA will miss the 1995 opening...we hope you can appreciate the spirit of this closing remark: half a weekend has been taken up in ensuring we met your deadline; please now meet LIPA's!

By the end of May, I was negotiating about the conditions of grant that Liverpool City Challenge was placing upon LIPA. We were relieved to note that Liverpool City Council/Liverpool City Challenge control had been modified in favour of a monitoring role to be placed on the hands of yet another reporting group: the Education Advisory Group, which, by a stroke of good fortune, was chaired by none other than...Mick Farley!

Grundig's London press conference

Away from public-sector accountability issues in Liverpool, the Mayfair Hotel, London, was the setting for (so in the midst of KMPG's review), Grundig finally to hold its press conference, announcing its support for LIPA. Johan van Splunter spoke on Grundig's behalf, I on LIPA's and Paul, always the main attraction, took questions.

Linda and the tour band also turned up, because it was hoped to announce the tour dates of the European leg at the same time. However, these had not been finalised, which was a happy result from the LIPA perspective since the entire press conference was about LIPA.

It was also announced that Paul was prepared, because of Grundig's exceptional participation, to agree for the first time in his career to allow 'C'mon People' to be used in a series of LIPA-related commercials that would also involve promoting Grundig's new 'Performing Arts' hi-fi range.

The thrust of the press stories that followed concentrated on the fact that a German company had seized the marketing opportunity rather than a British one. One headline read 'Shame School, not Fame School'.

Dieter had spoken to the local *Liverpool Daily Post*, saying, 'We have been involved in a long-term search for something fascinating for our clients in the area of culture. I was astonished that nobody took this idea for their commercial interests. It is ideal for Grundig because it is our target group and helps us establish ourselves as a European company against all these Japanese and Koreans.'

I had commented that 'Grundig have grasped the opportunity that we offered to nearly 600 British companies. I suppose there might have been a perception in people's minds that with McCartney behind the project, why do they need us? It's surprising really, because I would have thought that to be in partnership with McCartney in supporting such a visible project would have been attractive for them.'

Since the MIDO Steering Group had given its approval, there did not seem much point in hiding that either, so the ERDF announcement was made at the same time. Knowing that the agreement with Grundig still rested on LIPA achieving Liverpool City Challenge's appraisal and that the MIDO Directing Group also was awaiting its outcome, I wondered if this wasn't jumping the gun, but Geoff Baker swept such reservations aside for me, which had not been unduly difficult to do.

The playground

This April was also the month when Paul Taylor, from Liverpool City Council's legal department, casually mentioned to me that the playground to the back of the institute building did not belong to the building. He also was unsure quite who it did belong to. However, if it belonged to the council, there were two options: a best price sale or transfer by permission of the secretary of state to LIPA.

We were amazed that matters had gone so far without such a crucial disclosure being made. Without the playground, it would be impossible for the scheme to progress; aside from needed parking space, there was the requirement for a scenery dock behind the new projected stage and fly tower. When the scheme had been published for prospective architects to bid, the playground had been part of the building; indeed, since the mechanics institute had been built, it was the institute's playground.

One side of the site was occupied by a building owned and used by the City of Liverpool Community College. Once this institution got wind of the lack of resolution over the playground, it decided that it too had an interest in the area, which it expressed to Liverpool City Council.

Since we were obliged to discuss our learning provision with the college, dovetail some aspects, and seek not to overlap others, its involvement in the playground issue did not help the relationship.

It seemed as if another saga was about to unfurl.

Japanese activities

The second (or maybe the first, depending upon how these things can be assessed) stronghold of Beatle support was Japan. MPL suggested that I wrote to Tetsuo Hamada, the person who managed the Japanese Beatles Cine Club, as well as being the managing director of a publishing company, which, amongst other titles, published many books about the Beatles. The 'Cine-Club' came from the early days when the Beatles could only be seen on film in Japan. A film club formed which later blossomed into an active fan club.

The letter I received in return was enthusiastic, warm and courteous. Within a few months, after a London meeting between us, Tetsuo Hamada had put together a fund-raising plan in Japan and a Japanese Support Committee. He was prepared to work on a voluntary basis, which turned out, like the work John Rago had undertaken in the States, to be extensive. Like John, he never complained.

From time to time, various institutions in Japan came forward with deals that involved them becoming preparatory schools for LIPA. Although not exclusive, the publicity and cachet would be paid for by way of cash to LIPA, in some cases up to £500,000. The precise details of such an agreement and its feasibility usually, as time went on, scotched the idea, but these were further counters that were discussed by the LIPA board and mentioned to those who were still wary of LIPA's ability to raise further finance, and so of the project succeeding.

By the summer of 1993, Tetsuo Hamada had produced a Japanese version of the appeal brochure, co-ordinated publicity for the appeal, personally donated, with his wife, a five-figure sum and sold fifty-seven seats and sixteen stair treads. He also achieved a sell-out for the Japanese LIPA Ticket – all fifty tickets were sold for each of the five concerts, realising £113,000.

This is why, if you visit the LIPA building today, you will see Japanese names on the main staircases and auditorium seats. Japanese, American and German names greatly outnumber the British.

Before the tour's New York date, I again met Tetsuo Hamada in his Central Park hotel and discussed the possibility of a McCartney-supported advertisement in Japan. There had been a history of both British and American celebrities allowing their name to be used to support a commercial product and in return receiving a handsome fee for doing so; occasionally this had included fronting a TV advertisement. The usual stipulation, however, was that the advertisement was limited to Japanese audiences and so was never seen in the West. I recalled that Sir Lawrence Olivier had done just this.

Paul had had an approach a few years back from a well-known Japanese whiskey company. While LIPA was hard to sell, Paul, of course, was not, so, from a LIPA perspective, this seemed both a painless, and – since it didn't involve asking Paul for further financial help and repeated his commitment for a TV spot involving Grundig – a reasonable idea.

On the other hand, all this came very close to product endorsement, an activity which Paul had resolutely refused from the early days and also came perilously close to marketing Paul, rather than LIPA – the latter, Paul often reminded me, was my remit, not the former.

Before it ended in July, discussions were not only underway, but had agreed to extend the initially planned tour, both in Europe and the Far East. The financial out-turn of the previous tour legs was exercising many minds and a thorough review included the LIPA Ticket. So, once again, its merits, in financial terms, were reassessed. Paul and I talked and faxed each other extensively. I maintained constant contact with Dieter. The issue was matching the maximisation of the financial benefit accruing to LIPA with the financial reality of managing such an exercise.

Meanwhile, there were still loose ends to be tied up with the public sector back in Liverpool. The first was agreement over the conditions placed upon LIPA by Liverpool City Challenge. By June, these, some forty, had been agreed. They needed to be forwarded to the Department of the Environment (and the minister) for approval. We were also required to go before the MIDO Directing Committee in mid-July. The playground issue continued its journey. The community college was effectively given three months to come up with a realistic scheme to develop part of the playground area and two years to begin serious work. Meanwhile, Liverpool City Council was putting through its committee systems a recommendation that secretary-of-state approval was sought to pass over the land to LIPA at nil cost, with the proviso that should LIPA fail, it would be passed back at nil cost.

The need for validated programmes (programmes that had been approved by a publicly funded degree-giving institution – in LIPA's case, Liverpool John Moores University) was also being actioned by a joint working party between the two institutions, as was the appointment of a director of learning for LIPA.

The pilot courses are delivered

The first pilot courses too were finally underway with six Liverpool bands covering a range of musical styles, including indie rock, soul, heavy rock and dance, taking part in the Demo Dilemma. Music, Image and Style was the second course and asked ten bands/artists to develop a coherent communications strategy for the band or the concept behind the music. Local graphic and fashion designers, as well as photographers, were set up to turn concepts into reality. Given Paul's concern over the courses, the possible impact, should they be rubbish, on both him and the LIPA-to-be, Liverpool John Moores University was approached and agreed to front the courses. So it was that the first LIPA provision came, disguised, to life.

As well as masterminding these, Denise began to have a crack at the curriculum with Bergen and David

Price (who was appointed later in the year as our first director of learning).

Although we had set up a transnational network of some forty institutions across Europe and although representatives from many met in Brussels to discuss a variety of initiatives, the network never really, in the fullness of time, took off. There was simply too much to achieve in Liverpool.

There was the building. There were agreements to be achieved with various planning authorities and the public publication of the plans; the need to ensure the building was totally accessible for people with disabilities; early advice sought about the specialist areas (stage workshops, lighting systems, acoustic properties of key performance and rehearsal spaces, music practice rooms, recording studios, computer networking and the ability to send sound and visual signals throughout).

There was drawing up an agreement to formalise the relationship between LIPA and LJMU. There was the writing of the first prospectus. There was the second edition of *NewsLIPA* – a magazine designed to keep donors, sponsors and friends up-to-date with the creation. There were the second stage pilot courses, dealing with producing a master tape and creating a marketing campaign.

Paul's concerns erupt

And there was the tour wending its way through Europe and about to give me a sharp reminder of the stakes as I joined the tour from time to time.

I was aware of a growing irritation emanating from Paul. A curtain-raiser, although I didn't realise it at the time, was delivered in Oslo, when, during the after-show get together, Paul asked me to act: 'Come on, man, you say you were an actor, do something now. Shakespeare, do me a speech from Shakespeare.' I was bewildered. I never saw myself teaching acting and tried to explain that my role was managerial. The conversation, if it could be called that, awkwardly continued until Paul sharply told me to 'get up and go and get a bevvy'.

The Frankfurt date was a week later.

When I arrived, the Grundig people were trying to cope with Paul's insistence that their banners (with their name on) would not catch his eye from the stage; tacked up as they were across the front of the first floor balcony, this presented a problem. In the end the banners were placed either side of the stage, facing the audience, which pleased Paul because he could not see them, and which delighted the Grundig people because the audience, while facing the stage, could not avoid seeing the brand name.

I was there partly to continue the dialogue with Grundig, promote Grundig's involvement with LIPA at Grundig-organised news conferences and interviews, and partly to talk with and thank the LIPA Ticket-holders. In fact during the time I sat with them listening to the sound-check and sitting on the control riser. Paul's bodyguard, emerged from the side of the stage, walked across the arena to the riser and silently shook me by the hand. I had the strong impression I was about to be beheaded.

Halfway through the pre-concert meal with the VIP ticket-holders, I was told to meet Paul in his dressing room. My sense of foreboding grew; I was beginning to feel all the comfort associated with a tax audit.

Linda was sitting down in their dressing room when I arrived. I greeted her warmly, as she did me. Paul entered. Linda gave us both glasses of water and left.

Half an hour later, I stumbled from the dressing room. I was so shaken that, putting my hand out to steady myself on the wall outside the dressing room door, I mistakenly placed it on Mary McCartney (Linda and Paul's first child) who was standing outside waiting to go in. And worse.... . I had placed it on one of Mary's breasts. Aghast by the ramifications, I sprang back, white with apology.

For half an hour, Paul had given me an unedited

expression of his pent-up concerns, which had been fermenting ever since that meeting with The Christians. He began by telling me that he totally disagreed with the subject-matter of the short courses. One in particular, the 'Image and Style' course had particularly infuriated and worried him: was this to be a taster of LIPA to come? Effectively teaching trivia, rather than the serious business of making music?

He then re-launched into the test courses as a group and into the heart of his concern: what was the practitioner standing of those delivering the courses? What relevance did the courses have to the needs of practising musicians? Without pulling punches, he had continued unabated in this vein to a point where he told me that more of same would run the risk of him leaving the project.

I had made my way to the back stage canteen, where crew and staff tucked into vegetarian food. I sat down beside the staff I knew and, shakily, tried to consider the issues, putting to one side the vehemence with which they had been expressed.

Stepping on to the aircraft back to England, I played out in my mind the nightmare of Paul's withdrawal, now that LIPA was so firmly on the road. If Paul decided to leave, I morosely pictured the press release which would express sorrow about leaving the project and also express sorrow in placing trust in Mark Featherstone-Witty who had, regrettably, proved not to be up to it. There would be a general sense of 'a good try, but there we are'.

Looking back, why wasn't I able to focus faster on the issues raised and put aside my own emotional reactions? Yes, I'd been caught offguard, which can knock me off target and, I suppose, personally attacked.

I was also trying to come to terms with one simple immaturity: I still expected heroes to be perfect people.

Once over that, didn't he have a point? What practical experience could LIPA's faculty bring? As Van De Snapscheut elegantly put it: 'In theory there is no difference between theory and practice, but in practice there is.' In an area of work where measurement of quality is constant, the best are stunning. If you are preparing the new best, it seems obvious: what better guide could you have but the current best? Wasn't there a sense in which institutions teaching the arts were filled by teachers who had never made it? On the other hand, who could match a Paul and how often could you find an institution, anywhere in the world, with an artist of his calibre on the regular teaching staff?

Teaching is a skill; the self-made artist, the autodidact, who has self-learnt, is likely, in my experience, to have developed a very particular way of achieving his or her eminence. This is not readily transferable, nor should it be. Everybody needs to make their own way. Or put another way, teachers open the door, but you need to enter by yourself. A teacher can offer choice by hiding personal taste. Equally, a teacher can offer choice by pushing a single line and it may be the reaction that the teacher is hoping to engender. The choices the self-taught have made are hard-learnt and so often feel immutable to them. Aside from this, the self-taught feel enormous pride, and are suspicious of straight teaching. It is a truism that most business entrepreneurs in the UK are self-taught and feel that business schools are pretty much a waste of time.

Understandable but wholly illogical. After all, the reduction of that argument is: why teach anyone anything? Let them learn it for themselves. And, actually, you do often find that the self-taught have, in fact, had teachers: not teachers in a traditional sense or in a traditional building where teaching is carried out, but as friends, contacts and associates. As you see car bonnets up over a weekend, do you ever wonder how many have actually taken a car mechanics course? Hasn't some mate shown them how to adjust the carburettor?

That aside, there's a real problem in being taught by people who only teach: quite simply, they lose touch; they lose touch with the world they are preparing students to enter. Their sources of insight can be other teachers or academics, who themselves have lost touch – nowhere is this more evident than in some areas of academic research. There are academic papers about business practices by people who have never had to meet an end-of-month payroll; you can be taught composition by someone who has never written a commercial song.

So what's the solution aside from appointing staff with professional experience? Many institutions (and LIPA is no different) replenish staff with work placements or encourage replenishing professional experience, as well as managing a guest or master class programme, where the Pauls of this world can spend time with students. And to those who question the educative value of such an encounter (and sometimes the educative value can be a bit marginal), I am reminded that Paul told me about a social worker in Chicago who when asked why he showed youngsters O'Hare Airport and who responded by saying: 'To show them it's there.' Simple proximity can be a motivator.

Within two weeks, I sent Paul a memo detailing the practitioners who either had been sent or were about to be sent the curricula for music, acting, dance, management and design performance and technology. Dame Judi Dench, Anthony Field, Pete Fulwell, Gillian Lynne, George Martin and Humphrey Walwyn responded warmly and with suggestions.

Before the end of the year, the tour reached Japan, with Paul agreeing to participate in a fund-raising lunch on a non-tour day. Tetsuo Hamada undertook the organisation, which quickly formed the centrepiece of the Japanese fund-raising effort. The recession in Japan was making private-sector donations hard to achieve, so a lunch with Paul was a bonus for waverers.

As the lunch was starting and I was attempting to socialise with the Japanese guests, I received a message to meet Paul and Linda as they left the lift, before reaching the lunch.

As I walked along the corridor, I wondered what I might have done wrong this time. All I could recall was a tricky conversation the night before when Paul had revisited the Grundig deal, replaying his concern about the commercialisation of LIPA and the cheapening of what was to be a prestigious institution.

As Paul stepped out the lift, he confided that he had found a solution to the problem – the problem, as he saw it, of the LIPA logo with Grundig's name beneath it. The solution was to avoid sending letters in favour of despatching faxes. Just as I was trying to grasp how he'd come up with this solution, then realising that Paul was probably assuming that faxes didn't use letterheads, and then wondering if this might work, Paul became even more enthusiastic. At that moment, we entered the lunch.

The negotiations with the possible feeder-college were to occupy much of my time in Tokyo and, in the end, a compromise could not be reached. But the negotiations were extensive. More people appeared to join in and previous conversations were repeated. Since conversations needed translating, the whole process took a while.

One night this meant missing the concert. As I walked away from the 45,000-seater Tokyo Dome, I heard Paul singing about Penny Lane – a road I now knew as not being particularly noteworthy – and wondered how some Liverpool people, often quite senior, could believe that the Beatles had left the city in the lurch. What city council in the world, I wondered, would not believe Christmas had arrived early with an ambassador of that calibre working without payment?

The audiences themselves were unlike any I had experienced before. Not only were they seated throughout, they simply clapped enthusiastically. As Mark Knopfler once described, for a performer it was like playing behind double glazing. It was in fact more like a concert than a gig and in some ways all the more refreshing for that.

The building contact is signed

The year ended with a number of landmarks. The City of Liverpool Community College did not pursue their interest in the playground. The secretary of state gave approval for its passing over to LIPA at nil cost. Trusteeship of the building passed over to LIPA. Planning permission and Listed Buildings Consent were attained. The roof-work contractors were leaving. Various sub-committees were meeting regularly and effectively. Grundig was rife with ideas for fulfilling the joint marketing of themselves and LIPA (which included the re-naming of a theatre in Berlin as The Performing Arts Theatre, establishing a LIPA Information Centre and using the current show, *Shakespeare Rock and Roll* – which began life as *Return to the Forbidden Planet,* co-incidentally in Liverpool).

English Heritage made two last-minute objections that threatened to jeopardise LIPA's planning application, the building programme and eligibility for the ERDF grant. A major one involved slicing off a part of the frontage of the annex building facing Mount Street to allow a particular perspective to be achieved when walking up the street. There was no chance for recourse. This also involved the designers in last-minute late nights that LIPA had to pay for.

In meeting the objections, one major piece of redesign work had to take place which helped to compromise how the contract (that was issued as part of the tendering process) was put out. The solution had been to go for what was called 'a bill of approximate quantities', since this did not tie the contractor to a fixed sum. This was to prove part of the beginning of a financial time bomb, which took a while to explode. Tenders had been received and Balfour Beatty Buildings was chosen.

Thomas arrives

The year began to end with the birth of our son. Such was the press of meetings and such was the opportunity given by a Caesarean section that, unbeknownst to Alison, I decided to attend a specific meeting at Liverpool University and so altered the planned birth day by a day. That night, expecting to go into hospital the next day, Alison was astonished to discover she needed to wait a further day.

When Thomas was handed to us in the delivery room, we looked at each other. We were speechless. I felt love I had not known before but which still seemed familiar. We knew, without knowing exactly how, that our lives had changed forever. Paul, then touring in South America and despite having achieved a world-record attendance at a gig, thoughtfully left a message welcoming Thomas to the world. So it was that I heard Paul alongside the messages from friends and family, when I returned from hospital the first night.

The contract with Balfour Beatty Buildings was signed four days before the year ended with the handover of the building two weeks before. The board of directors was told that the contractors would be on site promptly after the New Year to achieve the seventy-week programme that would mean building occupancy by the end of May 1995.

There seemed no reason not to feel optimistic.

1994 was about to begin.

12 Above—The LIPA Design Group. Top row: Bergen Peck, Peter Carmichael (Brock Carmichael Associates), architects; Roy Billington (Roy Billington Associates, structural engineers); Richard Spencer (Walfords, quantity surveyors); Mark Featherstone-Witty. Bottom row: Geoffrey Manning (C E Griffiths & Son, mechanical and electrical engineers); David Watkins (Brock Carmichael Associates, LIPA architect); Paul Cleworth (E C Harris Project Management, project manager); Brian Edmondson (Roy Billington Associates, structural engineer) and Peter Thomas (Walfords, quantity surveyor). Not present: Collin Thompson (Walfords, quantity surveyor).

13 Below—One of the pilot courses.

14 &15 Just two of the pictures which sum up the scale of renovation; this is all that was left of the four floors to the back of the buliding and three floors to the front.

16 Above—Back of the building after renovation.

17 Right—The multi-purpose performing arts studio on the front top floor.

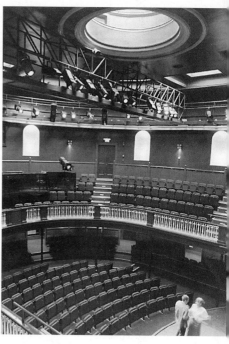

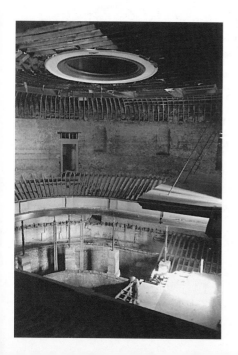

18, 19 and 20 The main
auditorium before (top left), during
(bottom left) and after (above)
renovation.

21 & 22 Inside the front door – before and after.

23 Above—Clare Wreath auditioning.

24 Below—Cutting the Inauguration cake with some first-year students.

25 Staff rejoice – the building is finally ours.

26 A moment during the Inauguration.

Chapter Seventeen

Approval of the institutional structure and the undergraduate curriculum – the involvement of strangers – the building delivers its first surprise – the first Monte Carlo simulation – Wayne's World 2 *premier and equipment donors – the funding of students – marketing a place which didn't exist – the Grundig spot*

There were four tasks to achieve in 1994: our institutional structure and internal processes and their approval by Liverpool John Moores University (LJMU); the building and its equipping, finance and fund-raising; the curriculum and its approval by LJMU; recruitment and financing of the first intake students, and marketing more generally, including pre-launch and launch publicity.

Approval of the institutional structure and the undergraduate curriculum

This was going to be more than two people could handle. Aside from the director of learning, the heads of the various subject areas needed to be appointed, as well as the director of administration, people to recruit students and meet their enquiries, as well as meeting the increased tempo of press work leading to the launch. Aside from the both massive and voluminous Gantt Charts needed to chart the building process, others (admittedly less impressive) were needed to manage these activities.

The involvement of strangers

This was inevitable, but it was also a feature I had to come to terms with quite quickly. I'd become used to the sudden change from managing three independent colleges with four managers to there being just Bergen and I as full-time employees. While I keenly felt the other part-time advisers were a team, the management was small and personal. This was the year when an embryonic structure needed to be born. The task facing many founders was similar: how do you get new employees to realise a stake-holding in the institution, while keeping the original vision? How do you encourage and stimulate discussion and fresh thinking, while maintaining the forward momentum characterised by the identity forged before the new employees came on board?

There was also the other element that I'd experienced with the CTC movement: it was a new enterprise and so everything could be questioned and, if possible, improved upon. This was both exhilarating and exhausting, since every decision had the potential for being policy. Everyone's hopes were constantly being negotiated. Since LIPA was a hybrid, the negotiations, at all levels within the organisation, could be intense – even heated. Two fundamental dichotomies were: was LIPA a higher education institution or a vocational training institution and did this matter? Was the underlying ethos private or public sector? At the curriculum level, the main tension was between specific subject-area provision and the core provision that was to be undertaken by all students, regardless of their chosen discipline.

There are moments when I wish I had the talent to be a painter or a novelist, when I would only need to struggle with my own ability to realise a dream. LIPA could only be realised through other people. The idealistic image I had of working relationships came from my late teens, watching Ingmar Bergman films. I'd spotted that Bergman had generally used a repertory company approach, both for the actors and technical staff. So, when every new project began, they all knew each other well; I imagined there would be no second-guessing, no questioning of motives – just a desire to create the best film. Now I found myself involved in the appointment of strangers to make my dream real.

I suppose this is no different from screenwriters or songwriters handing their work across, so perhaps this is why I found working with David Watkins, our architect, so satisfying – it was often just him and me, particularly when we came to consider the building finishes and colours. When I was considering the colours for my Toxteth house, I'd come across a painting by Andre Derain, *Turning Road, L'Estaque*. The vitality of his palette was just what I wanted to surround myself with. It was one thing for me and Alison to live amongst his colours, another to ask LIPA staff and students to do the same, so I realised I could be making a mistake on a scale that could not be disguised. But there are moments, I believe, where a single vision, rather than a committee's selection, needs to be given its head. The colours, I felt, expressed warmth, light and joyousness – experiences I was hoping people would sense entering and working in the building. I was also trying for a remembered sense of European and Mediterranean stone.

One exercise I remember our performance design students were set, encouraged them to translate the sensations they felt on the journey from their accommodation to LIPA into a series of colours. I was delighted to see one student had begun her journey with warm colours, which moved from blue (as she shut her front door and began her journey) and then through a spectrum until she entered LIPA when her colours matched the exhilaration she felt; colours which matched the colours in the building.

There was too much going on for me to be present at all the meetings where ethos and philosophy would be turned into concrete activities with the structures to support them, so I felt some aspects of LIPA slipping away, but there was nothing I could do except plough on with the tasks most immediately at hand.

Up until now, I've tried to give you some sense of what work-life was like: turning to one task after another, juggling a number of elements at the same time, which is familiar for business start-ups when staff levels are low. With an emerging structure, whole areas of work were now to be the responsibility of new staff members.

The building delivers its first surprise

First out of the box was the building – an early sign that this was to dominate the next two years. As it happened, the first problem was work not undertaken by LIPA. The roof stumbled towards a conclusion, without being wholly completed.

Even for this, Birse, the contractor, discovered they were facing £103,000 of cost above contract. The reasons for this were never clearly revealed, although I needed to react firmly when Liverpool City Challenge informed LIPA in January that the overspend might have to be taken out of the £3.4 million LIPA allocation. A month later, I was to discover that a further £169,000 would be needed to give us the roof we wanted. A year later I heard that Birse was taking action against Liverpool City Council (the client for the roof works). It crossed my mind that if this was just for starters, what else was about to be in store for the main body of the work? Although Bergen was less sanguine, I put the roof muddle down to misunderstandings. In time, this cost was met by City Challenge.

Balfour Beatty placed their first portacabins on the upper former playground in January and set to work with demolition, services diversion and work on the substructure. By July, the first extension to contract was allowed, but there was still confidence that practical completion would not hinder the projected 11th September 1995 opening. Despite the six-week extension, this was going to be achieved by allowing phased access to key parts of the building for fit out.

A month later, this ploy lay in tatters as Balfours and the architects appreciated the full decay of the brickwork at the back of the building. Initially it was thought that the solution was relatively straightforward – the demolition and reconstruction of what was to become the stage area. Then poor brickwork was discovered at high levels across the length of the back of the building; by poor, this meant bricks could be squeezed and water emerge; by poor, this meant that unfired bricks had been used for sections of the brickwork. So extensive was the brick failure, that a month later the cost of the building refurbishment had risen from £10.1 million to £12.5 million.

Although the major reason for the cost increase, this wasn't, as it happened, the only reason. The late changes to the frontage, the even later achievement of Planning and Listed Building Consent for an internal (but externally completely visible) staircase on the corner of the building, which arrived six months after submission, a late increase in the size of the scheme at our request and a rise in fit-out costs helped the figure rise.

The first Monte Carlo simulation

At this point, LIPA's board of directors decided they needed to have some certainty that this would not reoccur, particularly since it was likely, to maintain momentum, that a bank loan would be needed. Jim undertook to supply a four-year business plan to determine both the latest funding requirements and the information needed for discussion with bankers.

In November, E C Harris, LIPA's project managers, produced what it called 'a probability analysis of the possible final account costs based on the contract documents and instructions issued to date'. The idea was to work through all the remaining elements of the project to identify and quantify the residual risks in each. This was achieved by bringing all the information into one overall schedule of cost probability using a Monte Carlo simulation technique. Some directors laughed. The technique sounded ironic, too prophetically ironic.

What was interesting was that the stimulation, when it appeared in November, offered a range of final cost probabilities from ten per cent to ninety per cent. However, it was apparently impossible to offer one hundred per cent certainty.

Despite this, we were able to take comfort from the further information that excavation work was complete, as was the stripping out, the foundations and steel frames of both the new building and the extension. In other words, there was nothing else likely to be discovered.

This was the message that I took to Paul, as I had to, along with details of the cost increase, knowing that the unfolding saga would shake his confidence in the Liverpool team. And it did.

An initially philosophical reaction transformed itself into an angry Saturday morning telephone call, when I was reminded 'to neither a lender or borrower be'. Aside from anxiety about the ineptness of the team, I could appreciate Paul's anxiety about the financial consequences – inevitably he would be a part of the solution, but, just as inevitably, he couldn't be all the solution or even an early part if it. There could be no impression that Paul was the pot of gold at the end of the rainbow.

While a bank loan was being discussed and negotiated towards the end of the year, Mary Allen, then the Secretary General of the Arts Council of England, had visited Liverpool, staying with her old schoolfriend (and now my wife) Alison. When visiting the embryonic LIPA site the next day, she confirmed that LIPA would be eligible for lottery funding. A month later, a LIPA National Lottery application was submitted.

As the year ended, Paul Cleworth for E C Harris Project Management informed LIPA's governing council members that Balfours were four weeks behind their granted extension of time and that it was likely further extensions would be granted to take account of the brickwork. So the 12th July was looking weak. There was no hint as yet of what was to come: that students would be unable to begin their academic year in September 1995 as planned, because the building was not ready for them.

LIPA staff ploughed ahead of course, not knowing this, settling down to the tasks needing to be achieved for that first September intake.

LIPA was to be an associate college of LJMU. An agreement had to be reached on the relationship between the two institutions, not forgetting what would happen if LIPA somehow failed to exist – after all the students would be registered as LJMU students.

LJMU also needed to be certain that LIPA could deliver as an academic institution. For most of the world, this simply meant that LIPA had to prove to the university, which was in turn responsible to the quangos that related to higher education, that it had a robust strategy, educational programmes and an administrative structure, underpinned by appropriate expertise, to operate effectively. The institutional element came first. Within half a year, this process was achieved.

By December, the academic element had been submitted. To achieve that, staff responsible for heading up the various subject areas had to be appointed. The idea was to appoint initially on a consultancy basis so that they could write the courses and, where possible, pilot them, with full-time employment beginning in September.

As it happened, it was difficult to find them. Part of the difficulty was finding people who had achieved industry expertise as well as an understanding of the mechanics of higher education as well as teaching ability. The other part was that Liverpool was a disincentive in that practitioners already in education, particularly in London, would be reluctant to lose some handy freelance earnings. Some directors wondered if LIPA, as a new institution, presented too great a sense of uncertainty. It was difficult to tell.

Both the selection process and the process to appoint all the subject heads took a while. Since applicants taught as part of the process (and, subsequently, a class was invited to reflect upon the teaching they had just received), it felt as if LIPA was starting.

The first subject heads were appointed just in time to join a residential away-weekend which cleared the time to consider fundamental curriculum issues. It was the last time Roger Williams, the redoubtable HM Inspector, who had been with the philosophy since BRIT School days and had guided the education/ training concerns of Liverpool City Challenge, actively participated in LIPA.

The undergraduate programme was uppermost in everyone's minds (with attendant matters such as sorting out the auditions process), but other provision was close behind: a range of European Social Fund funded courses, the possibility of putting material onto a CD ROM (or CDi, as Philips was encouraging and funding) and the possibility of dual accreditation of courses through National Vocational Qualifications (NVQs). There was also the testing of courses with partners in Barcelona, Amsterdam and Dublin, as well as with Grundig in Berlin.

What with one thing and another (and more often than not simply maintaining the terms of the Grundig/ LIPA agreement), fund-raising took a relatively back seat, except for three activities.

Wayne's World 2 *premier and equipment donors*

The premier stemmed from Paul's approach to Lorne Michaels who had promised Paul that he would donate the premieres of *Wayne's World 2* to LIPA.

So it was that I found myself back again in the Empire, Leicester Square in January – this time addressing a cinema audience with news about LIPA and conveying thanks to the producer. I could never have imagined that I, the audience member, who had been inspired by *Fame*, shown in the same cinema, would, twelve years later, be explaining where the adventure had now taken me.

Before I did that, I'd gone for pre-performance drinks to a little ante-room. Aside from Paul and Linda and a smattering of their friends, a variety of what seemed to be a London party crowd turned up with many comedians (like Paul Merton and Angus Deyton). My most abiding memory was seeing Jerry Hall sitting on a sofa, smiling; often alone and smiling.

A day later, there was a Liverpool premier with tickets a third of the London price. The Cannon Street cinema, opposite Lime Street was packed. Michael Myers had been good enough to attend both events – the Liverpool one topped up by his relatives who lived in the city. It wasn't often that Hollywood actors graced the city, although had Cathy and her cousin, Mike, been successful there might have been more.

It was the first time she'd managed this kind of event. The idea was to sell tickets, which meant celebrities. They began with Liverpool and then trawled further to include the North West. 'M People' and 'Simply Red' were big (and Mick Hucknell did turn up and distinguished himself by showing everyone how a pop star behaved...not...), but the list petered out after them. What next? The industry bible – The White Book! On what basis? Anyone they'd like to meet! While Mike picked Madonna amongst others, Cathy picked Robert De Niro amongst her favourites and was astounded when his secretary thoughtfully rang to decline.

The London event was notable for the acceptance of a cheque for LIPA by Paul and Michael from the Hard Rock Café Foundation; the restaurant hosted the after-film event.

Backstage events behind the acceptance of the cheque had proved a mini-nightmare – how could Paul accept a cheque from a chain that sold burgers? On the other hand, they were also selling Linda's veggie burgers. There had been one attempt in Paris during the 1993 tour when Geoff Baker in an excess of enthusiasm had leapt forward just prior to the presentation and altered the cheque by felt tip putting the words 'Going Veggie' next to Hard Rock Café's name – a move that backfired, since the Hard Rock Café were not used to lively publicists, whoever they might be representing, personalising a carefully crafted piece of artwork.

The third task was to start the trek around hardware suppliers to achieve discounts and, where possible, sponsorship of equipment. As the building budget overflowed its boundary, the achievement of world-class facilities at a feasible cost became a pressing issue. Aside from genuine achievements, there was also luck. Lowell Fowler, the head of High End Lighting Systems, Texas and a lifelong Paul McCartney supporter, was prepared to provide the intelligent lighting that his company created and manufactured.

The funding of students

From the start, the founders had decided that LIPA should be available to all, regardless of parental background or income. This took us into the public sector, while being a private company. One of the City Challenge requirements was that courses should be eligible for funding from public sources, including the Higher Education Funding Council (HEFCE) and the Further Education Funding Council (FEFCE).

Sitting alongside this was another requirement which stated that 'at least a hundred full-time students and 1,000 part-time students of LIPA to be drawn from the Liverpool area, as detailed in LIPA's business plan. The Endowment Fund be established and operated by LIPA to support this target.' The next requirement asked for 'an agreed contingency plan for LIPA to meet revenue funding and offer places to students from a variety of backgrounds, in the event of HEFCE and/or FEFCE funding not being available. This is to be agreed with City Challenge by 1st September 1994.'

Since this became yet another central issue, it may be worth just briefly outlining how state-funding for higher education worked at the time and how the then government's 1994 budget critically moved the goalposts and put us on the back foot.

Essentially, higher education institutions received their funding from two main sources. The first were student fees, which started from a base level and were varied according to the discipline studied, and which were paid across by local education authorities. The second was core-funding, which was designed to help institutions achieve standards and resourcing, and which were paid across by the HEFCE. In rough terms, core-funding accounted for one-third of a given student's costs, while fees accounted for two-thirds.

There were two further details: if a course was validated and recognised by the Department of Further Education (DFE) as being of degree or Higher National Diploma status, then it automatically qualified for a mandatory award (tuition fees) from the local education authority concerned. So, mandatory awards and core-funding were not wholly connected. The second was that bidding for core-funding took place every year with the rules for the auction changing each year. So institutions did not know the outcome of the auction and therefore their revenue-funding until a few months before the beginning of the academic year.

The 1994 Budget expressed the government's wish to see a three to four per cent reduction in intake enrolments in higher education and the possibility of withholding core-funding if this was not achieved. There was another manoeuvre: to switch funding from tuition fees to core-funding, essentially reversing the existing percentages.

The problem facing us was: where were we going to get student-funding from? In addition to the reduction in the budget, there was another mechanism that set a strict limit on student recruitment to any given higher education institution. Either under- or over-recruitment brought cash penalties down on a 'transgressing' institution.

LJMU could 'donate' places to LIPA, but, without additional numbers, this would effectively mean removing places from their schools at a time when reductions were being sought anyway. Our 'success' would be at the expense of either LJMU or another university. Without detailing every option, it was clear that failure to secure HEFCE core-funding would take us down the road of some performing arts academies where students were reliant on discretionary awards from local education authorities and applications to trusts and foundations – as LIPA directors had pointed out to KPMG.

The need for resolution was being forced by the need to recruit students and, in so doing, inform them what the fees were and how they would be met. What was to appear in the prospectus? Despite the uncertainty, we decided to present the degree programme as eligible for the available public awards.

Discreet lobbying failed. Robin Squire, then Parliamentary Under-Secretary of State for Education (and such was life: he was Susan Fey's husband), John Patten, the Secretary of State for Education and Tim Boswell, then Parliamentary Under-Secretary of State for Further and Higher Education batted the ball back to LJMU and HEFCE.

The big guns were needed, in particular, our big gun. I contacted Paul and he agreed to host a lunch in London which eventually took place on 19th October 1994 attended by Tim Boswell, Peter Bounds, Graeme Davies (then the CEO of HEFCE), Stephen Dunmore (from the Government Office on Merseyside), Tony Field, Jennifer Latto (the Provost of LJMU), Robin Squire and Dieter Schneider (representing Grundig).

I met Paul before the lunch to brief him, once more, over the main issues. For some reason, Paul began the meeting by reflecting upon the advice his father had given him, which boiled down to the sentiment that Jews were the best in business, so he'd better have a

Jew on his side, if he entered business. He went on to note a line of Jews who had failed him in his business life, notably Brian Epstein and Allen Klein and rounded the list off by saying, 'And now I've got you.' I wondered what had prompted this reflection and concluded that it was probably the overspend on the building, which was clearly worrying him more than I had anticipated. I also suspected that this observation had no real depth, since, after all, Linda was Jewish. It was probably just a hangover from the past.

But I couldn't ruminate for long. I had to achieve a positive outcome from the lunch and Paul was a major participant, so I pressed on.

I had asked the LIPA supporters to share with the two ministers why they had become involved in the LIPA project. That much was orchestrated. What people actually said was not and it was difficult not to have felt enriched and energised by the simple enthusiasm expressed by such high-level people. Next on the agenda was the issue of student-funding. Graeme Davies, perhaps finding little room for manoeuvre, suggested private-sector bursaries. The private sector present felt they had done their bit; it was now government's turn. Paul put this at its simplest best: 'I'm not responsible for this country's education, you are. I don't even quite know why I felt the need to secure a future for my old school, but I have and it's for the public. Now, please help them get in.'

The ministers listened attentively and promised to do what they could.

'What they could' appeared in a guidance letter sent to HEFCE shortly after another budget, this time in November. While the covering letter was careful to point out that 'the guidance is necessarily expressed in general terms since the secretary of state is not in a position to influence the funding of individual institutions. It is now up to the Funding Council to decide its funding policies in the light of the secretary of state's guidance', there was a key piece of guidance under the sub-heading of 'Urban regeneration' that read 'The Council should take account, in its funding allocations, of the Government's City Challenge initiative where there is an acknowledged higher education dimension and an existing commitment'.

It seemed all was set fair again.

Marketing a place which didn't exist

How LIPA would be marketed to students was another immediate challenge. How could you market a place that didn't exist? Which didn't have any history? Any former students? And, from a design point of view the most demanding: what single image could be used to sum up the institution?

Billy Mawhinney, who had worked for Paul on album covers and posters, wrote in to see if he could help. An engaging gentle-hearted enthusiast, I met him many times. Eventually, he hit on the idea of an empty stage illuminated by a single spot and what was specifically illuminated was a cross on stage, a mark where very aspiring students could imagine their place.

I was also aware that some emphasis, some judicious emphasis, had to be placed upon Paul and his support, which meant discussing the design thoroughly with Paul. The basic concept was to provide a piece of arts and entertainment industry software: a video box containing a prospectus, an application form and an audio tape (one side explaining LIPA with commentary from Paul, Joan Armatrading, Cameron Mackintosh, George Martin and David Puttnam); the other, an aural prospectus), which was narrated by Peter Sissons with his usual grace and aplomb. Peter had been a contemporary of Paul's at the institute and had kindly agreed to help, uncomplainingly and diligently devoting a whole day to providing the narrative.

Billy also included delightful, quirky items like a 18-certificate (since you had to be above eighteen to apply), a running time of three years and a bar code grouped like the four pillars of the LIPA frontage.

Some staff wondered if it was all worth it. I'd argued

that a memorable item was needed and this was supplemented by a lively prospectus launch, although a live band followed by worthies in suits signalled a balance that LIPA had to address again and again: liveliness and gravitas.

The Grundig spot

There was also one element of the Grundig agreement that Paul had to fulfil; a LIPA spot. For the creators, this was quite a challenge since Paul would not endorse merchandise. Back and forth went suggestions. In the end two versions were agreed upon: a thirty-second stand-alone spot about LIPA with 'supported by Grundig' framed as an ending, and a visually arresting additional fifteen-second addition advertising Grundig merchandise.

One October morning it was shot in what seemed to me to be a large converted garage in South London. The thirty-second version featured Paul talking about the various subject areas covered by LIPA and as he moved from one subject area to another, he gained a new piece of clothing. He ended up perched on a stool wearing a mortar board and gown, over part of a business suit, part of a paint-splattered suit, Elizabethan ruffs and holding a microphone. I watched the filming, feeling awkward that Paul had been asked to caper around in such a fashion, although he seemed to be taking it in good heart.

It so happened that *The Beatles: Live at the BBC* was being released with fifty-six songs from thirty-nine radio shows made between 1962 and 1965. About thirty had never been studio-recorded for EMI and most were rock and roll classics.

The spot cost Grundig a small fortune, not so much to make as to distribute. It appeared on MTV, Eurosport, cinemas in Europe. Since this was the first time Paul had agreed to feature in a commercial, albeit for LIPA, it ensured more press coverage than LIPA could have afforded (maybe even Oxford and Cambridge too). Every UK tabloid and broadsheet covered the story. WENN produced a TV news item about the commercial, which was shown in France, Spain, Germany, Switzerland, the Middle East, South Africa, USA and Asia. UK TV coverage included Channel 4, the BBC and Granada. Given the staff resource at LIPA, this mass media coverage was a godsend.

Chapter Eighteen

Two particular scousers

Gabriel Muies was the man who spoke from the audience at Paul's *Let It Be Liverpool* press launch, when Paul announced his intention to campaign for LIPA; even now, his name conjures up a mixture of emotions in me. The arrival of LIPA conjured up a mixture of emotions in him.

One of the last group of the Liverpool Institute's parent-governors, Gabriel had never forgotten his keen sense of disappointment for what had happened to his son. Living, as he did in L8, Gabriel saw the institute as a doorway through which his son could be best prepared to face the adult world. Pride and pleasure when his son gained a place at the school turned to dismay and resentment when the school closed before his son could take up his place.

From that moment on and unemployed, he devoted his life to re-opening the school in its original capacity, despite steadfast refusals from Liverpool City Council to consider such a petition.

He got wind of our arrival in Liverpool (as he seemed to get wind of everything we did, sometimes we felt, even before we'd decided to pursue an idea) and presented himself at the LIPA offices in the Hahnemann Building. Stocky, talkative, dark-haired and capable of rough charm and dogged rants with a twinkling eye, Gabriel began by outlining his campaign for the restitution of numerous valuable statues and paintings, which he alleged had been moved from the abandoned building without consent, along with fireplaces, furniture, spiral staircases and other artefacts, including £30,000 of mountaineering equipment that the school had bought. He confided that council officers and employees were not above suspicion.

Without having the time or inclination to investigate his claims, Bergen and I made sympathetic noises. But, by way of response, this fell far short of what Gabriel wanted.

It turned out that he had written to Paul in the mid-eighties who, interested as he was in the future of the building, asked to be kept in touch with developments since he was concerned about the building. This innocent response was the charter that kept Gabriel writing to Paul to enlist his support for reopening the school and doorstepping us.

The arrival of LIPA was an opportunity and a threat; here was the possibility of enlisting a powerful public figure in his campaign; on the other hand, the powerful public figure was supporting plans of a somewhat different nature. So, whenever Gabriel met me, the possibilities ranged from a cheery drink in a pub to shouting threats ('There's no point in buying a house here; I'll have you back in London within days') in the street.

Since many of meetings between LIPA and the public, LIPA and public-sector officials, LIPA and public-sector grant-giving bodies, were of course public and since Gabriel had remarkable access to information, we were never able to discount the fact that he might be there and, equally, go up like a rocket when we described the plans for the institute.

Despite the growing support for LIPA, he never dropped his hopes. Aside from seeing LIPA personnel as Johnny-come-latelys, and overtaking his campaign, he felt there was still a possibility of both dreams being realised, *in combination*. If he had to, he could live with a performing arts institute, just so long as there was a secondary school running alongside. When the CTC movement saw possibilities in Liverpool, few could have been more overjoyed...and few were.

There were surreal moments. Securing money from the UK national environmental partnership, Civic Trust as part of their Action for Earth project, Gabriel, with a team of volunteers, set about clearing the weeds from the playground, but not before writing to Paul, Derek Hatton and Peter Sissons asking them to join in. So it was that one weekend in 1992, the playground was cleared (only to regenerate later) and I was handing across book tokens to the helpers.

Within days, Gabriel was claiming that the Charity Commission was seeking details of his plans in preference to LIPA's; weeks later he was sending me letters demanding restitution of artefacts within the building (forgetting the gymnastic equipment had been fatally used by woodworm), demanding meetings with Paul, LIPA's council, Tony Field, and adding in a PS: 'As Paul McCartney is a vegetarian, he will soon be biting his nails.'

Gabriel was part of a Liverpool backdrop for us, never absent, ever potentially present. The last I heard of him was his temporary arrest for causing disruption to the peace during the Queen's visit to LIPA in 1996. In many ways a noble man (he fought the drug peddlers on his estate), Gabriel was a nemesis in my spirit should the project fail. My internal reaction to him rested much on my morale at a given moment.

Adi Ogungboro was another figure – although not in the Gabriel mould, just as unpredictable. He suddenly appeared in the autumn of 1994 and identified himself as the person who had suggested to Paul that Liverpool needed a fame school; principally he saw this as 'a school for channelling the talent amongst the unemployed in places like Toxteth, especially for black, working-class people'. LIPA was designed to allow access for everyone, so there was a sense in which he felt his idea had been purloined. One question was: who had done the purloining? The regard he held for Paul meant it had to be me. His pleasure at his idea coming to fruition was balanced by his anger at his own lack of recognition.

The next question was: what are you going to do about it? Short of funds because of the building, the only thing we could think of was a bursary in Adi's name, which transmuted itself into an award that enabled the winning band in an emerging Merseyside Black Achievement Award ceremony to have free studio and even tuition time. Unfortunately it appeared that the idea of these awards had, he felt, also been purloined. At the first ceremony, Adi and his supporters were protesting outside the building while a brilliant capella group who had participated in our pilot courses, 'Sense of Sound', were singing in front of us. This was surround sound with a difference.

Chapter Nineteen

The first undergraduate student auditions – the building costs climb again – a bank loan – student-funding achieved – the true awfulness of the building problems – the staff and the directors decide to delay opening – managing the repercussions – further huge cost rise – Paul's solution – Induction Week

1995 began peacefully. The approval of the degree programme was achieved, the first round of overseas auditions, the setting up of a LIPA endowment trust and a pilot project with the Royal Liverpool Philharmonic Orchestra. Four more senior staff members joined.

The first undergraduate student auditions

UK auditions also began in a nearby set of rehearsal rooms, a part of the Liverpool Everyman Theatre. Teaching staff had decided to make the process a day-long affair for students to shadow the unique programme they were hoping to undertake. So the morning began with group endeavours, regardless of subject specialisation. Performers, possibly to their surprise, found themselves, amongst other tasks, getting down to the detail of setting up a charity concert for peace in Northern Ireland.

As in mainland Europe, the auditions were used to market the degree, both locally and nationally, which meant strategies had to be adopted to ensure that every student had the same experience.

For me, it was the first time I could begin to experience the reality, rather than the dream. All the committees, meetings and general foreplay had blurred the reason for undertaking the enterprise. Here, for the first time, were the people everyone had been labouring for. The world of words, laptops and faxes was vanished in the face of human encounter.

For one student, Richard Boschetto, it was his tenth audition and he told a journalist, 'I would like to say I was one of the very first students to come out here. It might go on for another hundred years and it would be great to be one of the first success stories.' (He was.)

It was also the first time I had seen teaching staff practise what they did – that is, aside from writing courses, handbooks and course materials. A member of staff said at the time, 'I find auditioning very difficult because I really feel for the candidate and I remember how nervous I was at my first auditions. You are sure everyone is better than you and that you are terrible. The candidate can forget that the panel is rooting for them and wants them to do well' – this was just the spirit which I hoped would typify the institute.

There was a concern about the relatively low level of applicants from priority areas around Liverpool and Knowsley. Within two months, there was a community liaison team to address this, alongside other local issues.

The extensive promotional work undertaken by Grundig meant auditions were also being held in Germany. Our head of publicity spotted the potential in Norway. Tetsuo Hamada helped student recruitment in Tokyo and we were also busy in the Channel Islands and the Isle of Man. Paul rang Lou Reed who then kindly headlined our US press launch. To give this event more publicity spread, Paul suggested that I informed the journalists about the imminent release of 'Free as a Bird'. This news ensured nationwide coverage.

While press coverage of the auditions was descriptive, *the Liverpool Echo* soon headed a piece

'Rock and Rubble at Fame School'. Although there had been some slippage, it was still anticipated that 11th September would be achieved. This did not prevent LIPA's board of directors from commissioning a further Monte Carlo simulation.

The building costs climb again

A month later, March, it was revealed that there was only a fifty per cent chance of containing the final cost below £9.6 million, with a ninety per cent probability of £9.9 million leading to a £2.8 million shortfall. There was also the possibility that BBBL would claim for prolongation and disruption costs that could run to a further £1,125,000.

It's worth just explaining that when delays hit a building programme, a client is hit twice: prolongation simply means that the contractors have to go on paying for working longer than scheduled, while disruption means a client has to pay for workers standing by to deliver their trade until the ones before them have delivered theirs. I was beginning to wonder if the building was about to turn into Maxwell's Law. This 'law' saw the light of day when Murphy's Law was described to the late Robert Maxwell. He'd explained that, in his judgement (as so 'law'), Murphy was an optimist.

At this point, speculation about how things had turned out as they had was a daily occurrence. However, for directors and executive managers, the key concern was to meet the shortfall. The train was running down the track; it needed to be fed. Halting the building programme was a cost beyond rational consideration.

A bank loan

Part of the answer, as Jim had advised, was to seek a loan of some £2,000,000 from our bankers, The Royal Bank of Scotland, secured on the building. Although this was achieved, I marvelled at the process which needed real or tacit approval from The Government Office on Merseyside (which monitored LIPA's European funding), Liverpool City Challenge (which monitored DfEE monies) and the Charity Commissioners (since LIPA was a charity), let alone the negotiations with bankers.

This was only a part-answer since the simple repayment (despite a capital holiday) could, if not supplemented, affect the very product that was being sold to aspiring students.

In the melting pot was a National Lottery application; a further European Regional Development Fund application for telematics, and Paul's potential agreement to advertise the Kumon Institute in Japan and donate his fee to LIPA.

Staff were also looking at strategies to reduce the cost of the operational programme since the recruitment of overseas students outside the EU was running at a lower level than budgeted for.

Student funding achieved

Five months after the London lunch, neither ministers nor HEFCE had decided about student numbers or the levels of core-funding. The strain of maintaining equanimity in the face of such uncertainty was draining.

I contacted Paul again. He grasped the situation immediately and agreed to telephone ministers, the chief executive of HEFCE, even the prime minister, pointing out that the delay was affecting our ability to achieve all the various public-sector outputs, the morale of staff and the confidence of our directors to continue to pay millions of pounds to the contractors on the expectation that we were a viable concern. This was aside from auditioning prospective students who would be entrusting their futures to teaching staff who were wondering how they could make offers to students when student-funding had not be secured.

Paul informed ministers that, if a satisfactory resolution was not found within three days, he would be interviewed in the *Independent* along the lines that we would survive by recruiting overseas students, but was this what ministers wanted, given the Liverpool/Merseyside focus of the initiative?

LJMU were unhappy about this action, but we felt it was impossible to simply sit and wait.

For the next three days, I was rarely off the telephone, co-ordinating and relaying the various outcomes. Paul too was sharing the results of his calls. Robin Squire (as Minister for Merseyside amongst his tasks) had apparently told Paul that there was nothing he could do. Paul retorted: 'Well, pass me over to someone who can! What does the Minister for Merseyside do anyway?'

This stroppy bluntness convinced me as never before that no project of any significant size could survive without a powerful lead patron who had ready access to the press and was prepared to act.

Within three days, HEFCE had agreed ninety-five core-funded places and LJMU had increased their offer of thirty fee-only places to fifty core-funded places from their allocation. The progression of mandatory awards from local authorities took a month longer.

The true awfulness of the building problems

At their May meeting, Paul Cleworth informed LIPA's directors and executive management that there was now a problem with the roof timbers. Some of the new timbers which had been put in under the Liverpool City Council contract were affected by rot, needed replacing and would, in parts, require more extensive work than the original undertaken by Birse. Completion date was now 18th October. He went on to comment on the lack of definition over twenty-seven miles of specialist cabling. Although this was denied by the specialist advisors, it was clear that core areas (even if LIPA inhabited a part of the building, which was one option being considered in detail) would be unlikely to be ready.

This was the first time acceleration of works was considered, despite additional cost (and therefore the additional burden on the institution operationally). The question was: what acceleration could actually be achieved, given the tasks that needed doing?

When pressed, Paul Cleworth stated that, in his opinion, we would not be in the building before Christmas. The room fell silent.

A staff member broke the silence: 'We'll need to look for another building, or series of buildings, then.' At once the worries started: if students realised they weren't coming to the expected building, would they come at all? Would overseas students react in the same way?

The meeting went on to discuss new issues: part-time numbers were now unlikely through government funding action; this radically changed the initial idea of 2,000 part-time students and so, inevitably, the percentage of Merseysiders – this wasn't to be the only time when one government department's actions effectively cancelled another's and left a receiving organisation in a quandary; a change of company name (as a restricted name, the use of the word 'institute' needed a special dispensation from the DTI); a new prospectus for the 1996 intake and the appointment of a finance director.

The LIPA team had to move from the old physics laboratories so that these could be destroyed, and temporary contractor's offices placed on this part of the site so that work could be progressed on the upper playground, shortly to be a carpark.

As LIPA staff moved to new offices a few hundred yards away from the site, some wondered when they would actually work on the site again.

The staff and directors decide to delay opening

On 13th July, the senior staff met to consider two options: start in alternative premises or start on 6th

January 1996. It was felt that absolute certainty had to conveyed to incoming students. Japanese and German students were booking flights, students were giving notice to their employers and, in one case, selling a business. Whatever option was gone for, planning had to take place if it was to be an alternative building (or set of buildings).

The first consideration was the quality of possible alternative accommodation. It wasn't there, which was the reason, as someone remarked, why LIPA was being built. While delay would be disappointing, this could be mitigated by an induction week before the new year; this would include lectures and workshops, and also work to be completed before the January start, a chance to meet other students, and to get some feel for the facilities to come.

Everyone felt that either option would mean some students would leave (a fear that later proved groundless).

Managing the repercussions

Staff considered the effect on student recruitment and in both cases felt that there could negative outcomes: in October, because students would not be experiencing the facilities and word would spread over the October-to-December application period; in January, because LIPA could not market the facilities as they weren't there. There was an advantage in January's favour: possible late recruitment of students.

The effect on student accommodation for a January start would mean LIPA meeting retainer charges. A January start was the preference when considering staffing, student welfare and administration issues. The thought of a multi-site enterprise, coupled with a run up to opening, commissioning and induction was a gloomy prospect. Financial issues also favoured a January start; October looked expensive, given hire, transportation and re-siting of equipment costs; as did learning resource considerations.

On balance, although it was felt there would be damaging press with either option, January would be preferable in that there would be no need to face student discontent with temporary facilities which could drag out for an entire semester.

The final vote, however reluctant, was for a January start.

The July board of directors' meeting was packed with twenty-one attendees. The journey staff had undertaken now had to be repeated with the people who carried the weight of our legal and fiduciary responsibilities.

However, the meeting began with Paul Cleworth informing it that the contractor was feeling that completion would be on 21st February 1996. He felt Balfour Beatty Buildings would be certain to prove delay was justified until Christmas; beyond that would need to further justified. He felt the contractor was hurting. The original tender, due to market pressures, was lower than reasonable and the contractor was paying sub-contractors more than they were being paid for the work. Sub-contractors were receiving delayed payments. All in all, there was a need to restore a degree of commercial incentive, which again touched upon an acceleration arrangement. Payments could be made for achieving intermediate stages with a final payment for achieving the due completion date.

The discussion was long. Rupert asked the question in most people's mind: could certainty of completion be bought? The answer was 'no'. The best chance was to encourage the contractor to perform to their full potential. I asked if another risk analysis was worth doing; again, the answer was negative.

At this point, the meeting was adjourned to consider the summary paper flowing from the senior management team's meeting over start dates.

After some verbal comments from staff, Tony told the meeting that he had experienced starting with an incomplete building, but he could see this was inappropriate and felt the January start was the right one. With the right spin, this would not be so much a delay as a compression of the first academic year (so ending in July, rather than May) and achieving a building with tip-top equipment.

Public-sector responses were all for opening, in some fashion, in October. Paul Winn, Paul's finance director and who represented Paul's commercial company, reported that I had informed Paul whose initial response had, understandably, been emotional. He naturally wanted the teaching to start on time. Paul Winn felt that, given a collective decision, Paul would accept the problem. Tony offered to join me in approaching Paul. I heaved a mute sigh of relief; a repeat of the telephone call I'd had was a cup that I was relieved not to drink from again.

The discussion covered, amongst other issues, the LJMU and HEFCE perspective, the possibility of running some elements of the degree programme (integration mitigated against this), running some elements within and without the building, cancelling the entire year; the possible loss of existing Grundig sponsorship; possible claw-backs from public-sector funders; the effect on students both in terms of morale and finance; the possibility of potential claims from students from a breach of contract and staff willingness to work an exceptional 1996 with just a month's break.

Everyone was invited to share opinions individually. The consensus was for a January start.

The next discussion centred on a strategy for informing and engaging the first students, as well as public relations. The meeting decided that whatever else happened, there would be no mud-slinging. The message would centre on unforeseen complications and the desire to ensure the best possible service when students joined.

However, the meeting did wonder what could be done to gain recompense for the early inadequate roof works. Rupert, once again, was instructed.

The meeting had to consider other issues, which included claims from local residents; the National

Lottery application; the changing of the company name; finalisation of the agreement between LIPA and LJMU; the ongoing fund-raising for equipment and software; a range of staff employment matters; inter-company work to finalise the bank loan; the inception of a large part-time programme covering September to December (Ged McKenna had now joined to manage this) and associated marketing issues; the success (and implementation) of four out of five of our European Social Fund Objective One bids; recruitment for 1996; corporate identity; the development of a student handbook and the latest edition of *NewsLIPA* (our newsletter to donors, amongst others).

Then three extraordinary pieces of timing: the project had this capacity: one moment – gloom, the next – sunshine.

Within days of the decision to delay the opening, the letter confirming a £2,000,000 National Lottery Award arrived. This news could be released to the press at the same time as the delayed start. Within a week, Paul, Linda and their son, James, were visiting the site, raising the morale of the builders, visiting the LIPA offices to raise morale there too, as well as calming the press: 'Anyone who has had the builders in knows this one,' as Paul unerringly said. As Paul Winn had predicted, he'd come to terms with the reality and wanted to help.

Earlier in the month, I had (along with the three main public-sector partners and Grundig) agreed a draft of the letter to students (which had included information about a helpline) and a press release. Local press headlines had been muted: 'Hitch on the road to fame' and 'Fame will have to wait'.

As it happened, the new 1996 prospectus came out two weeks later, which Paul hated and rang me to tell me in no uncertain terms. The challenge, yet again, had been to promote a concept, without a building and without students. The design was again influenced by a piece of the industry (this time, the magazine *The Face*) and it provoked quite sharp like and dislike. I had agreed with Paul the page where he welcomed the students, but had simply forgotten to clear the remainder of the design. (A few months later, Paul was open and generous enough to tell me that younger members of his extended family thought it was 'the thing'.)

A further huge cost rise

The gloom was that yet another rise in costs was reported to the wilting executive management and directors. Putting aside their dismay, funds had to found. The bank loan was spent, the lottery money was spent, so the only choice was to go cap in hand to MPL.

Paul's solution

Paul Winn had shared this news with his boss who had decided, with complete secrecy and so through a shell company, to loan the project £1.5 million that would be secured by a further charge on the building. This manoeuvre was critical. The public story was that a third part-investor had approached Paul's commercial company. The investor was prepared to loan money so long as he could be convinced that the project was do-able; in essence, would this solve the building problem once and for all? To that end, he had insisted on the appointment of a quantity surveyor to audit the project and have access to every member of the design team.

A range of detailed negotiations took place between Paul's team, LIPA's bankers, and the project managers, as yet another set of quantity surveyors came on board to monitor progress. As further costs emerged in September, confidence in Paul Cleworth declined sharply to the point where the head of E C Harris's Liverpool operation was asked to attend the LIPA council meetings in his stead. Paul Cleworth did not attend again.

Returning a month later to the possibility of some claim against the roof works, Rupert began by explaining that, when you purchased a building, it was normal to have collateral warranties in place so that the buyers could ensure the building works have been adequately done. Since Liverpool City Council preferred writs and since LIPA's request for warranties had been turned down, there was no direct legal relationship to Birse Construction who had probably done the best they could with the job. The members considered the possibility of involving Liverpool City Council, Liverpool City Challenge, The Charity Commission, aside from Birse, in some as yet unclear legal tussle and decided not to.

The next item was the remainder of the building, with me reminding the meeting that there was a two-way strategy in place: to get into the building by the 15th December, subject to snagging and outstanding items; the other part had to do with the quality of service received from members of the design team. The conclusion was to do all that could be done to achieve the former and to let the latter wait.

Induction Week

November had seen the student induction week for our undergraduate students: a mix of work, play and reassurance. On the final night, students presented the results of three days of practical workshops and the quality was there – as was drink and dancing shortly afterwards. The teaching staff had handsomely delivered. Every one, it seemed, bubbled with effervescence.

Thus had the communications staff delivered. They treated the management of the event as a dry run for opening. Sixty journalists, from print, TV and satellite, radio media attended various press events.

In between the work, students took a ferry across the Mersey (accompanied by Gerry Marsden), helped switch on the town's Christmas lights, ate at the Beatles Story, participated in a press conference and first student body meeting in the Cavern Club, as well as a reception in the grand and ornate Liverpool Town Hall, where the 'Sense of Sound' again captivated everyone.

I spent my time taking students on building tours and contrived each time to visit the dressing rooms that served the second auditorium, casually switching on all the make-up lights for a bit of dazzle. The days had ended with me bidding the students farewell and ending: 'You are now LIPA. Hold it close to your hearts and bring it back to us safe in January.' Fortunately, most of the staff were present, which allowed me to scurry back to the offices and weep unseen.

It was a weepy time for me, tired as I was. A BBC programme was being shot about the project and three students who were preparing to join. I was being filmed in the main auditorium and was simply asked about my feelings now that the institution was about to start. I just sobbed.

On the 15th December 1995, practical completion of the building was achieved and staff were photographed throwing their hard hats into the air outside the building by the *Liverpool Echo*.

There was much to co-ordinate for the launch. 160 press and media representatives, together with 21 camera crews needed to be accommodated. It was to be the first practical example of what the extensive cabling could achieve. While the event took place in the main auditorium, journalists were able to watch on full screen in the second. Nearly 900 people in all had to have a memorable day.

Chapter Twenty

The Inauguration

On the 8th January 1996, students attended their first whole institute meeting in the building.

Twenty-two days later, they found themselves on risers on stage, in darkness behind the curtain, awaiting the start of the launch, which had been called a variety of names and was now being called the Inauguration. The reason was confirmation that HM the Queen was going to open the building officially on the 7th June, so the precise naming of each event became a surprisingly lively issue between LIPA and the Lord Lieutenancy Office in Liverpool.

This was the moment when all the people who had contributed to it came together in the completed building. There were many people close, in or beyond tears.

The curtain rose.

LIPA's first students looked out from the stage at their benefactors; the benefactors gazed back. For a moment, some of the audience thought they were looking at a mirror and were seeing reflections of themselves; for them, the swift recognition that this was not so, brought a sharp intake of breath.

As so often, the profound response was silence. Although music was being played, in their hearts, the two groups simply mutely stared at each other.

After a light-show, I started the talk-show by sharing a notice I'd seen pinned up in an office headed 'The Six Stages of a Project'. I ran through the six: enthusiasm, disillusionment, panic, search for the guilty parties, punishment of the innocent, honours and rewards for the non-participants. I thanked the benefactors for not making that scenario come true.

I linked the story of the creation of LIPA with the speakers, so it was inevitable and right that the first speaker was George Martin, followed by Tony (who described LIPA as one of the three impossible dreams in his life), then came Peter Bounds, followed by John Flamson who stirringly ended by expressing his pride – as a scouser – in the achievement; next came Peter Reichardt, managing director of EMI Music Publishing (recalling that first fund-raising lunch), followed by European Commissioner Padraig Flynn (by then a trustee); than came Hans Bartel (for Grundig), Brigitta Unger-Soylka, for the German State of Baden-Würrtemberg, who, and which, had raised money for its students to attend LIPA; Sir Paul Beresford followed, representing the Department for the Environment. Peter Toyne was the last before I introduced Paul.

I did so by asking a rhetorical question: 'When you are trying to sell a dream, how do you encourage people to put their faith in something that doesn't exist?' The answer of course was Paul, who, above everything, had given the project credibility. I finished, 'Paul, welcome to your new old school.'

After acknowledging that the moment was all too much for him, Paul went on to describe the hope the school had given him as a lad from Speke and how you could succeed 'given enough love, passion and prepared to put in enough hard work'.

He went on: 'Obviously one of my feelings now is how proud my mum and dad would have been if they could have been here.' He stopped, thumped the lectern and said, 'But I won't get into that because I'll start crying.'

I wound up by also acknowledging how difficult it was to grasp all the emotions I felt with the words and energy available to express them. I ended by turning my back to audience and addressing the first student body directly: 'My only hope is that you, at some point in your career, will experience what I am experiencing now. After all this time, now that LIPA is finally here, now that you are LIPA, my dearest wish is that you will achieve your dreams as well or a reality that you'll enjoy just as much. We'll be here, doing our best, to help you on your way.'

Postscript

It would be satisfying to end this book at that shining moment. Although I still believe in 'living happily ever after', it can be tough to achieve. Although effectively there is no ending, because LIPA was just beginning, how was the building overspend solved? Since much of the final stage leading to the opening was concerned with this issue, you'll probably want to know what happened next. In fact, 'the next' became the key task for the next three years and, like many, I've come sadly to realise that you may start with the comet of an idea, but you'll spend much (if not most) of your time searching out the fuel of money.

It's worth recapping how dire the situation actually was. In January 1996, Jim wrote a strictly confidential paper to the board of directors. He began by summarising what had happened in pure cash terms.

He then reminded everyone how the VAT scheme worked. To separate the property from LIPA's education/training activities and facilitate the recovery of VAT on the costs of refurbishing the building, LIPA had set up a wholly owned subsidiary, LIPA Holdings Limited. Holdings was responsible for the refurbishing programme and had contracted directly with Balfour Beatty Buildings Limited (BBBL), the professional advisors (including the design team) and the suppliers of equipment needed to deliver the teaching programmes.

LIPA Holdings was VAT-registered and so received repayment of the VAT incurred on the refurbishment and fit-out programmes. LIPA was also VAT-registered, but, because of its main activity (the provision of

	Original anticipated cost	Spent to date	Final estimated cost	Possible further expenditure
	£m	£m	£m	£m
Building costs	7.8	10.3	12.3	2.0
Professional fees	1.1	2.2	2.8	0.6
Fit out costs	1.2	1.4	2.7	1.3
Other costs	–	0.6	0.6	–
Total building costs	10.1	14.5	18.4	3.9
Development costs to opening	2.1	2.1	2.1	–
Total expenditure	12.2	16.6	20.5	3.9

education), it could not recover the majority of the VAT it suffers as input tax.

LIPA had a freehold interest in the building and granted LIPA Holdings a twenty-five-year lease of the building at a commercial rent. To ensure LIPA's continuing tenancy of the building, LIPA Holdings entered into an agreement with LIPA to lease back the building for a term of twenty-five years less three days – again at a commercial rent. In the event of LIPA Holdings running out of money, the building would revert to LIPA.

The idea was that the rent LIPA Holdings received from LIPA was going to match the interest payable by LIPA Holdings to LIPA, since LIPA was the recipient of charitable donations (thus enabling gift aid to operate).

All this was hunky-dory until the amounts of money LIPA was loaning LIPA Holdings to enable the refurbishment to continue climbed beyond a point where its rental income could in no way meet the loans

LIPA was making. Effectively, LIPA Holdings was insolvent and, at the rate things were going, was in danger of bringing LIPA down as well.

The overwhelming need was to find cash which could be applied to LIPA Holdings. BBBL had decided early in 1996 to issue a statutory demand, which was a precautionary move to protect its position and would enable it to sue the directors of LIPA Holdings and effectively liquidate the company.

Three strategies were chosen: return to three of the main funders, determine the sums the suppliers would settle for and pursue a claim against the advisors, essentially E C Harris Project Management, for negligence.

The main three funders were Marfold (effectively Paul), The National Lottery and the European Regional Development Fund (it had been rumoured that, in the course of totting up expenditure of the agreed projects, there was an unspent amount). All three needed to be co-ordinated into a coherent approach and that took some doing.

Paul was the first to jump in by turning his loan into a gift, with the condition that a funding plan had to be achieved by the public funders. This was a profound and generous shift, not least because LIPA could recover £0.5 million of gift aid.

We were extraordinarily lucky in the timing of our approach to the Arts Council, which managed arts-based national lottery projects. Two weeks later the funding shutters came down. The Arts Council had two main concerns: the quality of LIPA's directors (they did not want to bail out ineffective management); the other concern was long-term viability. Accordingly, investigators were appointed, who came to the view that LIPA management had done the best it could in difficult circumstances; it was the advice they were receiving that was poor quality. Assuming an award was granted, their investigators recommended that all outstanding claims should be ditched and the money applied to redeeming the bank loan, so securing LIPA's future. We did not feel BBBL deserved such treatment, but the next potential public-sector funder was about to prevent that happening anyway.

The Government Office for Merseyside (which administered ERDF grants) sent along Coopers and Lybrand. Their main interest was LIPA's long-term future, rather than apportioning blame. If further public money was applied to the problem, would LIPA's future actually be secured?

As it happened, the two accountants were impressive and helpful, but it surprised me that yet again the public sector was sending in accountants at public cost to investigate a project that was rich in qualified accountants (Jim Dimmock, Tony Field and Paul Winn) whose loyalty to professional ethics overrode their loyalty to a specific enterprise. It seemed to me a waste of taxpayers' money and still does.

In the end, one of the conditions for further grant was settlement with BBBL and proper resolution of other claims. The frustrating slowness of resolution – some within LIPA said 'prevarication' – effectively reduced a final contribution by a third (and we are talking about a sum in region of £400,000, through movement of the EU currency unit, the euro). While Coopers was part of the solution, it was noticeable that the Government Office on Merseyside regularly seemed to approach LIPA as an adversary, much as the DES had treated the BRIT School. There were notable exceptions, but, equally, there were too many senior public servants whose motivation, it seemed, was to catch you out in some way, rather than work alongside. You came away with the impression they thought you were on the scrounge and that you would do and say just about anything to achieve your objective.

We were also extraordinary lucky with BBBL's two senior managers (Ken Winter and Ken Tait) who were trying to resolve their problems with us, under, we imagined, board pressure. As it happened, the relationships between the two Kens and Jim and I were frank, trusting, tolerant and cordial. BBBL was prepared to settle at £12.3 million – the last figure reported by LIPA's own quantity surveyors. With accrued interest, this figure came to £12.6 million, which we felt was not an unreasonable settlement. In the end, BBBL settled for £11.6 million (the ERDF funding achieved). Although this was less, this was all LIPA Holdings could offer so as not to compromise the fundamental objective of meeting LIPA's long-term future. But BBBL extracted their own price: there would no recourse to them, should a part of the building prove to be fundamentally unsound and all snagging works had to be met by the LIPA Group. However, they also met the claims of sub-contractors.

A further grant of £1.3 million from the National Lottery and the gift-aid on Paul's additional donation was applied to meeting our bank loan.

Now, the third strand of the strategy. The nub of our claim is what we would, could or should have done if we had known what the financial outcome was likely to be. In retrospect, things had drifted from the start with the £600,000 spent 'on our behalf' on the roof by Liverpool City Challenge. The next biggie was the recommendation to sign a bill of approximate quantities, rather than a fixed cost, which meant we were exposed to paying whatever it cost to renovate the building. We weren't blameless though. We changed our minds (particularly as we began to employ subject-specific staff). However, we couldn't understand why we were supposed to shoulder all the increased cost.

Of course, if these sums had been estimated from the start, LIPA would never have been allowed to leave the starting blocks, but then that's true of many building projects.

When the legal advice came in, counsel opinion was that we had 'a *prima facie*' case against E C Harris Project Management; however, the cost of pursuing such a claim was large, in the £100,000s. Companies can't apply for legal aid and LIPA advised the directors of LIPA Holdings that it wasn't prepared to forward any money for this purpose. There was no certainty of achieving a reasonable settlement so it couldn't take the risk with what was also public money after all.

It's also worth recording that, although the financial over-run on the building was solved, and that we now have a magnificent home, the possibility of failure was haunting. This had to be kept from staff; undergraduate-teaching staff who were running on reserves (running the first year of a new degree for the first time, after just a month's summer break; preparing for the second year, supporting independent student work and auditioning a high number of applicants) and administrative and support staff (who had also had a short break and were shaping new systems). Executive management had to maintain morale and appear chirpy. Didn't someone once point out that the difference between an amateur and professional performer was that the latter had to be spot on, regardless of what he might be feeling? Well, there are similarities. And because staff are also not aware of the management time being absorbed, you also have to take the brunt of their frustration at the seeming slowness of resolution attached to other matters.

What lesson can be drawn from this? I feel that the way in which the Treasury allocates spending is where the lesson starts. Liverpool City Challenge had a funding timescale that meant projects had to begin on a specified date, which encouraged all sorts of professions to take a more than reasonably optimistic view of delivery dates (if we had been able to delay a year only a fraction of what we went through and spent through would have come to pass), and which also meant that spending had to have taken place within financial timescales, not building or developmental timescales. I also feel that governing bodies undertaking building work should have a qualified advisor, preferably a quantity surveyor, as a governor. And, finally, I also feel that having a project manager, whose function it is to be the sole conduit between client and design and building teams, is not an effective model.

This was not the postscript I ever thought I would write, because I had no idea the building would be such a major pre-occupation.

I imagined I'd be writing about the destinations of our first graduates and the moment when, four years after we opened, we placed an advertisement in the official programme of 'In the City', the annual get-together for the music industry and a chance to debate the latest issues through seminars and informal meetings, linked with a programme of unsigned band evenings. And so I shall, because the variety of employment seemed to be the culmination of that practical philosophy which was first expressed in the early 'eighties.

The advertisement was based around the theme of 'Who's working? LIPA is working'. The text ran like this: Liam is working as a writer, musician and director with MTV USA; April is working with Greater London Arts Disability Unit; Emma is working, appearing in *Blood Brothers*; Jude is working in The Manchester Corner House; Kevin is working, appearing in *Miss Saigon*; Gail is working on a national tour with *A Slice of Saturday Night*; Elizabeth is working as a director with Norwegian TV; Sarah is working with Joan Armatrading; Chandra is working with the BBC; Amanda is working with Liverpool Probation Service; Lisa and Andrew are working, appearing in *Mamma Mia*; Anne is working with Warrington YMCA; Rachel is working, appearing in *Spend, Spend, Spend*; Nick is working on a tour with Eddie Izzard; Sara is working as editor *of International Line Dancer Magazine*; Rachael is working with the Liverpool Philharmonic Hall; John is working as a promoter and VM at L2 The Lomax; Julie is working at LIPA Positive Action Pathways; Jesse is working as a composer for *Playstation*; Ben is working for his own company, Wireless Imagination; Mark is working with Everton Football Club; Penny is working as Policy Officer with West Midlands Arts; Paul is working on tour with Finley Quaye; Matt is working with Zomba Records;

Russell with working with Yahama Kemble Music; Jutta is working managing a European gospel tour; Michele is working as an audio engineer with Mersey TV; Elina is working as a designer with The Finnish National Opera; Gerd is working as a creative director for a German fashion house; and in this year's 'In the City': Julie is working, appearing with 'Oceana'; Miriam is working, appearing with 'Lamen'; Stephen is working, managing 'Spoonwagon'. LIPA's 'Get Serious Programme' is active and one of the bands appearing is 'Maevella'.

Also in the official programme was a insert about our 'Music Industry and Media Innovation Centre' (MIMIC) – a research and support facility for music enterprises which included: 'Get Serious' designed to help local musicians become more aware of some of the skills and issues which could help and enhance career prospects in the music industry (thirty-seven bands listed, one named by NME as one the country's best unsigned bands of 1999 and a research projected headed by the same Pete Fulwell to assess the impact of the World Wide Web on the local industry in collaboration with a variety of local agencies and with a focus on the future of e-commerce. As it happened, MIMIC was but one of some twenty initiatives with local clients of most age groups.

OK, back to the pre-opening: the press were always close behind. Because of our association with Paul, ups and downs were news. I'm recalling a piece in *The Sunday Times* that described our building problems and inferred this was hardly surprising, given the past business history of the person running the place, i.e. me. Although the paper later conceded that the inference it was my fault 'was unjustified' and apologised, it's a possibility that's worth keeping in mind: opening your Sunday paper and finding yourself being undermined, just when you are launching forth to seek further financial backers and recruiting overseas students.

Ah well, you have to move on. I thought the creation

was the hard part. Running a performing arts institute where a higher education ethos can mean nothing is taken at face value, and where the performing arts ethos does not immediately imply moderation or restraint let alone rational debate, and where some staff appear unaware they are employees, is a tougher task that I'd imagined.

Despite seeing further hills (even mountains) beyond, I can now look back and survey the scenery through which I've travelled and tried to describe to you. Looking back, you slowly gain a sense of perspective. This often happens when I take visitors round the institute.

To those who helped: without you, LIPA would not be in existence and could not expand the horizons of the people who now study with us – and this book, if it had been written at all, would have told a different story and it would be hard to end feeling optimistic, even now.

And no, I don't agree with Don Marquis who said that 'an optimist is just a guy who has never had much experience'.

Appendix One

The Blueprint for the British Record Industry Trust School

THE BRIT School, the first City College for the Technology of the Arts (CCTA), presents an added dimension to the City Technology College programme. This document outlines the aim areas of the curriculum.

Our aim is to provide an education programme, designed in such a way that students achieve a variety of attainments to recognised standards, within the school setting, and be as prepared as possible for the world of work.

Our skills programmes are, of course, directed towards performing arts and their attendant technologies. It is here that the school has a unique educational mission. Within a broad and balanced curriculum, there are four skill areas that will be taught to all students:

> ➤   dance
> ➤   music
> ➤   theatre
> ➤   electronic media

Following years of research, both in this country and overseas, we are convinced that there is a need for the education and training of entrants to the arts and entertainments world who can demonstrate:

- ➢ versatility across the four skill areas
- ➢ extensive practical performance training
- ➢ experience of the application of technology to the performing arts
- ➢ preparation for the world of work and for links to industry
- ➢ appreciation of the popular and contemporary in performance arts

We aim to deliver a response to this need.

We are ensuring that the courses offered are relevant to the needs of industry by extensive consultation in the planning process. We will invite professionals from the arts and entertainment industry to contribute to or teach the vocational courses. We aim to place students within a work-setting as a part of their education.

Links with Croydon College

The BRIT School sees natural good sense in maximising the potential relationship between itself and Selhurst Tertiary Centre, with whom it will share the same site. The school aims to share its specialist facilities (recording and video library, video studio, performance areas, foe example) and consult fully with Croydon College on shared teaching facilities to the mutual benefit of both institutions.

Monitoring of student achievement

The BRIT School is aware that a school record should contain a profile of its students' personal attributes. While helping students achieve their goals and the appropriate qualification, we are also keen that due recognition is made of each student's personal and professional development. The school will provide its own profiling system to which each student will actively contribute, leading to entries in their Personal Record of Achievement.

Preparation of the curriculum

The BRIT School's curriculum is undergoing constant development. Liaison with Croydon College, negotiations with examining boards and validating bodies and talks with the arts and entertainment and other industries will all play their part in enhancing the effectiveness of the curriculum before September 1990.

The education advisers will be pleased to discuss progress towards a working curriculum. They are Mark Featherstone-Witty and Bergen Peck. They may be contracted at the school's offices.

The curriculum for thirteen to sixteen year olds

The BRIT School will adhere to the substance of the National Curriculum. Students will follow the core subjects – English, mathematics and science; the foundation subjects – design & technology, history, geography, a modern language, physical education, art and music. A second modern language, home economics and computer skills will also be available.

All these subjects will make maximum use of syllabuses, which allow a bias towards the performing arts and technology. For example, an English class might choose texts that can be acted; a GCSE art student might use computer graphics to create a lighting design.

A programme of short courses in dance, music, theatre and electronic media will contribute a significant proportion to the curriculum for all students. Combined with GCSE studies in a variety of performing arts, and the biases within other subjects, some students may find up to sixty per cent of their curriculum devoted to performing arts and technology. Additionally, musical instrument tuition will also be widely available.

Provision will be made for religious education and collective worship. There will also be personal, professional and social development courses, which will deal with moral, health and personal issues, as well as careers advice, entrepreneurial skills and understanding of commercial enterprise, which will be encouraged across the curriculum.

Student in this age range will be subject to national attainment targets and assessment arrangements. Student will be expected to study up to eight subjects at GCSE, including aspects of the performing arts. Foundation courses, validated by the Joint Unit for 14-16 Pre-Vocational Education, will be available alongside GCSEs for some students.

Enrichment activities

The BRIT School will provide opportunities for activities such as sport, outdoor pursuits, recreational clubs and community service.

The curriculum for sixteen to eighteen year olds

The BRIT School has adopted a very flexible approach to learning opportunities, It will offer a wide range of subjects at GCE 'A' and 'AS' levels, in English and RE; modern languages; humanities and social sciences; mathematics and pure and applied sciences; computing and electronics; design and technology; and arts and the performing arts.

Moreover, there will also be a wide range of unit-structured courses in the fields of performing arts, design, engineering (electrical & electronic – arts and media), and business and finance (arts and media). These will be validated by BTEC and lead to National Vocational Qualifications (NVQs), which are designed to recognise achievement to the standards required in industry and the professionals, set out by the Industry Lead Bodies (ILBs).

The individual units may lead to Certificates of Achievement and may be built up towards the awards of BTEC First and National Diplomas, Courses validated by the City & Guilds of London Institute will also be available, as well as the Joint Board's Certificate of Pre-Vocational Education (CPVE).

All students will take some of these modules in order to retain a breadth of work in technology and the performing arts. Thus, a student taking a BTEC National Engineering course will also study certain elements of dance, theatre and music (whether performing or not); and a student taking GCE 'A' levels in double music, art and history will also study units in dance, theatre and electronic media.

As all students complete vocational units, they begin to build up their National Record of Vocational Achievement (NROVA). This provides a lifelong portfolio of learning and achievement that may be added to throughout adult life. It may be shown to prospective employers and colleges and anywhere a personal record is needed.

All students will take a Professional Preparation course. Thus will deal with self-employment, contracts, personal finances, venue management, etc. and will develop the qualities of enterprise, self-reliance and responsibility. These will be support tools for finding a route into any industry or profession. Our students will be aware of the value of personal achievement.

Showcase

The BRIT School will initially develop two innovations.

The Showcase Afternoon will take place every week. The whole school will be involved, regardless of age, and timetables courses in a variety of possible activities:

> ➤ work on shows/guest artists or speakers
> ➤ visits to theatres (backstage or performances)
> ➤ productions in local schools, for example

The Showcase Term will be a short term during each academic year (the school will operate a four-term year). It will provide the opportunity for a variety of more extensive projects, large or small. They may be major productions, involving a hundred students and aiming at public performance; or they may be smaller-scale projects in the video studio; a musical group may spend some time in the recording studio, supported by other students in the control room; or a group of dancers may work towards the development of software for computer-aided choreography.

Appendix Two

*The LIPA Bachelor of Arts (Honours)
in Performing Arts*

Year 1	Semester One	Semester Two
Core	All Performing Arts students take Professional Development Information and Performance Technology	All Performing Arts students take Performing Arts and Popular Culture Collaborative Performance Project (24 Credits)
Options	Alexander Technique, Management Workshop, Acting Workshop, Movement Workshop, Singing, Percussion Skills, Video, Music Theory, Design for Performance, Community Arts Workshop Skills, CAD and DTP for the Performing Artist, The Life Class	(All Performing Arts students must also choose an Option Module from this list of Options)
Routes		
Acting	Acting Fundamentals Performance Skills Fundamentals	Text and Performance Voice and Movement
Community Arts	Introduction to Community Arts Skills. Choose one module from: Performing Fundamentals or a module from the Music Route	Introduction to Community Arts. Choose one module from: Voice and Text or a module from the Music Route
Dance	Dance Fundamentals Dance Narrative	Dance Performance Skills Choreography and Repertoire
Enterprise Management	Management Skills Culture and Structure	Winning Resources and Support Ownership and Investment
Music	Choose two modules from: Performance Skills, Harmony, Songwriting, Sound Recording and Production Technology	Choose two modules from: Composition and Arranging, Text and Performance, Music Technology and MIDI Systems, Performance Styles
Performance Design	A Visual Vocabulary Performance Design Technical Skills	Performance Design Making Skills Design for the Stage

Year 2	Semester Three	Semester Four
Core	All Performing Arts students take Performing Arts in the 20th Century Performance Workshop (24 Credits)	All Performing Arts students take Performing Arts and Popular Culture Collaborative Performance Project (24 Credits)
Electives	All Performing Arts Students must also choose an elective module from the following list or (timetable permitting) from a range of electives offered by JMU	Introduction to Directing, Singing and Performance, Touring and Working Abroad, The Artist as Educator, Dance Techniques, Performing Arts in the Heritage Industry, Acting Technique, Enterprise and Self-Employment, Art, Site and Performance, Introduction to the Music Business, Alexander Technique, Creative Lighting for Performance and Performers
Routes		
Acting	Applied Acting Skills Choose one module from: Musical Theatre Workshop or Creating Narrative Performance	Advanced Acting: Shakespeare Acting for Screen and Radio
Community Arts	Community Arts Since 1945 Choose one module from: Musical Theatre Workshop, Creating Narrative Performance (Music) or a module from the Music Route	Applied Workshop Skills (24 Credits)
Dance	Applied Dance Skills Choose one module from: Dance in Context or Musical Theatre Workshop	Experimental Dance Applied Choreography
Enterprise Management	Applied Management Skills European Cultural Industries	Managing Cultural Industries (24 Credits)
Music	Choose two modules from: Performance and Repertory, Applied Music Production and Recording, Musical Theatre Workshop, Applied Harmony	Choose two modules from: Applied Songwriting, Composition and Arranging, Advanced Music Technology, Advanced Performance Skills, Singing as Performance
Performance Design	Applied Performance Design (24 Credits)	Performance Art Production (24 Credits)

Year 3	Semester Five	Semester Six
Core	All Performing Arts students take Professional Preparation Cultural Realpolitik	All Performing Arts students take Final Dissertation (48 Credits) or Final Practical Project (24 Credits) plus Final Research Project (24 Credits)
Routes		
Acting	Voice and Character Choose one module from: The Director (24 Credits) or The Theatre Company (24 Credits)	Professional Presentation Skills
Community Arts	The Community Artist (24 Credits) Advanced Support Studies	Arts in Institutions
Dance	Advanced Performance Skills Choose one module from: The Choreographer (24 Credits) or The Dance Company (24 Credits)	Professional Presentation Skills
Enterprise Management	The Arts Manager (24 Credits) Managing Innovation and Change	Advanced Marketing and Communication
Music	Choose one module from: The Musical Director (36 Credits), The Performer (36 Credits), The Composer/Songwriter (36 Credits), The Music Producer (36 Credits)	Professional Presentation Skills
Performance Design	The Performance Designer (36 Credits)	Advanced Visual Presentation

Appendix Three

The cast lists

The Schools for Performing Arts Trust

Trustees

Michael Church, Patricia Clayton, Mark Featherstone-Witty, Anthony Field, Joanna Moriarty, Bergen Peck

Initial Patrons

Joan Armatrading, John Barton, David Bedford, Leonard Bernstein, Sir Richard Branson, Graham Collier, John Dankworth, Dame Judi Dench, Richard Eyre, Bryan Forbes, Lenny Henry, Dr Richard Hoggart, Glyn Johns, Mark Knopfler, Gillian Lynne, Sir Cameron Mackintosh, Sir George Martin, Sir Kenneth MacMillan, George Melly, Jonathan Miller, Dudley Moore, John Mortimer, Robert North, Lady Olivier, Dame Merle Park, Alan Parker, Monica Parker, Andre Previn, Lord David Puttnam, Alpana Sengupta, Paul Scofield, Ronnie Scott, Carly Simon, Wayne Sleep, Tom Stoppard, Pete Townshend, Toyah Willcox, Victoria Wood, Vangelis

Main participants

Margaret Bown – secondee from Prudential plc
Susan Davenport – freelance fund-raiser
Denise Fiennes – freelance fund-raiser
Veronica Jobbins – creator of the dance curriculum

Nigel Morgan – creator of the music curriculum
David Self – creator of the acting curriculum

The British Record Industry Trust School

Main participants

Kenneth Baker MP – Secretary of State for Education
Lord Michael Birkett – president, the BRIT School
Richard Branson – founder, Virgin Group
Shirley Burns – PA to George Martin
Alan Callender – Her Majesty's Inspectorate
Maggie Crowe – PA to John Deacon
John Deacon – director general, the British
    Phonographic Industry
Susan Fey – chief executive, the City Technology
    Colleges Trust
Neil Flint – senior officer, the Department of Education
    and Science
Coleen Hue – PR officer, BPI
Maureen Milgram – project director, the BRIT School
Donald Naismith – chief education officer, Croydon
    Council
Bergen Peck – education advisor
Anne Rumney – first principal, the BRIT School
Jeremy Silver – PR officer, BPI
Alan Stephenson – curriculum advisor
Alex Stewart – head of City Technology Colleges Unit,
    the Department of Education and Science
Sir Cyril Taylor – chief executive, the City Technology
    Colleges Trust
Brian Taggart – the BRIT School architect
Gillian Weldon – PA to Terry Ellis
William Whitehorn – corporate relations director,
    Virgin Group
Roger Williams – HMI Inspector

The Liverpool Institute for Performing Arts

Trustees, directors and advisors for the start-up

Main participants

Jeremy Harrison – director, EU technical assistance unit
Philip Hart – Harman Pro Group
Gerlinde Heckenblaikner – sponsorship and marketing officer, AMC, Germany
Alison Holbourn – LIPA's first marketing manager
David Jones – Yamaha-Kemble Music
Shelagh Jones – PA, Paul McCartney
Tim Johnson – accountant, KPMG and City Challenge assessor
Steve Lipman – Berklee College of Music
Neil Mackenzie – Charity Commission, Liverpool
Terry Marshall – Marshall Amplification
Billy Mawhinney – freelance graphic designer
Bill Maynard – city planning officer, Liverpool City Council
Shirley McLean – freelance music industry acquisitions consultant
John Morley – head of division, DGV
Gordon Newbury – my stepfather
Richard Ogden – manager, Paul McCartney
Toomas Paiste – Paiste Cymbals
Simon Prentice – English/Japanese translator
David Price – director of learning, LIPA
John Rago – American lawyer, LIPA fund-raiser in USA
Dieter Schneider – sponsorship manager, Grundig AG
Gerhard Seiferth – marketing and sponsorship manager, AMC, Germany
Cathy Skelly – first full-time LIPA employee
Adrian Simmons – buildings manager, Liverpool University
Christian Simon – German freelance journalist and LIPA fund-raiser in Germany
Johan van Splunter – board member, Grundig AG
Denise Stanley – freelance training advisor
Barbara Stewart – freelance feasibility study compiler
Sir Jack Stewart-Clark – European MEP
Paul Taylor – solicitor, Liverpool City Council
Peter Toyne – vice chancellor & chief executive, Liverpool John Moores University
Ken Tait – Balfour Beatty Buildings Limited

Collin Thompson – partner, Walfords
James Warnock – head of City Action Team, Merseyside
    Task Force
David Watkins – architect, Brock Carmichael and
    LIPA's architect
Kate Willard – freelance arts consultant
Paul B Winn – finance director, MPL
Ken Winter – senior manager, Balfour Beatty Buildings
    Limited
Robert Wiczling – Avedis Zildjian Cymbals

LIPA Staff List on opening in 1996

Ray Adams, Mike Barker, Susanne Burns, Helen
Davies, Katharine Dimmock, Christine Elwin, Mark
Featherstone-Witty, Iain Griffiths, Paul Grimshaw, Jill
Halstead, Alison Holbourn, Ruth Jackson, Robert Jeal,
Paul Kleiman, Helen Matthews, Ged McKenna, Rachel
McLean, Bob Memery, Maureen Newport, Paul
O'Donnell, Ken O'Donoghue, Iain Ormsby-Knox, Nick
Owen, Tim Pike, Mary Prestidge, David Price, Susie
Quinsee, Irene Richardson, Sue Roberts, Phil Saxe,
Cathy Skelly, Agnes Skelly, Donna Soto-Morettini, Jon
Thorton, Graham Williams

Index